The sinews of the spirit

The ideal of Christian manliness in
Victorian literature and religious thought

William Holman Hunt, *The Shadow of Death* (1869–73)

The sinews of the spirit

The ideal of Christian manliness in Victorian literature and religious thought

NORMAN VANCE

Lecturer in English, University of Sussex

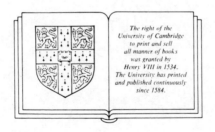

The right of the
University of Cambridge
to print and sell
all manner of books
was granted by
Henry VIII in 1534.
The University has printed
and published continuously
since 1584.

CAMBRIDGE UNIVERSITY PRESS

Cambridge

London   New York   New Rochelle

Melbourne   Sydney

Published by the Press Syndicate of the University of Cambridge
The Pitt Building, Trumpington Street, Cambridge CB2 1RP
32 East 57th Street, New York, NY 10022, USA
10 Stamford Road, Oakleigh, Melbourne 3166, Australia

First published 1985

Printed in Great Britain at
the University Press, Cambridge

Library of Congress catalogue card number: 84–28593

British Library cataloguing in publication data
Vance, Norman
The sinews of the spirit: the ideal of
Christian manliness in Victorian literature
and religious thought.
1. English literature – 19th century –
History and criticism 2. Masculinity (Psychology)
in literature
I. Title
820.9′352041   PR468.M3
ISBN 0 521 30387 7

SE

Contents

Illustrations

Acknowledgements

I am grateful to the staffs of the Bodleian Library, Cambridge University Library, the British Library, the Working Men's College Muniment Room and the libraries of the University of Sussex and The Queen's University of Belfast for their help in locating books and unpublished materials.

I would like to thank James Johnson for first interesting me in Charles Kingsley. I am indebted to Geoffrey Rowell and Dorothy Bednarowska for expert guidance in the early stages of this project. More recently I have benefited from the knowledge and interest of my Sussex colleagues, particularly John Burrow, Laurence Lerner, John Lowerson, Norman MacKenzie and Stephen Medcalf. To my parents, for their encouragement, to my aunt, for her meticulous typing, and above all to my wife Brenda Richardson, for her patience, support and shrewdly perceptive commentary I am deeply grateful.

Some of the material of this book has appeared in different form in *Notes and Queries*, *Theology*, *Yearbook of English Studies* and *The Victorian Public School*, edited by Brian Simon and Ian Bradley (Gill and Macmillan, Dublin 1975).

Abbreviations

BL   British Library, London
Bod.   Bodleian Library, Oxford
CUL   Cambridge University Library
DNB   *Dictionary of National Biography*, compact edition, 2 vols., Oxford 1975
LM   [Fanny Kingsley] *Charles Kingsley, Letters and Memories of his Life*, 2 vols., 1877
OED   *Oxford English Dictionary*, compact edition, 2 vols., Oxford 1971
PG   *Patrologia Graeca*, ed. J.P. Migne, Paris 1857–66
PL   *Patrologia Latina*, ed. J.P. Migne, Paris 1844–55

References to the novels of Kingsley and Hughes, except where indicated, are to the one-volume Macmillan electrotyped editions, which are the most widely available.

Introduction

Christian Manliness was the title of a popular and representative religious work published by the Religious Tract Society in 1867. This 'book of examples and principles for young men', compiled by the Revd S. S. Pugh, draws attention to a much wider range of concerns than its title suggests. 'Christian manliness' was a common Victorian preacher's catch-phrase. It represented a strategy for commending Christian virtue by linking it with more interesting secular notions of moral and physical prowess. 'Manliness' in this context generously embraced all that was best and most vigorous in man, which might include woman as well. Pugh holds up the example of Christ and St Paul who combined the virtues of both sexes in their manly energy and gentleness.[1] Most of Pugh's material came from the Bible, but he enlivened it with allusions to secular literature and references to General Havelock, a conveniently Christian hero of the Indian Mutiny, and to Wilberforce and other heroes of the abolition of the slave-trade. It is this attractive but vulnerable blend of perennial religious principle with contemporary heroisms and concerns that this study seeks to explore, especially in the work of those supremely manly Christians Charles Kingsley and his close friend Thomas Hughes. Seen in its historical context their Christian manliness gives the modern reader unexpected access to the whole Victorian age.

The nineteenth century began with heroic acts on land and sea. Wellington and Nelson between them refurbished the age-old tradition of military glory. Wordsworth's poem 'Character of the Happy Warrior' (1805), inspired by the death of Nelson, helped to wreathe patriotic duty in a mystic aura, appropriating religious language to assure every true soldier of applause in Heaven and 'comfort in himself and in his cause'. But the circumstances of peace required a different heroism. At the beginning of *Don Juan* (1819) Byron tried to back away from the strident militarism of the Napoleonic era: tongue-in-cheek he selected not a soldier or a sailor but a legendary aristocratic libertine as the hero of his poem. The

Victorians developed more respectable and more democratic approaches to the heroism of peace without ever completely abandoning the heroism of war. The most influential discussion was Thomas Carlyle's lectures *On Heroes, Hero-worship and the Heroic in History* (1844), which will be considered in a later chapter. But Elizabeth Barrett Browning's moralizing comment in *Aurora Leigh* (1856) strikes a characteristic note: 'all men [are] possible heroes.'[2]

In the years between the two great reform bills, between 1832 and 1867, Kingsley and Hughes adapted this emerging sense of individual possibility, moral and political, to their own profoundly religious confidence in personal and social salvation through service and strenuousness. The so-called 'Age of Equipoise'[3] in which this manly Christian ethic was developed and publicized in popular novels and other writings loses much of its bland serenity on closer examination. Even after the last Chartist demonstration of 1848 which prompted Kingsley's first 'social-problem' novels the era was embittered by religious controversies, by growing unease at the political and economic position of labour in town and country, and by the continuing revelation of urban squalor. As if this was not enough the sense of national emergency which was registered during the Napoleonic wars was reawakened by a series of cholera epidemics, by the threat of French invasion in 1853, by the Crimean War and the Indian Mutiny. Kingsley and Hughes responded to all these disquiets intellectually, imaginatively and practically. It is a pity that the vigorous, socially aware Christianity which they preached and practised against this background has attracted the trivializing label 'muscular Christianity', first applied by indolent reviewers.[4]

The trouble with the phrase 'muscular Christianity' is that it draws attention more to muscularity than to Christianity. The self-consciously anti-Christian Algernon Swinburne rather improbably described himself as in 'a rampant state of muscular Christianity' merely because he had been riding and swimming.[5] The alarmingly brutal and effectively godless Philistinism of school life at Westminster was described as 'muscular Christianity' in 1858.[6] Wilkie Collins' novel *Man and Wife* (1870), attacking excessive devotion to athletics, was regarded as an onslaught on the 'muscular Christians' of the time.[7] It was not surprising that Kingsley tried to dissociate himself from the term in his Cambridge sermons on *David* while insisting on his own ideal of a 'healthy and manful Christianity'.[8] Kingsley and Hughes have been underestimated by posterity because persistent attributions of a merely muscular Christianity ignore the liberal religious awareness which crystallized with them into a vigorously combative Christianity involving urgent ethical and spiritual imperatives.[9] This religious dimension, which has never been seriously examined, needs to be investigated if either writer is to be fairly assessed and if the atmosphere of mid-Victorian England is to be fully understood.

For many prominent Victorians the anxieties of contemporary living were symptoms and episodes in a general sense of religious and social crisis. God and Mammon had always tended to pull apart, but things seemed to get much worse in the 1840s and 1850s. The attempt to open the Great Exhibition on Sundays, to display the mighty works of man on the Lord's Day, was frustrated by the Sabbatarian lobby. This was symptomatic of the growing tendency to drive a wedge between secular and sacred, between an increasingly complex industrialized society with its special leisure-needs and an ever-more rigorous and exclusive sense of religious obligation.[10] Victorian organization-mania was part of the problem: at the very moment that the wonders of science and technology were being organized into the greatest exhibition of the age in Hyde Park individual consciences were being organized into aggressive or defensive religious movements in Exeter Hall. Sabbatarian rigour, pious philanthropy, the evangelical missionary impulse, the formerly private sense of necessary separation from a fallen world were articulated and co-ordinated at mass-meetings, formalized into societies, petitions and subscription-lists, and publicized through a partisan religious press. A stream of published sermons and pamphlets denounced Sabbath-breaking and commended African missions, supported the Sunday School movement and condemned Puseyism and the Pope. Puseyism had had its part to play as well, for in the 1830s the influential series of *Tracts for the Times* represented a well-organized Puseyite campaign against ecclesiastical laxity and compromise with the world.

All this self-conscious, public religious discussion tended to separate religious awareness from everyday practical concerns. The climax was reached in Newman's intemperate statement of the religious worthlessness of the merely moral citizen, the State's pattern-man, in his *Lectures on Anglican Difficulties* (1850).[11] The uneasy relationship between church and world embarked on a new phase when the new biblical and historical scholarship and the new geology and biology were perceived to challenge popular, literal-

minded readings of the Scriptures. Religion was driven onto the
defensive as churchmen had to vindicate or revise previously
unquestioned assumptions which had been the common ground of
secular and sacred discourse. The Revd Charles Kingsley rose to the
occasion: he actually welcomed the publication of Darwin's *Origin of
Species* in 1859.[12] But his friend Philip Gosse, a distinguished marine
biologist, ruined his scientific reputation with his book *Omphalos*
(1857), an ill-judged attempt to reconcile a literal interpretation of
the Genesis creation narrative with scientific fact. These uneasy and
self-conscious oppositions of Science and Religion, Church and
World, were bound to cause anxiety and divided loyalties for
thoughtful and earnest men of the world. They represented a major
crisis in Victorian culture insofar as it laid claim to a religious basis.
If man was created in the image of God, if Christ Himself was made
man, surely there must be some vital connection between the
hectically busy world of men and the spirit of God, but where was it
to be found? Kingsley and Hughes and their spiritual mentor Revd
F. D. Maurice sought answers to this question, which was
fundamental to all their religious and practical endeavours. The
cultural problem which they tackled in their writings is perhaps
most clearly illustrated by some of the paintings of the period.
Holman Hunt's famous *Light of the World* (1854) attracted praise for
its aestheticized and spiritualized Christ-figure, abstracted from the
world of contingency and practical necessity and presented in terms
of generalized allegory. But the very unworldliness of the painting
attracted criticism. It appalled Thomas Carlyle, the secular prophet
whose gospel of heroic moral activism deeply impressed his
contemporaries, including Kingsley and Hughes. For him this was
'a mere papistical fantasy ... a poor misshapen presentation of the
noblest, the brotherliest, and the most heroic-minded Being that
ever walked God's earth'.[13] This humanly heroic Christ, type of
toiling and suffering humanity rather than ethereal icon, had been
commended in Carlyle's writings years before.[14] Holman Hunt
must have been impressed by Carlyle's protests, for his later painting
The Shadow of Death portrays Carlyle's Christ, strong but vulnerable
and intensely human, a weary carpenter whose outstretched arms
cast a shadow suggesting the crucified Christ.

   This painting antagonized the severer sort of churchman because
it transgressed the carefully guarded frontier between secular and
sacred. Millais' earlier painting of *Christ in the House of His Parents* had
run into the same difficulties. The full implications of the Incarna-

1   Ford Madox Brown, *Jesus Washing Peter's Feet* (1852)

tion were found to be embarrassing, a 'pictorial blasphemy'. *The Times* was appalled at the association of the Holy Family with 'the meanest details of a carpenter's shop, with no conceivable omission of misery, of dirt, or even disease.'[15] That Christ should have been associated with everyday activity, with muscular exertion and fatigue, was somehow visually unacceptable though a religious commonplace. Rossetti's Llandaff Cathedral altarpiece *The Seed of David* was less controversial. Like Kingsley he found David a manly subject. He associated Christ as Good Shepherd and King with David as a finely-muscled shepherd boy and as King of Israel. It was safer, perhaps, to interpose typological distance between vigorous physical masculinity and the figure of Christ. Ford Madox Brown

was not so prudent. He too caused offence when he tried to bridge
the widening gulf between human realities and religious awareness
by painting a strong but humble and unromantic Christ in *Jesus
Washing Peter's Feet* (1852) (illustration 1).[16]

All these paintings represent the intensely human manly Christ
who dominated the thinking of the mid-Victorian manly Christians.
They offer a visual counterpart to works such as Thomas Hughes'
The Manliness of Christ which spells out the gospel of *Tom Brown's
Schooldays* in a series of homely talks. Hughes insists on the
connections between a vigorously human Christ and a vigorously
humane Christianity, opposed to ascetic otherworldliness and
earnestly committed to work in the world. *Work*, by Ford Madox
Brown, is the supreme manly Christian painting. It shows men
working in different capacities: there is a 'young navvy in the pride
of manly health and beauty', and Thomas Carlyle and F. D.
Maurice are represented as bystanders, brainworkers striving to
improve the social and moral conditions of the age. The painting
also shows a poster for the Working Men's College, where Hughes
and Maurice and their associates conducted a typically strenuous
programme of adult education. It is interesting that Charles
Kingsley was originally suggested instead of Maurice as a suitably
vigorous worker for a better world.[17]

The manly work of social improvement can be regarded as God's
work only if one believes in God: otherwise it can be a laudable but
entirely secular undertaking. This draws attention to a central
difficulty in the manly Christianity of Kingsley and Hughes. For
them the manliness and the Christianity were inextricably bound
up with each other, and their novels project an imaginatively
compelling synthesis of the two elements. But the synthesis is
unstable and intellectually vulnerable. Manliness or man in his most
vigorous aspect and the liberal Christianity which seeks to improve
the present world have largely separate histories, each of which will
have to be considered in some detail in the following chapters, and
the alliance between them has always been intermittent at best.
Kingsley tried to intellectualize the alliance by invoking the
Platonic notion of *thumos* or 'spirit'. By *thumos* Plato had meant a
combative righteous indignation which could provide the social
reformer with energy, an energy of the spirit arising from a
judiciously balanced mixture of the rational and the passional
faculties in man.[18] But what secured the judiciousness and the
balance? What regulated and controlled the indignation and
guaranteed its righteousness? For Kingsley and Hughes what kept

manliness Christian? The conventional answer might be 'the grace of God', but grace is often considered as something which imposes itself from outside upon the ordinary activities and endeavours of men. This dimension of transcendence sat uneasily upon the shoulders of writers committed to celebrating ordinary humanity as religiously significant in itself.

Popular novelists can often side-step such problems. In *Westward Ho!* and *Tom Brown's Schooldays* Christian manliness seems to fit snugly into the secular format of the outdoor adventure-story or the fictional biography enlivened with hearty games. But what about the factor that makes manliness specifically Christian, the moral and spiritual regulator that sanctifies manly adventure and disciplines passion and prowess, dedicating them to God's causes? This had to be derived from dogma, from an intuition that of course God was the living energy of the universe and the sanction of righteous causes and that ordinary experience revealed His priorities. Once accepted, this made sense of everything, but by its very nature such a dogma was incapable of proof or systematic demonstration within the confines of ordinary realistic fiction. It is not surprising that the conventional novel-form gradually collapsed under the weight of manly Christianity entrusted to it. Dream, myth and fable tend to take over from straightforward realistic narrative carried forward by the initiatives and responses of the characters themselves. The gradual military collapse of Kingsley's Hereward, for example, is not accounted for in conventional historical terms though the structure of the novel is that of sequential historical narrative. Instead, Kingsley turns his tale into dogmatic moral fable, blandly assuring us that 'The grace of God had gone away from Hereward as it goes away from all men who are unfaithful to their wives.'[19]

It was inevitable that manliness and Christianity should be sometimes uneasy together. The entertaining and healthy activism of the manly hero, whether in fact or fiction, was bound to jar with the less vivid religious imperatives: patience and heroic martyrdom, self-abnegation and the discipline of the will. The secular hero is captain of his fate and master of his soul, confidently dominating the action. But sooner or later the Christain hero must acknowledge Christ as captain and master. The literary and social antecedents of the notion of 'manliness' could make such allegiance difficult. The tradition of liberal religious thought through which the consecration of manliness was attempted will be considered in a later chapter. The idea of manliness itself now calls for closer examination.

I

Varieties of manliness

'Manliness' has almost always been a good quality, the opposite of childishness and sometimes of beastliness, counter not so much to womanliness as to effeminacy. It brings with it connotations of physical and moral courage and strength and vigorous maturity.[1] But since man is a complex and contrary being the precise qualities appropriate to a man as opposed to a child, or a beast, or an effeminate person have been much discussed. In consequence the term 'manliness' trails after it a motley collection of camp-followers, additional nuances of meaning generated by context and reflecting what might seem in a given time and place to be specially appropriate to the dignity of a man. The manly man may be patriotic, generous, broad-minded, decent, chivalrous and free-spirited by turns.

When Sir Walter Scott describes the character of Scotland as 'independent and manly' in *Waverley* the context indicates that he implies not merely moral and political maturity but also the nation's capacity to bear arms in her own defence. Later in the same novel the Jacobite Fergus MacIvor answers the judge who has condemned him to death in a 'manly and firm tone': here there is a similar nuance of embattled patriotism for the suggestion is not merely of courage and moral resolution but also of a warrior's pride in dying for the cause of his country as he perceives it.[2]

But there are different kinds of manliness in death as in life. The critic Leslie Stephen described the dying Fielding as 'manly to the last'.[3] This use of the word 'manly' does more than describe the ailing novelist's unflinching courage: it implicitly pays tribute to his imagination, registering appreciation of the unabashed rumbustiousness of the novels, the generous, uncomplicated ethic of the good-hearted man and the unfailing energy of the human comedy which they portray.

'Manliness' in the novels of Anthony Trollope means something slightly different again. Trollope's shrewd moral realism tends to exclude the extremes of moral heroism and depravity so that when

8

'manliness' appears as a term of praise it implies a pragmatic moral decency, doing the best and bravest thing a man can reasonably do in the circumstances. The selfish and unprincipled Lopez in *The Prime Minister* simply gives in too easily, committing suicide because he is 'utterly unmanly and even unconscious of the worth of manliness'. In *The Duke's Children* the determination with which Frank Tregear defies the wrath of the Duke of Omnium in demanding his daughter's hand is described as a 'manliness' which wins the Duke's grudging respect. Lord Silverbridge, the Duke's son, defends his love for Miss Boncassen with a comparable courage and spirit and is similarly praised for his 'steady manliness'.[4] The context of romantic love between aristocrats and commoners ensures that the primary meaning of 'manliness' as fortitude in difficulties is enriched with a hint of chivalric devotion to a fair or noble lady. Dickens, self-consciously a man of the people, achieves a similar effect in *Bleak House*: the aristocratic Sir Leicester Dedlock nobly shields and protects his erring wife, conduct which is 'honourable, manly and true', though Dickens democratically insists that the 'commonest mechanic' may often do the same.[5] Dickens and Trollope, like their contemporaries Kingsley and Hughes, tried to make manliness an up-to-date practical ethic for everyman, supplanting the old aristocratic ideal of chivalry but retaining something of its glamour and moral grandeur.

As the novelists well knew, Edmund Burke had linked manliness and chivalry, heroism and generous feeling, in his famous elegy for Marie Antoinette and the *ancien régime*, lamenting the passing of the age of chivalry and of 'the nurse of manly sentiment and heroic enterprise'.[6] That may have been true in France, but Englishmen liked to think of themselves as more enduring in their manliness. As soon as Byron's Don Juan reached England from the continent 'his mind assumed a manlier vigour' from the prevailing moral atmosphere, or so the poet, tongue-in-cheek, would have us believe.[7] A generation later the desperately serious Mr Gladstone described his morally resolute sailor-brother as gifted with a manliness higher than his own.[8] The very fact that the brother was a sailor somehow ennobled his manliness with the best traditions of the senior service, the dauntless courage and enterprise of Drake and Nelson.

The Nelson touch dignified manliness in the works of Pierce Egan, the Regency sporting journalist. Egan insisted on pugilism as a very English sport, cultivating manly courage of the kind displayed by the sailors and soldiers who fought with Nelson and Wellington in

the long war against France. Military and patriotic feeling is
subsumed in the epithet 'manly' so that when a prize-fighter's
'manly heart' is grieved by the taunt of cowardice and he lunges at
his opponent's left eye one is encouraged to feel that a plucky blow
has been struck for England. Tom Cribb, champion of England,
won Egan's admiration chiefly for beating a Frenchman. When
'manliness' is attributed to the great pugilist 'Gentleman' Jackson
along with integrity, impartiality and good nature it is clear that
Egan means more than physical prowess: he has endowed his hero
with moral stature and essential Englishness.[9]

Egan's manly chauvinism has a pedigree. Milton the embattled
champion of the Commonwealth indulged in a comparable rhetoric, describing England under the Stuarts as a degenerate nation
fallen away from 'the apprehension of native liberty and true
manliness', now happily restored under Cromwell.[10] Burke's more
conservative vision of a disciplined national liberty attracted the
same language: 'I flatter myself that I love a manly, moral,
regulated liberty as well as any gentleman.'[11] Here 'manliness' and
'manly' register both a sense of achieved moral and political
maturity and a sturdy independent-minded individualism.

All these added layers of meaning complicate and enrich the basic
meaning of 'manly' and 'manliness' as physical and moral strength
and maturity. It may be helpful to inspect the varieties of manliness
more closely under different headings. As it has emerged 'manliness'
may relate to physical vigour and prowess like that of Egan's noble
prize-fighters, or to patriotic and military qualities, or to the
traditions of chivalry, or to a variety of moral qualities ranging from
Fielding's genial benevolence to the most awe-inspiring moral
rigour which could command the respect of a Gladstone. Each
nuance of meaning mingles and overlaps with the others, so when
the Victorians preached a gospel of 'Christian manliness' almost
every good and perfect thing was potentially included under that
generous label. For the purposes of the present discussion 'manliness' can be summarized as physical manliness, ideas of chivalry and
gentlemanliness, and moral manliness, all of which tend to
incorporate something of the patriotic and military qualities which
'manliness' may also connote.

PHYSICAL MANLINESS

One of the unflattering descriptions of the merely muscular
Christianity attributed to Kingsley and Hughes asserted it was the

capacity to 'fear God and walk a thousand miles in a thousand hours'.[12] Kingsley and Hughes were certainly God-fearing, and no mean walkers, but the specific reference is to the not particularly pious pedestrianism of one Captain Barclay, who did it for a wager at Newmarket.[13] Newmarket, betting and physical hardihood denote the slightly raffish outdoor atmosphere of the English tradition of physical manliness. Overseas visitors like the American writer R. W. Emerson and the French critic Hippolyte Taine were fascinated by what seemed to be a national habit of 'manly exercises' which fostered the indigenous 'constitutional energy' and contributed to the physical and moral vigour of the race. Pierre de Coubertin, founder of the modern Olympic games, saw the athletic traditions of England, perpetuated in schools and colleges, as a model for the rejuvenation of France after the humiliations of the Franco-Prussian War. His book on this subject paid tribute to *Tom Brown's Schooldays* as a classic of physical manliness, among other things, by quoting extensively from it.[14]

English sturdy manliness is at least as old as mediaeval hunting and falconry. King James' book of sports (1617) regulated rather than instituted archery practice and the games of the village green. Traditional village cricket has continued down to our own day. While cricket as 'the gentleman's game' has been much praised as a model of fairness and itself a moral discipline, other traditional sports have been less respectable. There was always the risk of corruption through betting and cynical professionalism. But even apart from this the pugilistic contests at county fairs, the gladiatorial football matches in Cumberland described by Hugh Walpole,[15] the casual brutality of unsupervised school games all involved the possibility of injury, cruelty and disorder. This seldom distressed the apologists of sturdy manliness. There is plenty of fresh air and physical knockabout in the earnestly Rousseauistic novels of Thomas Day and Henry Brooke published in the later eighteenth century but still read and admired by Victorians such as Kingsley and Hughes. Alexander Macmillan, their publisher, even proposed a series of articles on eighteenth-century 'muscular Christianity' which would include Day and Brooke.[16] Maria Edgeworth, a friend of Thomas Day and a nursery favourite with the Hughes family, was less aggressively in favour of sturdiness for its own sake but even she made a model father insist on his son Frank learning to ride and being sent off to school to be 'roughed about among boys, or he will never learn to be a man, and able to live among men'.[17]

Throughout the nineteenth century this rough and ready

tradition of physical sturdiness persisted at different levels of society, with varying degrees of formal organization, and often in the teeth of dominant or 'respectable' public opinion. Miss Edgeworth's *Frank* was published in 1822. Angus Wilson has described how in the 1890s the old and rather brutal world of prize-fighting and the turf and manly exercise chiefly as a spectator-sport enjoyed a new lease of life, a return almost to the raffish 'Corinthianism' as it was sometimes called of the Regency era.[18] There are passing references to this 'Corinthianism' in the poetry of Byron and his Irish friend Tom Moore,[19] but the Homer of Regency manliness who conferred epic status upon sporting events was Pierce Egan. His *Life in London* (1822) (sometimes known as *Tom and Jerry* from its central figures) celebrated the dissipations and sporting diversions of the metropolis in a tiresome canting jargon embellished with details of the reckless wagers and wild drinking-bouts which tended to be associated with sportsmen or 'the Fancy'. Pugilism was Egan's main interest, but he made space for other sports and diversions such as dog-fighting and cock-fighting. In a later book, *Pierce Egan's Book of Sports* (1832), he covers a wider range of activities: horse-racing, hunting, cricket, angling and shooting among others, and adopts a more defensive tone. He is anxious to point out that sporting occasions bring all classes of people together:

the money is continually changing masters at such times – the rich man spends it freely, and the poor fellow finds the advantages resulting from these sort of amusements for the sale of his wares.

He still writes best about pugilism but now goes out of his way to defend the prizefighters as men of scrupulous integrity, incorruptible even when large sums are risked on their prowess. He commends their courage and chauvinistically champions sturdy English pugilism against French dancing and duelling which he sees as more frivolous and more dangerous forms of exercise.[20]

Sturdy manliness needed more defence as the unregenerate aristocratic Corinthianism of the Regency fell under the shadow of more domestic values, an easy victim of middle-class morality. The schoolboy Thackeray had loved Pierce Egan, for the illustrations as much as for the text, but by 1860 he felt the world had changed utterly. While the pictures were still entertaining the writing now seemed a little vulgar and flashy and the descriptions of Regency London 'more curious than amusing', a lost world and a different age.[21] That earlier age lived on in memory, crystallized into myth, a brilliant and brittle Vanity Fair, as Thackeray's most famous novel had demonstrated, coarser but possibly gayer than the present.

The Duke of Wellington was the most celebrated figure of the Regency era to survive into the middle years of Victoria's reign. As long as he lived no Englishman could forget the remark (which he may never have made) that the battle of Waterloo was won on the playing-fields of Eton. Even before Waterloo he had helped to secure the English legend of sporting manliness in his enthusiastic hunting expeditions behind the lines of Torres Vedras in mid-campaign during the Peninsular War.[22] The connections between sporting and military manliness were already well-established. The eighteenth-century poet William Somerville had celebrated the chase as '. . . the sport of kings; / Image of war without its guilt'[23] and this was repeated, with ironic qualification, by the nineteenth-century novelist R. S. Surtees as 'the sport of kings, the image of war without its guilt and only five-and-twenty per cent of its danger'.[24] War could be regarded as the image of sport, particularly when boxers fought for their country as nobly as for their prize-money. Tom Moore's poetic 'Epistle from Tom Crib to Big Ben' (1815), a satire on the unsporting punishment and exile of Napoleon, is couched in the boxing slang of the day and acknowledges indebtedness to *Boxiana*, Pierce Egan's annals of the prize ring. Moore's satire pays tribute to Lifeguardsman Shaw, the 'Cheesemonger', one of the finest prizefighters of the age, who died heroically at Waterloo after inflicting almost unbelievable damage on the ranks of the French.

> Oh, shade of the *Cheesemonger*! you, who alas,
> *Doubled up*, by the dozen, those mounseers in brass
> On that great day of *milling*, when blood lay in lakes,
> When Kings held the bottle, and Europe the stakes.

Sir Walter Scott, who had met Shaw in London, was so moved by his heroism that he arranged to have his body brought back to his native Nottinghamshire. A generation later Thomas Hughes found a place for Shaw in *Tom Brown's Schooldays* as the opponent of the gentlemanly former champion of the west country.[25]

In the 1830s and 1840s, in the wake of Waterloo, sport and military heroism were often associated. Charles Lever's popular novels of sporting and military adventure kept harking back to the Napoleonic wars for examples of sturdy heroism and a consummate horsemanship first learned on the hunting field. In *Yeast*, Kingsley's first novel, this rather rollicking world of physical adventure on horseback is deliberately evoked, but already with a certain nostalgia. Railways, respectability, the growth of organized institutions and social change gradually altered the nature of mid-Victorian sporting manliness. School sports lost their innocence when they came to be organized by the masters to keep boys out of trouble and began to form part of the official school curriculum.[26] The hunting field became less ribald and less exclusive when ladies and Londoners were able to travel to it by train.[27] R. S. Surtees' popular novels about Jorrocks the sporting grocer demonstrated that the old-fashioned gentry no longer had the monopoly of the chase. An increasingly democratic age responded less favourably to privileged self-indulgence in manly exercises. For Matthew Arnold the sporting diversions of the aristocracy were no substitute for intellectual culture, a merely barbarous activity when sweetness and light were in such short supply.[28]

By the beginning of Victoria's reign the Master of Foxhounds was bound by regulations to protect farm land and deal fairly with farmers. The old-fashioned manly bully was no longer allowed to have it all his own way, as the Hon. Grantley Fitzhardinge Berkeley discovered to his cost. A blundering and blustering aristocrat who spent his childhood 'seeking sport wherever it was attainable' and who learnt the art of self-defence as a way of dealing with his inferiors 'when the latter were insolently aggressive', he found himself facing court-proceedings in 1836 when he savagely horse-whipped the proprietor of *Fraser's Magazine* for publishing an unfavourable review of his novel.[29]

Aggressive manliness, whether civil or military, was more manageable as myth than as a habit of life. G. A. Lawrence, son of a clergyman with aristocratic connections, wrote a series of novels which glamorized a vanishing world, the hard-riding, hard-living, brutal world of Berkeley and the sporting aristocracy. Five years Tom Hughes' junior at Rugby, Lawrence produced his first novel *Guy Livingstone* in 1857, the same year as *Tom Brown's Schooldays*. Guy is physically indomitable and has never learnt to submit to anything or any man. Horses, hunting and fighting are his chief interests. His agonizing death after a hunting fall may demonstrate his 'brave heart and iron nerve' at its best, but he dies a sinful and essentially unrepentant hero, though the author has no reproaches for him.[30] Royston Keane, 'the best swordsman in the Light Brigade', reproduces this amoral heroism in *Sword and Gown* published two years later. His death at Balaclava crowns a passionate, sinful life, but Lawrence indulgently hopes

> That heaven may yet have more mercy than man,
> On such a bold rider's soul.[31]

Once Tennyson had celebrated the charge of the Light Brigade the Victorian public perversely began to regard the disaster of Balaclava as another Waterloo, a yet more glorious achievement of British manliness under arms. Lawrence's hard-bitten lawless adventurer is actually an unusual Crimean hero, for by the 1850s the glamour of military achievement was often a starting-point for homilies on Christian heroism and soldiers of the cross, a theme which will be discussed later. Frankly impious military novels such as *Sword and Gown* were conspicuous against this background, and Lawrence was accused of founding a school of 'very muscular literature'.[32] The allegations of merely muscular Christianity in the novels of Kingsley and Hughes began to circulate about the same time, and inevitably, if unfairly, some of Lawrence's reputation for celebrating brutal lawlessness rubbed off on them. Other writers who had no claim to moral or religious seriousness added to the corpus of 'muscular literature' for which Kingsley and Hughes were held responsible. Henry Kingsley, Charles' impecunious, scapegrace younger brother, is a case in point. He drew on his experience as a trooper in Australia to produce *Geoffry Hamlyn* (1859), a tale of adventure and physical hardihood in the Australian outback. One of the minor characters of the novel, the Revd Frank Maberly, is introduced tongue-in-cheek as 'a very muscular Christian indeed', though he has no special message to preach.[33] An earlier novel, F. E. Smedley's *Frank Fairlegh*, celebrates a similarly secular physical manliness and hardihood. One of the book's heroes is Harry Oaklands, who has 'a proud consciousness of power in his every look and motion, which possessed for me an irresistible attraction'. There is a generous allocation of daredevil horsemanship and some rowing and boxing to add to the interest of the novel.[34]

The morally ambiguous myth of sporting manliness and physical hardihood celebrated in popular novels and sustained by the combined efforts of Pierce Egan and the Duke of Wellington's foxhounds truculently outfaced all criticism in the middle years of the nineteenth century. Insofar as the apologists of Christian manliness sought to incorporate aspects of it this represented an act of defiance. Life was earnest in mid-Victorian Britain and manly recreations might well appear a waste of valuable time even if the moral dangers were disregarded. No one ever wasted less time than

Anthony Trollope, but there is something defiant and self-conscious about his love of hunting. He certainly enjoyed the exercise, but self-congratulation may have had something to do with it as well. After the poverty and difficulties of his early life it must have been specially pleasing to ride to hounds like an old-fashioned English man and gentleman. Cheerfully, though not altogether convincingly, Trollope championed the morality of fox-hunting against the onslaught of the historian E. A. Freeman in the columns of the *Fortnightly Review*.[35] He made a point of indulging himself with hunting scenes in many of his novels. He had no doubts that hunting was a healthy and wholesome occupation but he was uneasily aware that it might not be quite respectable enough for a clergyman to be seen taking part. In the first half of the nineteenth century it was increasingly customary for the clergy of the established church to identify with the landed gentry and sometimes to share in their sports and amusements. But 'serious' clergymen, especially Evangelicals, had always dissociated themselves from this. Henry Philpots, the notoriously High Church Bishop of Exeter, had tried unsuccessfully to ban his clergy from hunting. In 1859 the *Saturday Review* was willing to approve of a hunting clergy only if this did not interfere with parish duties or scandalize the parishioners.[36] Trollope tackles the issue in *Framley Parsonage* (1861) and leaves the reader to wonder whether it is legitimate for the Revd Mark Robarts to spend quite so much time hunting in the occasionally ungodly company of the gentry.

As the influence of the Oxford Movement spread there were frequent attempts to foster a more exclusively clerical consciousness, a sense of the clergyman as primarily a priest of God rather than a gentleman with an education and a black coat. College sports, though harmless in themselves, might perhaps be rather time-consuming and frivolous pursuits for those preparing themselves for the Christian ministry, it was argued.[37] This new clericalism, which frowned not only on clerical sportsmen but on any kind of clerical worldliness, appalled that manly clergyman Charles Kingsley, who rode to hounds himself on occasion and whose funeral was attended by the local hunt. He found this religious exclusiveness theologically repugnant as it enshrined a distinction between secular and sacred, world and spirit, which his manly Christianity manfully opposed. The ostrich-hunting Bishop Synesius in his historical novel *Hypatia* represents a deliberate taunt at clerical exclusiveness. He would have been well pleased by Dean Stanley's judgement at his memorial service that his life had proved 'that a Christian clergyman need not be a member of a separate caste, and a stranger to the common interests of his countrymen'.[38] Kingsley's personal receptiveness to the tradition of sturdy manliness, and his literary exploitation of it, enabled him as a clergyman to become a particularly effective advocate of a Christianity which could be demonstrated to be manly. Thomas Hughes offered a similar combination of manliness and Christianity, enriched by the experience of a practising sportsman well aware of the English traditions of physical manliness. He wrote not as a clergyman but a layman, a Christian gentleman imaginatively and practically responsive to the ideals implicit in the time-honoured notions of chivalry and the gentleman.

CHIVALRY AND THE GENTLEMAN

Pierce Egan's manly and disciplined pugilists, the manly heroes of Waterloo or Balaclava, Trollope's manly lovers and Dickens' manly aristocrats and mechanics all help to democratize and domesticate the traditional notion of chivalry with its associations of dedicated courage, loyalty, unselfish devotion and protection of the weak. In nineteenth-century England and in America, as recent studies have demonstrated, chivalry enjoyed a new lease of life.[39] By the 1850s chivalry had come to be regarded as one of the attributes of the true English gentleman. The knight of mediaeval chivalry and the gentleman of earlier times had fused in the popular imagination into a conventional moral ideal democratically applicable to all classes of society. But knights were originally a warrior class of mounted and fully-armed fighting men; gentlemen were originally those heraldically entitled to bear arms though not among the nobility. The shift of meaning of both terms from description of military and social status to ideal of conduct conveniently allowed virtue to retain something of the dignity and glamour of high social standing. From New Testament times the image of the whole armour of God has invested righteousness with romantic dash and spirit, but in the rapidly changing social, economic and religious conditions of mid-Victorian Britain the classless and timeless moral possibilities of true knightliness and true gentility were particularly useful to the preacher and the moralist. It was natural that they should pass into the preaching of attractively manly Christianity.

Questions of class, individual conduct and public duty might seem to be characteristically Victorian obsessions but they were fundamental also to mediaeval discussions of the nature of knightliness. The nineteenth century was not the only epoch of social change: the epidemics of fourteenth-century Europe had decimated the ranks of hereditary knights and nobles and inaugurated a redistribution of wealth, particularly in the Low Countries, which permitted *parvenu* families to purchase patents of nobility. The military life had been both the occupation and the *raison d'être* of the old nobility, the basis of an intricately evolved code of honour. But the new nobles had neither the traditions nor the enthusiasms of an hereditary warrior-caste, which presented their rulers with certain problems. A ducal ordinance of Philip the Good of Burgundy, issued in 1438, enacted that the children of new nobles were liable to taxation unless they followed a military career. Increasingly the military necessities of individual princes required knightliness to be the service of the prince and the public good as well as a code of personal honour, an ambivalence which persisted to later ages. The pressures of the time renewed the age-old debate about the nature of true nobility, discussed in works such as Jean Miélot's *La Controverse de Noblesse* (1449), translated for Philip the Good from an Italian source.

This work is in the form of a dialogue between an idle man of noble birth and an active citizen of humble birth, rival claimants for the hand of a lady. Their rivalry is left unresolved, but true nobility emerges from the discussion not so much as an hereditary right or an individualistic ethic as a quality of life achieved through active participation in politics, public office and war. Jean de Bueil's *Le Jouvencel* (1466) proposed an even more explicitly moral definition of knightliness as unselfish sacrifice for a comrade, loyalty, self-forgetfulness in the heat of battle.[40]

Elsewhere in fourteenth- and fifteenth-century Europe, in Provence, Italy and England, the argument recurs with varying emphases. In the *Roman de la Rose*, an influential work translated for English readers by Geoffrey Chaucer, Nature insists that true gentility is meaningless without an accompanying goodness of heart.[41] Early Italian poets such as Guido Guinizelli of Bologna had insisted that proper nobility or gentility was not to be found even in a king 'except the heart there be a gentle man's'.[42] Guido's disciple Dante drew on Juvenal and Aristotle in his treatise on *Monarchy* to make the point that nobility, whether hereditary or not, was essentially a moral quality. In the third canzone of the *Convito* Dante returned to the theme, insisting that neither ancestry nor riches on their own could constitute true nobility, which by definition connoted goodness of heart in him who had it.[43] Chaucer's *Wife of Bath's Tale* follows Dante in the pious observation that

> Crist wole we clayme of hym oure gentillesse
> Nat of oure eldres for hire old richesse.[44]

By the end of the fifteenth century, notions of chivalry, gentility and nobility had come to connote personal honour and public and patriotic virtue as well as, and sometimes instead of, hereditary privilege. This affected Victorian notions of chivalry and the gentleman and of manly conduct in two ways, both directly and through the subsequent history of ideals of honour and noble conduct in the Italian courts, in Elizabethan and Stuart England and in the eighteenth century. The direct influence of mediaeval chivalry will be considered first.

The Victorian cult of chivalry and Victorian mediaevalism generally have been affectionately surveyed by historians of art and architecture as well as of literature.[45] The enormous popularity of Scott's novels, especially *Ivanhoe* (1819), helped to make the old chivalry a valuable imaginative resource in the midst of the social and economic dislocations of the industrial revolution. Disaffected Tory noblemen grumbling at the Whiggish economies of Queen Victoria's rather prosaic coronation organized the elaborately authentic Egremont Tournament (1839) as an aristocratic extravaganza.[46] In *The Broad Stone of Honour* (1822) the dreamy idealist Kenelm Digby had pleaded eloquently for a new knightliness. Benjamin Disraeli, romantic, opportunist, ambitious, attempted to exploit Digby's enthusiasm in his 'Young England' novels, presenting the young Queen Victoria as the source and object of knightly service, presiding over English chivalry. His fictional hero Coningsby, an aristocrat born to a tradition of public and political service, is required to prove that he has intrinsic as well as merely inherited nobility and personal worth before he can marry his beloved Edith.

Much of this revitalized chivalry was amiably preposterous. The beginning of the Egremont Tournament was ruined by bad weather and greeted with howls of derision. The youthful artist Dicky Doyle produced maliciously accurate sketches of knights in armour sheltering under large umbrellas. Middle-class common sense was unsympathetic to backward-looking aristocratic extravagance. Novelists such as Disraeli who celebrated it were mercilessly treated by later and greater writers: Thackeray's wicked parody *Codlingsby*, a tiny neglected masterpiece, suggested that Coningsby and his associates were anachronisms in the nineteenth century.[47] Thackeray's literary disciple Anthony Trollope cast a cold eye on obscurantist Tory mediaevalism in *Barchester Towers*: the ultra-conservative Miss Thorne of Ullathorne has organized a *fête champêtre*, as she calls it, for the local tenantry, with a quintain for modern knights, or at least gentlemen, to tilt lances at. Even her brother grumbles that the quintain is a 'rattletrap'. Only a farmer's son can be persuaded to take part, and his horse trips over the trailing lance before he can get anywhere near the target.[48] In Cardiff William Burges might design a pseudo-mediaeval castle with chivalric trappings for the wealthy and eccentric Marquess of Bute,[49] but chivalry as a diversion and an idle dream seemed to find little favour with the earnest and energetic Victorian middle classes. They could respect mediaeval knightliness and savour something of its glamour and glitter only by insisting on chivalry as a timeless and classless moral ideal.

Prince Albert, noble and romantic but also practical and public-spirited, a man of science interested in drains and the Great Exhibition, helped to link essentially bourgeois values with the traditions of chivalry. Landseer painted him many times, in the robes of mediaeval chivalry and in the garb of any respectable Victorian gentleman.[50] The greatest work of ethically self-conscious Victorian mediaevalism, Tennyson's *Idylls of the King*, was dedicated to Albert's memory in 1862 and E. H. Corbould's Memorial Portrait of the Prince Consort (1863) depicted him as a mediaeval knight who had nobly fought his last battle.[51] The *Saturday Review* caught the tone of this updated chivalry in its obituary notice for Prince Albert by depicting him as an example of honour and manly virtue prominent in

all those benevolent enterprises for the relief of misery, and for improving the lot and character of the people, which are the prosaic but solid substitutes for the visionary enterprises of knight-errantry in forming the character of a gentleman at the present day.[52]

Very much in the same spirit Charles Kingsley and Thomas Hughes, manly Christians too brisk and busy in the real world for the fantasies of Cardiff Castle or the Egremont Tournament, were able to indulge an imaginative sympathy for the knightliness of old romance by linking it with the practical and contemporary concerns of the heroes of their fiction. In Kingsley's novel *Two Years Ago* the mediaeval fortress of Ehrenbreitstein which had allegedly inspired

Kenelm Digby's *Broad Stone of Honour* forms part of the setting of a
book whose hero is not a knight-errant but a doctor. Thomas
Hughes' hymn 'O God of truth' contrived to make the manly figure
of Christ simultaneously an energetic Christian socialist and a
mediaeval chevalier crusading for truth and right.[53]

But chivalry as a moral ideal also filtered into the Victorian
notion of the gentleman and the manly Christian by more indirect
means. Late mediaeval notions of knightliness, nobility or gentility
as personal honour and public virtue rather than hereditary right
passed over from the Burgundian Court and elsewhere into the
Renaissance cult of honour and fame associated with the courts of
Italy. Castiglione's *Il Cortegiano* (*The Courtier*), an influential work in
England in Sir Thomas Hoby's translation (1561), suggested that
on the whole it was better that a courtier should be of noble birth,
but came to terms with moral and social realities by admitting that
'in men of base degree may raign the very same vertues that are in
gentlemen'.[54] The book as a whole was devoted to identifying and
describing these distinguishing courtly virtues. A generation later
Spenser's *Faerie Queene*, Charles Kingsley's favourite poem,[55] aimed
'to fashion a gentleman or noble person in vertuous and gentle
discipline'. In Book III the knights of an already past age were
invested with an ethical purpose which made them exemplars for
posterity. Spenser exclaims

> O goodly usage of those antique times,
> In which the sword was servant unto right;
> When not for malice and contentious crimes
> But all for praise, and proof of manly might,
> The martiall brood accustomed to fight.[56]

This chivalrous, noble and virtuously disciplined 'manly might'
appealed strongly to the imagination and the moral instincts of the
Victorian manly Christians, and to Kingsley in particular. In
Westward Ho! Frank Leigh, Kingsley's euphuistic Renaissance hero,
is a reconstruction of the literary image of knightliness or gentility
given currency by Spenser and by his contemporary Sir Philip
Sidney, courtier, poet and soldier. Edwardians as well as Victorians
fell under the spell: as late as 1913 the highest praise Sir Arthur
Quiller-Couch could bestow on Scott's last expedition was to link it
with the spirit of Sidney.[57]

But the gentleman or noble person, like the Victorian manly
Christian, had to achieve virtue in the affairs of society and the state
as well as in himself. Spenser's original scheme for the *Faerie Queene*
was to idealize the private virtues as Aristotle describes them and

then to explore public virtue through the experience of Arthur's kingship. The second part was never accomplished, but there are traces of the scheme in Book V, which describes the adventures of Artegal, representing justice. Spenser had encountered harsh political realities in Ireland, some of which are reflected in *Westward Ho!* His patron Lord Grey's ruthless suppression of the Desmond rebellion provided a model for the activities of Artegal and his henchman Talus with his iron flail. The best Victorian account of the *Faerie Queene*, by Dean Church, dwells on this severe and practical aspect of Spenser's vision, attributing to him 'his full proportion of the stern and high manliness of his generation'. Church was a devout but thoughtful clergyman who saw a lesson for his own time in Spenser's combination of chivalric and ethical idealism with a more rugged practical manliness, 'the quality of soul which frankly accepts the conditions in human life, of labour, of obedience, of effort, of unequal success'.[58]

High-minded gentlemen and noble persons imbued with the spirit of Sir Philip Sidney or Edmund Spenser might unhappily find themselves on different sides in the English Civil War half a century later. Clarendon's lament for the Royalist Viscount Falkland, killed at the battle of Newbury, is an elegy for one of the last of the Renaissance heroes. He was

a person of such prodigious parts of learning and knowledge, of that inimitable sweetness and delight in conversation, of so obliging a humanity and goodness to mankind, and of that primitive simplicity and integrity of life, that if there were no other brand upon this odious and accursed civil war than that single loss, it must be most infamous and execrable to all posterity.[59]

The Cavalier Lovelace could proclaim the chivalry and honour of his cause in 'Lines to Lucasta, on going to the wars'. But the Roundheads represented an alternative virtue, no less noble but grimmer, often less aristocratic, stiffened by recollections of the sword of the Lord and of Gideon, and this prevailed for a time. The victorious Roundheads found themselves involved in the affairs of the Commonwealth, and this drew attention once again to the tensions between individual and public virtue, the strenuous private morality of Puritanism and the requirements of the state to which John Milton devoted creative energy and his eyesight. The Rule of the Saints involved a measure of tyranny in England and massacres in Ireland. But at least it showed that spiritual fervour and moral energy could be harnessed to the service of a whole society.

This had its effect upon the Victorians, conscious of the romance of the Cavaliers and the legend of quixotic loyalty which they enshrined, but impressed by the Puritans and deeply influenced by Carlyle's rehabilitation of Oliver Cromwell. Ford Madox Brown, who had painted a manly Christ washing Peter's feet, also painted *Cromwell on his Farm*, brooding and awaiting his destiny.[60] When the old Roman Catholic hierarchy of bishops was restored in England in 1850 it gave the House of Commons an opportunity to fight the Civil War all over again. Lord John Russell was convinced that this so-called 'Papal Aggression' threatened liberty and invoked the moral authority of Hampden and Pym. Gladstone, who thought it did not and was afraid that anti-Catholic measures would strain the loyalty of Catholic citizens, countered with the Royalist principle of loyalty represented by Clarendon and Newcastle.[61] Romantic loyalties and moral protest, the spirit of Clarendon and the spirit of Hampden, can be found side by side in the manly Christians Kingsley and Hughes, often in unresolved tension, as it will appear.

It is usual to see in the eighteenth century a period of reaction from the excitements of the Civil War. Eighteenth-century moral theory tends to be purged of the 'enthusiasm', the sectarian fanaticisms which had driven men to arms and wrought havoc in the state. Instead of the loneliness of Puritan introspection or the courtly grandeurs of Renaissance gentility practical benevolence and rational virtue supported by generous and honest sentiment were advocated by the optimistic latitudinarian preachers of the age. Sir Richard Steele's *The Christian Hero* (1701) helped to set the tone. Charity and 'walking as Christ did' were incumbent upon all Christians, but the gentleman had a special responsibility in this respect since his superior wealth and social position gave him better opportunities to do good and set a good example.[62]

Samuel Richardson's *Sir Charles Grandison* (1754) is perhaps the supreme work to commend this intensely social conception of virtue. M. A. Doody has pointed out that the name 'Grandison' and other names in the novel can be found in Clarendon's *History of the Rebellion*, a discreet method of linking the new world of social benevolence with Clarendon's Royalist heroes representing older and more individualistic types of honour and nobility.[63] But if Richardson wants to exploit the heroic glamour of the Cavaliers he is embarrassed and constrained by the lingering influence of the morality of the Roundheads, derived ultimately from the Gospels. M. A. Doody argues that it is an article of faith with Richardson that the rational code of worldly social virtue and the code of the Gospel must ultimately be one and the same for Grandison, but the Gospel imperatives of unworldly self-abnegation, humility and meekness do not come easily or naturally to the great and good man of the world.[64]

Richardson's almost offensively virtuous hero had a mixed reception among the Victorians. The novel was often reprinted,[65] but in Charlotte M. Yonge's *The Heir of Redclyffe* (1855) Grandison is linked with the pseudo-hero rather than the real hero. Philip Morville is a priggish and unattractive moralist lacking the self-awareness which the events of the novel slowly teach him. The true hero, his much more attractive cousin Guy Morville, is linked not with Richardson but with the rehabilitated chivalric tradition. He is considered as a modern Sir Galahad and finally emerges from moral testing as a proven knight of the round table.[66] George Meredith, more severely, saw in Grandison an example of dangerously impractical moral system in *The Ordeal of Richard Feverel* (1859). The system-obsessed Austin Feverel considers one of the daughters of the Richardson-obsessed Mrs Grandison as a bride for his son, but this is just one of the many damaging mistakes which needlessly create the ordeal of Richard Feverel.[67]

The main legacy of Richardson's Grandison to Victorian novelists, particularly the manly Christian novelists, seems to have been an object-lesson in what to avoid. To be successful in worldly terms, and to be interesting in fiction, the Victorian hero needed qualities of self-assertion and determination rather than the humbler, more passive qualities of patience and heroic martyrdom. His inner life and inner dilemmas could not be ignored but Kingsley and Hughes in particular found it prudent to concentrate much more on the life of action, endowing their heroes with social virtues which were an energy as well as an ornament in their society. In effect if not always literally they were Christian soldiers on active service for the benefit of the whole nation.

This strenuous ethic of service, which extended democratically from gentlemen like Tom Brown to tailor-poets like Kingsley's Alton Locke, can be partly explained in historical and secular terms. Richard Shannon has argued that mid-Victorian reforms in the universities, the Civil Service and the army all reflected a self-conscious liberal theory of the state which was beginning to establish itself at the time. Indolence and irresponsibility were gradually outlawed. Gone were the palmy days of gentlemen-idlers in the universities and government offices, derided in *Tom Brown at Oxford* and *Little Dorrit*. They were being swept away on the same tide of reform that abolished military commissions by purchase. In every case new standards of professionalism and service to the nation were established. The modern meritocracy envisaged by John Stuart Mill had begun to evolve. In theory at least education and social position were no longer of much account unless they were accompanied by integrity and a capacity for social usefulness.[68]

Mid-Victorian fiction reflects the changing atmosphere. Given the right opportunities and enough talent and determination, any man could succeed and do the state and his fellow men some service, irrespective of birth or rank. Mrs Craik's hero in *John Halifax, Gentleman* (1856) grafts the tradition of moral gentlemanliness on to the contemporary ethic of self-help popularized by Samuel Smiles. John Halifax, once a penniless orphan in a provincial town, heroically works his way into a position of considerable power and influence. His son Guy, embarrassed by tales of his father's early struggles, observes 'we are gentlefolks now', to which his father replies 'we always were, my son'.[69] Charles Dickens, a self-made man himself, was impatient with the incompetence of effete aristocrats and 'gentlemen' in high places and in the Circumlocution Office in *Little Dorrit*. Pip's ill-founded gentlemanly aspirations in *Great Expectations* are sardonically treated. The plot evolves to embarrass Pip by revealing that the mysterious income which sustains his illusions comes from the good-hearted but socially disgraceful escaped convict Magwitch. The closing stage of the novel somewhat hastily outlines an alternative moral gentlemanliness based on an ethic of unselfishness, generosity and patient hard work. The most influential attempt to substitute ethical (and religious) values for merely social qualities in the definition of the Victorian gentleman is represented by Thomas Arnold's labours at Rugby school, which will be discussed later.

Moral gentlemanliness of the kind explored by Mrs Craik, Dickens and Dr Arnold was at least notionally classless and contemporary. Elizabeth Barrett Browning's comment that 'all men [are] possible heroes' reflects the same attempt to modernize and democratize chivalric and gentlemanly heroism. Charles Kingsley and Thomas Hughes develop the manly Christian heroes of their fiction in the same idiom. But the glitter and the glory embedded in the long history of chivalry and gentlemanliness linger seductively in their writings. For all their professions of Christian socialism they avail themselves of the romance and the implicit class-distinction of older tradition as a tactic for commending Christian manliness.

MORAL MANLINESS

The traditions of physical manliness and of chivalry and gentleman-liness which helped to mould mid-Victorian Christian manliness were social and literary phenomena. They have obvious relevance to those aspects of manly Christianity which reflect and operate in terms of the general social and literary atmosphere of the day. But they belong to the village green and the market-place, the houses of the great and the humble, rather than to the pulpit. Moral and religious considerations frequently arise, as we have seen, but in the context of the world rather than the church. Since Kingsley in particular felt uneasy about hard-and-fast distinctions between church and world this may hardly seem to matter, but the preaching of Christian manliness in his novels and in those of Thomas Hughes related to a tradition of preaching moral manliness as well as to more secular traditions.

St Paul can probably take the credit for inaugurating this tradition of moral manliness. Athletic and military imagery enliven his account of the Christian life: he often uses the term *agon*, 'race' or 'contest', and describes running the race for the prize of the high calling of God as well as fighting the good fight of faith.[70] This strenuous version of the spiritual life was reflected in the religious writings of Coleridge and his disciples Thomas Arnold and F. D. Maurice, who in their turn influenced the work of Kingsley and Hughes as it will be shown. But it persisted in popular preaching and religious apologetic at a much less sophisticated level. C. H. Spurgeon, the great Baptist preacher, roundly asserted

When I say that a man in Christ *is* a man, I mean that, if he be truly in Christ, he is therefore manly. There has got abroad a notion, somehow, that if you become a Christian you must sink your manliness and turn milksop.[71]

This robust rhetoric might have come from Thomas Hughes' *The Manliness of Christ*. But Spurgeon operated in terms of a fervent Evangelicalism which the more liberal-minded Thomas Hughes and Charles Kingsley rather disliked. It was all very well to insist that Christianity was manly but examples were needed to get the message across. The greatest hero of the age, the Duke of Wellington, might have been useful in this respect, but unfortunately his manly exploits in the field could not disguise the fact that he was a little lax in private life. When he died in 1852 he rather embarrassed the preachers who would have liked to exploit the occasion. Newman Hall, a prominent Evangelical, pointedly said nothing of Wellington's Christian character 'because I know nothing' and went on to discuss Christian as opposed to military warfare, the campaign against 'all that dishonours God, and degrades and oppresses man'.[72] This was rather dull stuff. Edward Hawkins, Provost of Oriel (Hughes' old college), was very little better though more flattering to the Duke. He took him as an example of the combination of moral and physical courage. In a sermon for the start of the university term he began promisingly by mentioning the hero the nation mourned in these terms, but this was only a pretext for preaching about courageous resistance to temptation and the importunities of evil companions.[73] Thomas Hughes made a much better job of the same theme in *Tom Brown at Oxford* by inventing an interesting manly hero and staying with him through thick and thin, through adventures on the river and adventures of the spirit.

Preachers could hardly be expected to invent heroes. If the Duke of Wellington obstinately refused to fulfil the role of Christian hero perhaps there were other great soldiers and patriots who might prove less intractable. Militarism was very much in the air in the 1850s, with the Crimean War and the Indian Mutiny and intermittent rumours of French invasion which led to the foundation of the Volunteer Corps in 1859. Kingsley and Hughes shared in the excitement and exploited it for their own ends in their novels, but the popular preachers of the day were there before them. They found several devout and heroic soldiers who had distinguished themselves in recent engagements and helped to give an attractively literal significance to the language of Christian warfare and the Church Militant. Major-General Havelock, hero of Lucknow in the Indian Mutiny, was one favourite example. Captain Hedley Vicars of the 93rd Regiment, killed in the Crimea in 1855, was another. Charles Kingsley was upset by his death and tried to wring from it the religious consolation that that doughty Christian hero had undoubtedly ascended into heaven to be with God.[74] But Havelock and Hedley Vicars and, some time later, General Gordon, were all Christian heroes of a decidedly Evangelical stamp, ruthlessly exploited in Evangelical pulpits and in the Evangelical religious press,[75] and Kingsley felt uneasy about this. In his Preface to the

1859 edition of *Yeast* he speculated as to whether Havelock and Hedley Vicars owed their gallantry to their arguably rather narrow Evangelical creed or 'to the simple fact of their being – like others – English gentlemen'.[76]

This rather equivocal attitude to the tradition of moral and religious manliness, seeking to merge it in the more secular tradition of the gentleman, neatly illustrates the dilemma of the Victorian manly Christians, caught on the fence between the church and the world while trying to deny that the fence existed. Carlyle was constantly singing the praises of secular heroes and religious writers such as the ultra-High Church Revd John Mason Neale produced popular books with titles like *Tales and Sketches of Christian Heroism* (1854). Both writers exploited the contemporary taste for literature of hero-worship, but for different ends. The different kinds of hero-worship were indicated in a series of historical sketches published by Revd J. Hampden Gurney, Thomas Hughes' vicar in Marylebone, under the title *God's Heroes and the World's Heroes* (1858). This volume gave pride of place to Wilberforce and Howard the prison-reformer in preference to Wellington and Gustavus Adolphus. Kingsley and Hughes would not have insisted on the distinction. They admired pious philanthropists and soldiers alike, seeing in their dedicated service to the social and military needs of their country a service well pleasing to God whether undertaken in a religious spirit or not. Their novels belong with the contemporary rhetoric of moral manliness and heroic religion, expressed in innumerable sermons, articles and books, but they transcend it. Where the details of military prowess and heroic endeavour which had no overtly religious significance were often hurried over in pious productions of this kind as unimportant window-dressing, the manly adventures and vigorous activities of Tom Brown or Amyas Leigh draw in an unembarrassed fashion on the secular traditions of physical manliness and gentlemanliness and are demonstrated to be valuable and significant in themselves. The liberal religious outlook which they exemplify must now be considered, both as a reaction against narrow notions of saintliness and as a creative embodiment of the theological tradition stemming from Coleridge.

Sturdiness and the saints

Kingsley and Hughes undertook to bring manliness in its various manifestations to church, and to keep it awake when it got there. Their novels can be seen as an extended demonstration of their own manly enthusiasms given dramatic shape and confidently if at times tendentiously justified in the name of the living God who created the world and saw that it was good. Both men inherited the sporting interests and the Tory paternalist instincts of English country gentlemen of the old school. Kingsley's father had been a New Forest squire until he lost his money and took Holy Orders, and Thomas Hughes was the son of a Berkshire squire of literary tastes who was steeped in the traditions of the countryside.[1] The religious atmosphere and the historical circumstances of the 1840s and the 1850s caused them to transmute this heritage into an embattled Christian activism. The baptism of manliness caused them to do battle with Evangelical and Puseyite or Tractarian notions of saintliness which sometimes tended to disparage the present world and energetic devotion to its concerns. It also led them to espouse the tradition of vigorous, socially concerned liberal religion which will be discussed in the next chapter.

In theological matters Kingsley the clergyman had always more to say than Hughes the layman. Enthusiastic, energetic, too easily inclined to dramatic exaggeration and simple rhetorical polarities, Kingsley carried on the manly battle against unsatisfactory saintliness largely on his own, though Hughes was with him in spirit. Hughes had perhaps never come close enough to Evangelical and Tractarian spirituality to be seriously bothered by it, but Kingsley was the son of a clergyman who ended his career by presiding over an Evangelical parish in Chelsea, and his wife had come under Tractarian influence in youth. At one stage Kingsley himself seems to have been attracted by Tractarian ascetic discipline and in matters of church order and devotion at least he identified more with the High Church party than with any other, though stopping well short of the Anglo-Catholicism imparted to old-fashioned High Churchmanship by the Tractarian or Oxford Movement.[2]

As early as 1846 Kingsley was trying to establish his own religious position by attacking Tractarians and Evangelicals. He wanted to establish a polemical religious magazine and felt that

Its two mottoes should be Anti-Manichaeism – (and therefore Anti-Tractarian, and Anti-Evangelical) and Anti-Atheism… [It ought] to show how all this progress of society in the present day is really of God, and God's work, and has potential and latent spiritual elements.[3]

Kingsley's vigorous temperament and his liberal theology drove him to find an ultimate sanction for the splendours and energies of human nature and all human activity in the person of Christ,[4] a view which he felt bound to champion against the traditional dichotomies of church and world, body and soul. The most striking contemporary example of this was the withdrawn, ascetic spirituality commended by the leaders of the Oxford Movement, reviving the severe ideals of sanctity which the early church had advocated, partly under eastern pagan influences.[5] It was tempting, though inaccurate, for Kingsley to assimilate this to the extreme dualistic, ascetic religion of Mani, the third-century Babylonian thinker who taught that the material world was essentially demonic and that the soul of man consisted of particles of divine light trapped in the darkness of totally corrupt physical nature.[6] St Augustine was the real seminal figure in the history of the Christian dichotomy of the world and the spirit, the earthly and the heavenly cities, and both the older generation of Calvinist Evangelicals and the Tractarians followed him in stressing the total depravity of ordinary human nature and the necessity for holy contempt of the world.[7]

Kingsley, however, more at home in the English Pelagian tradition of practical good works in terms of the present world, dismissed all this as an ultimately unchristian rejection of what God had created. He was hardly the first to identify it with non-Christian eastern religions like Manichaeism: the early Coleridge and his friend Southey, for example, had repudiated such views as a pagan contamination of Christian doctrine. Southey's strident protests against celibate and ascetic religion rival Kingsley's own.[8]

The Tractarian and Evangelical ideas Kingsley lumped together in his condemnation of modern 'Manichaeism' repay investigation not only because they illuminate his radically different understanding of man but because they illustrate the real basis of his fundamental disagreement with John Henry Newman, once the most eloquent of Tractarian apologists, later a Roman convert. This finally issued in the famous controversy of 1864. Kingsley rather rashly claimed that 'Truth, for its own sake, had never been a virtue with the Roman clergy' and cited Newman as a case in point.[9] Newman retaliated by writing his spiritual autobiography *Apologia pro Vita Sua*. Kingsley's truculence was shamed by the dignity of Newman's prose and his reputation as a religious thinker has never recovered from Newman's withering dialectic. But perhaps Kingsley was rude rather than wrong. He was quite prepared to admit that full and absolute truth on all occasions was not necessarily a good idea and had said so in print in 1852.[10] But he felt that there was something evasive and morally unsatisfactory about Roman Catholic preaching and practice in relation to 'truth for its own sake' and to that extent he was simply articulating a commonplace of Victorian anti-Catholicism.[11] More specifically he felt that both as an Anglican and as a Roman Catholic Newman had been less than straightforward in his polemical writing which tried to claim that the ideals of unworldly sanctity and celibate and ascetic discipline had a central place in the teaching and tradition of Anglicanism and the Christian Church. His real quarrel with Newman had more to do with his 'Manichaeism' than his mendacity. The controversy was in effect a battle between different religious temperaments with different views about the nature of the religious character. The ostensible issue of the virtue of truth, which hinged on some passages in the moral theology of St Alfonso Liguori, canonized as recently as 1839, was never really settled. Liguori maintained that equivocation might be permitted to churchmen in special circumstances.[12] Newman may or may not have been an equivocator in his public life but he was equivocal about Liguori. He could not and would not disavow a saint of the church, and claimed that Liguori was a very moral man, but he would not admit that he felt bound by all his teaching and managed to avoid saying whether or not he agreed with him about equivocation.[13]

CONTEMPTUS MUNDI

The 'Manichaeism' Kingsley loathed needs to be examined in some detail. The 'Manichee' contempt of the world characteristic both of the older generation of Evangelicals and of Newman and the Tractarians tended to involve a rejection of ordinary human nature 'in the flesh', a rejection of everyday human society as the proper sphere of Christian activity, and a rejection of the physical world as of no consequence in comparison with the heavenly world which

forms the goal of Christian aspiration. This ran counter to
Kingsley's insistence on a healthy body as well as a healthy mind. It
struck at the roots of his emphasis on Christian action in the world,
and the whole Christian Socialist endeavour to institute a more
equable society on earth. It also seemed to outlaw his scientific
interests. He had found that his own Evangelical upbringing had
provided him with no real theological basis for his early fascination
with the physical beauty and the scientific principles of the natural
world, and it was this that had helped to drive him to the
metaphysical despair from which he was rescued by Fanny Grenfell,
later his wife, and by the writings of Coleridge, Carlyle and
Maurice.[14]

Henry Venn's *Complete Duty of Man* (1763), the popular classic of
early Evangelical literature, is an eloquent testimony to the
'Manichaeism' Kingsley rejected. The only basis for the biblical
doctrine of atonement and redemption, Venn insists, is the entire
corruption of human nature.[15] This emphasis on the hopelessness of
man's estate sometimes leads him to reduce human misery in the
present world to a mere rhetorical foil to the transcendent glories of
the world to come. He once visited a young man dying of fever and
ulcers in a wretched hovel, and drew religious comfort from his
otherworldly resignation and calm where the more practical
Kingsley would have soundly rated the landlord for criminally
neglecting the premises.[16] But such sublime disdain for man's sinful
physical nature was an Evangelical commonplace: the *Evangelical
Magazine* for 1800 placed at the top of its 'Spiritual Barometer' the
satisfactions of 'Glory; dismission from the body'.[17]

The Friendly Visitor, edited by William Carus Wilson, the original
of the sternly Evangelical Mr Brocklehurst in *Jane Eyre*,[18] was
prepared to retail a little practical advice during the 1848 cholera
epidemic, but commented severely that 'These things relate to the
poor dying body' and abruptly transferred its attention to the
'never-dying soul', anticipating the contemptible preacher in
Kingsley's *Two Years Ago* by suggesting that the epidemic could be a
divine visitation warranted by 'our aggravated transgressions', and
possibly adding to the general panic and even hysteria of the time by
urging spiritual revival before it was too late.[19]

Human society and the ordinary interests and enterprises
connected with it had not appealed to the rapt, even ascetic
spirituality of Henry Venn: when he could not enjoy the conversation of the godly he took solitary, meditative walks.[20] The Evangeli-

cal 'religion of the heart' was a strongly personal affair between the individual soul and the Creator. For some Evangelicals any social gathering not specifically for 'prayer and experience' tended towards the 'carnal' or unacceptably 'pleasure-seeking'.[21] The retreat from the world was deliberate: Evangelical zeal and Tractarian fervour alike sought to recapture the spiritual urgency of the apostolic emergency when the early church had to struggle against fearful odds for survival, and even in a later age compromise with an ungodly generation seemed unthinkable. *The Friendly Visitor* proclaimed 'The world, is the Christian's grand enemy ... We have to meet the day in which we live, with its errors and evil customs.'[22]

Kingsley's generously comprehensive theological, social, patriotic and scientific concerns represent a radically antagonistic religious spirit. Not all Evangelicals were equally oblivious to the world's problems, of course. Kingsley always admired the devout Lord Shaftesbury and took part in his manful and prayerful campaigns for sanitary reform and against the use of climbing-boys in the sweeping of chimneys. It was said that Shaftesbury's 1858 address in Liverpool on preventable disease preached the Kingsleyan gospel: certainly Kingsley admired him for it and spoke more kindly of Evangelicals in consequence.[23] Later Evangelicals such as the Baptist preacher C. H. Spurgeon to some extent followed Kingsley in insisting that Christian living must come to terms with the world, spiritualizing rather than shunning the secular,[24] but the old inflexibility died hard. As late as 1856 the *Record*, a partisan Evangelical organ, was roundly condemning religious liberals like Benjamin Jowett for daring to re-state Christianity in terms of 'humanity' and 'the world's opinions' to the detriment of biblical truth.[25]

It was in the Evangelical teaching of his youth that Newman found support for his imaginative retreat from the world around him, for the doctrine of final perseverance and individual assurance of salvation left him with 'the thought of two and two only absolute and luminously self-evident beings, myself and my Creator'.[26] In later life this issued in a rare contemplative spirituality which he and his fellow-Tractarians were anxious to see more generally restored to the religious life of the Church of England. A sermon on 'The Good Part of Mary' which he preached in 1836 urges that 'quiet adoration' is as acceptable a service to God as 'active business', and slips easily into special pleading for what soon becomes 'the more favoured portion of Mary'.[27] Edward Bouverie Pusey, another

leading Tractarian, took it as axiomatic that the devotional spirit
would be at odds with the 'self-corrupting world'. In a moving
sermon preached in 1848 he recommended an unworldly religion
which stands at the opposite pole to Kingsley's Christian socialist
gospel, outlined in *Yeast* which appeared the same year. For Pusey
the perfection of the soul is not work in the world but the withdrawal
from the transience of all created things to commune with the
Creator, hidden from the world in the vastness of God.[28] At times,
however, this emphasis on withdrawal could issue in absurdity.
Newman's project for a complete series of *Lives of the English Saints*
provided opportunities for his spiritual protégés to investigate and
apply the lessons of saintliness. The biographer of St Ebba, known to
posterity as Father Faber of the Oratory, gave grounds for
Kingsley's anger against otherworldly 'Manichee' churchmen in his
characteristically intemperate prose. So far from urging Christian
intervention in society he blandly tells his readers:

> to forget the world or to hate it are better far than to work for it. One is the
> taste of ordinary Christians; the other the object of the Saints.[29]

This implicit slight on the activities of the great majority who must
work in and for the world only reflects Newman's own stated
rejection of ordinary human society and all merely humanitarian
schemes for social improvement and reform as an ultimately Satanic
conspiracy against God.[30] This dualistic rhetoric brings him
momentarily within striking distance of the teaching of Mani, and at
one point he seems to deny the incarnational religion of redemption
completely, stating baldly that 'Satan is the god of this world'.
Kingsley attributed this astounding doctrine to Conrad the spiritual
director in his verse-drama *The Saint's Tragedy* to strengthen his
polemic against 'Manichee' religion. In the context, of course, it
appears that Newman means only that 'at first sight' the whole
world seems alien from God, though it can be sanctified through
Christ. Even so, for Newman all the ordinary activities of the world
are 'evil unless they have become good'.[31] His contempt for the
world is sometimes petulant, self-righteous, even arrogant, reflecting a pardonable exasperation with the unbridled hostility with
which the Oxford movement was greeted by the world in general,
and Evangelicals and bishops in particular. One can understand
that for him at least 'the gross, carnal, unbelieving world, is blind to
the peculiar feelings, objects, hopes, fears, affections of religious
people'.[32] It was in the same sermon that he commented wryly that

the wisdom of serpents was often needed by the religious, a remark Kingsley was to use in evidence against him.[33]

KINGSLEY AND NEWMAN

Newman triumphantly vindicated his personal integrity in the *Apologia*, but it is not always remembered that both he and the other writers of *Tracts for the Times*, persecuted and reviled as they were, appeared at the time to display serpentine wisdom, unscrupulous evasion, and an equivocal attitude towards the Church of their baptism. In their zeal to revive the Catholic traditions of the Church of England, and to attack the liberal accommodation of Christianity to everyday work in the world represented by staunch Protestants like Kingsley, they sometimes engaged in sophisticated special pleading on the basis of ambiguous historical evidence. Pusey's tract *Thoughts on the Benefits of the System of Fasting, Enjoined by our Church*, to take one example, shamelessly begs the question. It begins by arguing that regular fasting is a desirable religious practice, finds some Anglican precedents for it, and implies that it is therefore a strangely neglected official Anglican institution, though obliged in the end to admit that it is not recommended on the direct authority of the Church.[34]

The most ingenious attempt to reconcile Catholic teaching with Anglican formulae was Newman's tricky Catholic interpretation of the Thirty-nine Articles in the famous Tract Ninety, which provoked a youthful Kingsley to protest indignantly 'Whether wilful or self-deceived, these men are Jesuits.'[35] Kingsley always resented the Tractarian attempt to impose upon the Church of England an apparently alien and, for Kingsley, totally unacceptable ideal of sanctity by seemingly unfair means. Newman's conversion to Rome only seemed to confirm this betrayal of everyday practical Protestantism.

Kingsley's initial remarks about Newman and the virtue of truth, which sparked off the whole controversy, muddle together this confused sense of tricky equivocation on Newman's part, resentment of his 'Manichee' religious beliefs, and traditional anti-Catholic prejudice against Jesuitical casuistry. The context of his famous gibe readily accounts for the protests against Catholic contempt for truth: he was reviewing those volumes of Froude's *History of England* which dealt with Papal politics and murky Catholic-inspired intrigue against the Protestant Elizabeth, especially in Scotland and Ireland, and Kingsley had already denounced such treachery in *Westward Ho!*[36] But this is in a sense almost a side-issue. More than twenty years of hostility to Newman's insidiously advocated 'Manichee' religion spills over into his hasty polemic when he makes Newman say 'cunning is the weapon which Heaven has given to the saints wherewith to withstand the brute male force of the world which marries and is given in marriage.'[37]

Newman deliberately excluded from his first published reply any answer to 'Mr Kingsley's accusations against the Catholic Church', and the *Apologia* itself is a personal rather than a doctrinal vindication. From Kingsley's point of view this largely avoided the issue, though it was his own fault as it was his gratuitously personal remark which had laid down the nominal grounds of the controversy. Newman's personal integrity and the virtue of truth were in a sense incidental: what really mattered was Newman's long-standing 'Manichee' opposition to 'the brute male force of the world' which seemed to deny the incarnational theology underpinning Kingsley's ideal of Christian manliness.[38] The apparently superfluous allusion to Catholic traditions of celibacy and the 'unmanly' religious life of 'the saints' reflects two specific aspects of unworldly withdrawn spirituality which he found particularly unacceptable.

CELIBACY AND THE FAMILY

Kingsley almost lost his bride Fanny Grenfell to one of the new Tractarian-inspired religious orders set up at Park Village under Pusey's spiritual direction, and his friend Froude the historian had a similar experience some years later when he planned to marry Mrs Kingsley's sister.[39] Kingsley stated bluntly that the Oxford Tracts had 'struck at the roots of our wedded bliss'.[40] This incipient frustration, which he felt keenly as an ardent and highly-sexed young man,[41] gave rise to a lifelong near-hysterical horror of celibacy. This is reflected in his partly autobiographical novel *Yeast*, in which the hero helps to rescue the heroine from a celibate religious life as he had rescued Fanny, and in *Hypatia*, his fictional indictment of the celibate and ascetic practices of the 'Church of the Fathers' which the Tractarians frequently invoked. *The Saint's Tragedy*, the story of St Elizabeth of Hungary, was an earlier and even more intemperate attack on Catholic notions of sanctity, and in this and in his poem 'St Maura' Kingsley deliberately and defiantly wrote about saints who were married. He vindicated his own domestic happiness by stressing the spiritual and symbolical significance of family relations as his friend F. D. Maurice had done, and contrasted this view of man as 'a spirit embodied in flesh and blood, with certain relations' with the 'Manichee' view that the flesh and the married state were unholy spiritual distractions.[42] He constantly maintained that Catholic teaching degraded the institution of marriage and despised the married as inferior Christians.[43]

This was of course flatly contradicted by the Catholic view of marriage as a sacrament. But Augustinian and scholastic traditions within the church, which claimed that original sin was transmitted through concupiscence, and that this could be institutionalized in the married condition, did supply some grounds for his attack.[44] The slightly smug rhetoric of the self-consciously celibate could provide further provocation. Newman himself occasionally came close to despising marriage. He argued that 'the humble monk, and the holy nun, and other regulars, as they are called', were 'Christians after the very pattern given us in Scripture'. He did qualify this by saying he was describing a model 'not commanding your literal imita-tion',[45] but Kingsley can perhaps be forgiven for drawing the inference that those who were neither monks nor nuns nor under any religious vow were, according to Newman, hardly Christians in the biblical sense.[46]

Newman in effect implied that there were two kinds of celibacy, which can be distinguished as the practical and the mystical. Practically speaking, missionary work among the heathen, or some other special kind of Christian service, could render marriage inexpedient, and Kingsley himself seems to have been perfectly prepared to accept this view. But celibacy as an aspect of the 'Manichaean' withdrawn spirituality, Newman's 'feeling of separa-tion from the visible world', was quite another matter.[47] Newman's personal preference for the celibate life on these grounds led him to grumble when one after another of his fellow-Tractarians decided to marry. This grumbling could be construed as a 'Manichaean' contempt for marriage though it related only to specific instances.[48] Other Tractarians, like Hurrell Froude, brother of the historian, and William Ward, carried this 'high severe idea of the intrinsic excellence of Virginity' to extremes. Ward managed to place himself in an amusingly awkward position when he suddenly married and had to disclaim ever having professed to lead a celibate life himself.[49] F. W. Faber, always a romantic extremist, actually feared that the devil might tempt him to marriage in 1844.[50]

The writers of the *Lives of the English Saints* were particularly prone to immature raptures about the celibate life, and the youthful Mark Pattison, in later years the morosely anti-Tractarian Rector of Lincoln College, found an opportunity in his *Life of St Ninian* to exalt the mystique of celibacy as 'his [Ninian's] special blessedness, as one of those virgin souls which follow the Lamb whithersoever he goeth'.[51] The extravagant Faber saw nothing incongruous or untoward in describing St Cuthbert's celibate horror of female company, 'characteristic of all the Saints', which led him to spend all night up to his neck in water after conversation with St Ebba, presumably to subdue unholy thoughts.[52]

This abhorrence of women, which Kingsley works into the opening chapter of *Hypatia*, was condemned not only by Kingsley but by Southey and other advocates of a more everyday religious spirit.[53] The normal social decencies and family life generally seemed to be called in question by the practice of celibacy, and the new Anglican religious orders often set up awkward tensions between natural family affections and the claims of the religious life, sometimes exacerbated by unwise or insensitive superiors and spiritual directors.[54]

But the Tractarian revival of Catholic ideals of sanctity affected more than domestic pieties. It set up an ideal of spiritual perfection which necessarily excluded not only the married but the great majority of mankind. Christian socialist principles supported by Maurice's theology of the Kingdom of Christ, to which all men belonged in the present world on the basis of their common humanity with Christ, naturally revolted against this 'aristocratic, exclusive method of soul-saving',[55] and in *Hypatia*, as it will appear, Kingsley tried to show true Christianity was essentially comprehensive and democratic.

ASCETICISM AND EFFEMINACY

Another serious objection to the 'Manichee' religious life from Kingsley's standpoint of Christian manliness was that it wilfully injured and suppressed man's God-given physical nature through ascetic privations,[56] and cultivated an unmanly 'fastidious, maundering, die-away effeminacy'.[57] Both Newman and Pusey had laid great stress on fasting and ascetic discipline, and Newman wrote a rather tendentious pamphlet on *Mortification of the Flesh a Scripture Duty* for *Tracts for the Times*.[58] The 'Manichee' Augustinian view of the total corruption of the flesh perhaps involved the corollary of voluntary affliction of the flesh, but some of Newman's associates took this to bizarre extremes. Faber, predictably, had to be restrained from excesses of ascetic rigour,[59] and Hurrell Froude, whose unwisely published *Remains* caused a public outcry which greatly embarrassed the Tractarians, tormented himself daily in his fanatical determination to 'chastise myself before the Lord'.[60]

This extravagant ascetic discipline, commended in women as well as among Tractarian clergy[61] and sometimes injudiciously practised in the new Anglican sisterhoods,[62] provoked a storm of protest. Sadistic and perverted behaviour in religious communities was almost a literary commonplace since the publication of Diderot's scandalous novel *La Religieuse* (1796, begun 1760).[63] Southey's notes for a projected *History of the Religious Orders* indicate he would have provided a compendious indictment along similar lines.[64]

Popular Protestantism found in tales of inhuman cruelty in the new religious orders a splendid opportunity to decry Tractarian spirituality in the name of ordinary humanity,[65] and Kingsley occasionally found himself in the role of chivalric champion called upon to shield and dissuade weak females from the ascetic rigours of the superficially attractive religious life.[66] In his pamphlet *What, then, does Dr Newman mean?* he made rhetorical capital out of this, thundering that Newman shared the blame for the degrading hysteria induced by severe conventual discipline and 'he will remain upon his trial as long as Englishmen know how to guard the women whom God has committed to their charge'.[67] It was a common objection that mortification of the flesh and other religious observances were often ultimately selfish will-worship in any case, a deliberate attempt to win to heaven by one's own efforts and by 'meretricious formalism' rather than through Christ, and Kingsley whole-heartedly shared this view.[68]

Devotees of this kind of religious life were easily recognized as emaciated and effeminate pale young curates, and the controversy which raged in the early days of Cuddesdon theological college near Oxford crystallized the debate between 'Manichaeism' and 'manliness', the esoteric, saintly, unworldly ideal and the more practical Kingsleyan ideal of Christian character. The Bishop of Oxford, Samuel Wilberforce, was finally driven to side with the latter, complaining to a friend 'Our men are too *peculiar* – some, at least, of our best men'.[69] H. P. Liddon, the first vice-principal of Cuddesdon, saintly but intractable, imposed his own almost fanatical standards of personal holiness on the college. He banned smoking, late rising, and the healthy manly exercises such as cricket and fives which the average English gentleman at college would normally pursue, and instituted regular religious offices and rules for meditation adapted from Roman Catholic practice.[70]This was extremely unpopular in the diocese, for the demonstrative piety and elaborate ceremonial of the Cuddesdon men seemed to be more in keeping with the baroque religious traditions of continental Catholicism than the simple, manly devotion of the Church of England.[71]

This vague association of extravagant and effeminate devotion with foreign religion, emotional restraint and practical, games-playing manliness with English religion, is really a commonplace of traditional anti-Catholic feeling in England. A writer in the *British Critic* replied to Cardinal Wiseman's criticisms of the English church in this vein, representing Roman proselytizers as

holding out tales for the nursery, and pretty pictures, and gilt gingerbread, and physic concealed in jam, and sugar plums for good children ... We Englishmen like manliness, openness, consistency, truth.

The writer was not Kingsley but John Henry Newman in his Anglican days, using the rhetoric of popular Protestantism, which he lived to regret, to justify the beleaguered Anglo-Catholic position and distinguish it from Roman Catholicism. Anti-Tractarian propaganda naturally assimilated Anglo-Catholic to Roman Catholic practices – the aim of Anglo-Catholics in any case – and visited on them all the same patriotic Protestant indignation.[72]

But there was a political as well as a theological objection to continental Catholicism. In addition to the 'miserable mockery of the Confessional', the dogmatic absolutism and the traditions of 'Manichee' religious devotion, which Anglo-Catholics and Roman Catholics held in common, there was the whole question of religio-political tyranny and persecution, relating to long-standing Protestant suspicions of the temporal power and influence of the Papacy. The restoration of the Roman Catholic hierarchy in England in 1850, popularly regarded as 'Papal Aggression', strengthened the patriotic element of manly Protestantism by reviving memories of the Spanish Armada and the hoary traditions of English liberty and freedom from invasion.[73] Kingsley's *Westward Ho!* and (to a lesser extent) *Hereward the Wake* exploit this anti-Catholic political excitement by adopting patriotic themes. But this is in a sense a turning aside from his habitual grudge against Catholicism, Roman or otherwise, for advocating an unworldly religion, celibate and ascetic and radically antipathetic to his own theological under-standing of man and the healthy, socially committed, domestic ideal of Christian manliness which he commends in his novels.

3

Liberal religion

Evangelical and Tractarian 'Manichaeism' was the principal negative influence on the Christian manliness of Kingsley and Hughes. The positive influences were the teachings of Coleridge, F. D. Maurice, Carlyle and Thomas Arnold. At first sight this seems a rather miscellaneous group: a poet, a saintly but often obscure theologian, a Scottish social prophet, a schoolmaster-historian. There is a fortuitous element in this assembly of influences: Kingsley happened to have been a pupil of Derwent Coleridge, the poet's younger son; F. D. Maurice happened to be Chaplain of Lincoln's Inn where Hughes was a barrister; earlier, Hughes had been a schoolboy at Arnold's Rugby. But there is some inner coherence as well. Like many of their generation, both Maurice and Arnold were greatly impressed by Coleridge's religious speculations, and Arnold knew him personally. Carlyle's presence in the group is hardly surprising since almost every important Victorian writer seems to have felt his influence at some point in his career even if disillusionment set in later on. Maurice acknowledged specific debts to him, and it will be recalled that it seemed natural to Ford Madox Brown to place Maurice and Carlyle side by side in his painting *Work*. At first sight Carlyle's acknowledged antipathy to Coleridge, dismissed as a purveyor of 'bottled moonshine',[1] seems to strike a discordant note. But in his helpful study *Coleridge and the Broad Church Movement* C. R. Sanders convincingly argues that, whatever he may have said, Carlyle's work creatively embodies much of Coleridge's abstract speculation. Sanders also demonstrates the nature of Coleridge's influence on Arnold and Maurice.[2]

Following Sanders, one can link Coleridge, Arnold, Maurice and Carlyle in a liberal or 'Broad Church' religious tradition. But the term 'Broad Church', apparently coined by Arnold's pupil A. H. Clough about 1850 and popularized in an article by the Revd Walter Conybeare in 1853,[3] covers a wide range of doubtfully orthodox theological possibilities. Maurice never liked it. Later in the century it was extended to include the new school of biblical criticism and various heterodox religious positions which might well have dismayed Maurice and Kingsley and Hughes.[4] To safeguard what he saw as the imperilled orthodoxy of the Church of England Kingsley actually joined a Committee for the Defence of the Athanasian Creed in 1872. Earlier in his career he suppressed slight misgivings about one of the clauses of this, the most elaborate and exacting of creeds. Characteristically, it related to the manliness of Christ: Kingsley could not quite understand how Christ was 'inferior to the Father, as touching his manhood', but even then he was content to trust to the wisdom of 'the magnificent metaphysician (whoever he was), who wrote that creed'.[5]

But if 'Broad Church' is too broad a term for the tradition of religious thought to which Kingsley and Hughes belonged how else can it be defined? The element of challenge to conventional religious and social thinking is certainly strongly present in Coleridge and Arnold, Maurice and Carlyle. Newman uncharitably wondered whether Dr Arnold was a Christian at all,[6] and Maurice was obliged to resign from his post at King's College, London, because his liberal views on Eternal Punishment ruffled the calm surface of that conservative reservoir of Anglican orthodoxy.[7] But in many respects both men were orthodox, even conservative. Arnold's moral severity and constant dismay at human wickedness participated in a long-established clerical tradition. Maurice based his teaching on the Bible, the prayerbook and the creeds in the traditional Anglican manner. Coleridge had strayed after the French Revolution, Pantheism and Unitarianism in youth, but *Aids to Reflection* (1825) and *On the Constitution of Church and State* (1830), his most influential religious works, were deeply inbued with the traditions of the Church of England and the former soon became standard reading for Anglican intellectuals.[8] Only Carlyle remained completely outside the fold of religious orthodoxy. But his Scottishness made a difference. The grim Calvinism of his upbringing, rejected in favour of a vague but earnest ethical theism compounded of German Idealism and the Old Testament, was not very close to English orthodoxies, so no offence was caused. In any case, it was Carlyle's religious-sounding rhetoric and social criticism rather than the precise nature of this quarrrel with the religion of his youth that made the strongest impression on his disciples. In social outlook none of these thinkers would qualify as a radical, or even a progressive, in modern terms. Discussing popular disturbances in *Culture and Anarchy*, Matthew Arnold recalled his father's draconian solution: 'Flog the rank and file, and fling the ring-leaders from the Tarpeian rock.'[9] Carlyle's hero-worship of dictators and his scornful atttitude to what he called 'The Nigger Question' offended liberals even in his own day. His defence of Governor Eyre of Jamaica, charged with murderous brutality in suppressing a riot, lost him many of his friends, including Thomas Hughes, though Kingsley took the same side as Carlyle.[10] F. D. Maurice was timid and conventional in many of his social attitudes and always needed to be spurred into action and then kept on a tight rein by his more vigorous reformist associates.[11] He rather tended to disapprove of democracy as 'the tyranny of the majority'.[12] Coleridge had collaborated with Southey in a revolutionary but worthless tragedy *The Fall of Robespierre* in 1794 but he had begun to write for the Tory press even before the end of the eighteenth century. Byron never missed an opportunity to taunt him with his earlier Revolutionary enthusiasm 'long before his flighty pen / Let to the Morning Post its aristocracy'. Southey's increasing diehard conservatism annoyed Byron even more.[13] But this was hardly a complacent and uncritical conservatism. Southey's affinity with Kingsley in condemnation of ascetic discipline and clerical celibacy has already been noted. Southey and Coleridge and Kingsley after them were all profoundly uneasy about the human consequences of contemporary economic developments and an increasingly industrialized society.

The apparent conservatism of Coleridge and his Victorian disciples actually represents a kind of traditionalist radicalism, challenging the social and political *status quo* and its apologists in fundamental ways. Coleridge's *Church and State*, Kingsley's Christian socialist journal *Politics for the People* and Arnold's *Culture and Anarchy* all pour scorn on the triumphalist gospel of material progress most eloquently stated by Macaulay and assert more important moral, spiritual and cultural values. But this critical dissatisfaction stems from a moralized vision of the past and from a reappraisal of the meaning and function of existing structures and doctrines rather than from a prophetic vision of some desirable future state. For the later Coleridge the health of the nation consisted not in revolutionary change but in an ideal harmony of permanence and progression. Once-healthy plants which have been blighted or badly pruned may grow again from the root if properly tended, and this conservative-radical method of cultivating improvement was the one Coleridge and his disciples preferred to uprooting or starting again from seed. Coleridge traces his religious and ethical musings back to their roots in seventeenth-century Anglicanism in *Aids to Reflection* and elsewhere. An idealized version of the mediaeval social and ecclesiastical order and a reading of Hooker lie at the root of *On the Constitution of Church and State*. The Bible, the creeds and the Anglican Prayerbook lie at the heart of Maurice's theological enterprise, which was to dig down to underlying religious truth as he perceived it and present his findings in challenging form rather than to venture self-consciously new ideas. Both Carlyle and Arnold were historians and moralists who saw in the French Revolution or the Peloponnesian Wars ever-recurring patterns of moral and social significance which could profitably be applied to the contemporary situation. Part of the attractiveness of this traditionalist radicalism was that it permitted its protégés to enjoy both the comforts of the past and present order and the exhilaration and self-satisfaction of condemning contemporary evils. Kingsley, like Arnold and Maurice, could continue to operate as a clergyman within the Church of England as by law established. Thomas Hughes, a barrister and eventually a county-court judge, was able to survive and attain modest success in a conservative profession and keep faith with his own past as son of a high Tory Berkshire squire. Yet both men were prominent Christian socialists allied with controversial causes. Kingsley's campaigns for sanitary reform and Hughes' political work on behalf of the early Trade Union movement are examples of their successes. The theological and ideological paradoxes of the traditionalist-radical school of thought which they inherited are homologous with the blend of perennial and contemporary of the Christian manliness they preached and practised.

This tradition, if it can be called that, must now be considered in more detail. Though close friends and involved side-by-side in many of the same causes, Kingsley and Hughes did not think alike on everything as their difference of opinion over Governor Eyre and Jamaica indicates. Neither did they respond equally to the same influences. Only their beloved master F. D. Maurice, perhaps, was regarded with equal veneration by both men. Hughes absorbed Coleridge's ideas chiefly at second hand through Coleridge's disciple Thomas Arnold, and through Maurice; Kingsley read and admired Arnold but was less influenced by him than Hughes was: after all, he had not sat under him in Rugby Chapel. But despite this Kingsley and Hughes achieved a remarkable degree of unity on important issues. Behind much of what they thought and felt, directly or indirectly, lay the strange fragmented genius of Samuel

Taylor Coleridge, 'a helpless Psyche overspun with Church of
England cobwebs' in Carlyle's view but still a formidable figure, 'an
Archangel a little damaged' in the more charitable opinion of
Charles Lamb.[14]

COLERIDGE

Coleridge's enormous influence on the intellectual life of Victorian
England has been amply acknowledged. Thomas Arnold described
him as 'a very great man indeed, whose equal I know not where to
find in England'. Writers as different as John Stuart Mill and John
Henry Newman learnt much from him.[15] But Kingsley's debt to
him, surprisingly, has been little explored. David Newsome, in his
excellent study *Godliness and Good Learning*, actually suggests that
Coleridge's notion of 'manliness' should be sharply distinguished
from that of Kingsley and Hughes.[16] While it is difficult to imagine
the dreamy metaphysician of Highgate as a Tom Brown figure,
particularly as his closest approach to practical manliness was his
comically short-lived enlistment as trooper Silas Tomkyn
Comberbacke,[17] Coleridge contributes more to Christian manliness
at a theoretical level than has been acknowledged. One of the books
given to Kingsley by Fanny Grenfell, his future wife, was Coleridge's
Aids to Reflection. Kingsley was a Cambridge undergraduate at the
time, severely troubled by religious doubt. The volume helped
convince him that 'there must be a God eternal in the Heavens to
which the world must be conformed'.[18] Coleridge, nature-poet as
well as philosopher, did more than anyone else to provide Kingsley
with a theology to unify his instinctive love of nature, his delight in
physical manliness, his scientific and humanitarian interests.

Even at an early stage in his career, while still committed to a
Unitarian religious outlook, Coleridge contrived, by his romantic
celebration of 'Science, Freedom and the Truth in Christ',[19] to
baptize the radical secular enthusiasms of the French Revolutionary
era into an idiosyncratic Christianized Godwinism. This included a
religious perspective on contemporary scientific discovery in which
he was influenced by the materialist philosophy of Joseph Priestley,
political radical, Unitarian clergyman and distinguished pioneer of
modern chemistry. Years later, by now a convinced Trinitarian,
Coleridge could still affirm that all organic life radiated, was in some
sense 'the translucence, of the invisible Energy'.[20] In his religious
understanding of man as individual and in society, as well as in his

views on organic nature, Coleridge held to a romantic intuitionism which challenged the rationalist traditions of the Enlightenment and Descartes in particular, dismissed as a mathematician who had attempted to geometrize the world:

instead of a World *created* and filled with productive forces by the Almighty *Fiat*, He left a lifeless Machine whirled about by the dust of its own Grinding: as if Death could come from the living Fountain of Life.[21]

Neither man in himself nor man in his social relations could be adequately assimilated to such a lifeless and godless 'mechanico-corpuscular Philososphy'. While there might be no mathematically conclusive demonstration of the existence of a 'good, wise, loving, and personal God' the moral conscience and the intuitive faculty of the Reason as opposed to the merely rational Understanding made it almost impossible not to believe in Him.[22]

This was the perception which consoled and encouraged Kingsley at a time when God seemed hard to find. One necessary consequence of this perception for both Coleridge and Kingsley was a profoundly Christian manliness. In *Aids to Reflection* Coleridge suggests true enlightenment comes about when man opens himself to and reflects the light of God as the seeing light of his existence. In this way he can realize his total personality and gradually cure his diseased moral will, cultivating his own Reason by participating in the Divine Reason.[23] This involves vigilance and effort, a resolute 'self-superintendence' as Coleridge calls it, for 'most truly does the poet [Samuel Daniel] exclaim,

> "Unless *above* himself he can
> Erect himself, how mean a thing is man!" '[24]

Self-indulgent sensibility, the 'sentimental Philosophy of STERNE', is futile in the circumstances, and so is the cold theoretical virtue of the Stoics. What is needed is

Manhood or Manliness ... strength of Character in relation to the resistance opposed by Nature and the irrational passions to the Dictates of Reason; Energy of Will in preserving the Line of Rectitude tense and firm against the warping and treacheries of temptation.[25]

Coleridge goes on to stress that the cultivation of this moral strength has precedence over mere 'strength of body, or even strength of mind'. The same thought is expressed in Hughes' *Tom Brown at Oxford*, mediated by Arnold of Rugby: the so-called 'muscular Christian' hero should discipline his body in the service of Christ and mankind: 'For mere power, whether of body or intellect, he has (I hope and believe) no reverence whatever.'[26] The atmosphere of the two remarks is different for Coleridge speaks from a position of intellectual strenuousness where Hughes represents physical strenuousness, but they agree on the need for moral energy as the supreme requirement.

For Coleridge the steps on the Christian way can be clearly marked: 'Add to your faith *knowledge*, and to knowledge *manly energy*.' He is quoting from Paul's second epistle to Peter, but 'manly energy' is his own translation of the word *arete* usually more feebly translated 'virtue'. He seems to be relying on a now discredited etymology which links *arete* with *Ares*, god of war.[27] This vigorous, aggressive definition of the moral life links Coleridge with the temperamentally bluff and aggressive manly Christians Kingsley and Hughes. So does its incorporation of 'knowledge'. Knowledge of the world's wonder and beauty was sought by Coleridge the poet as well as Coleridge the philosopher, and Kingsley shared his enthusiasm. For Coleridge in his later, Trinitarian, phase, all being, all existence with its patterns and causal relationships, can in its totality be attributed to the *Logos* (i.e. 'Word') or objective expression of God. The *Logos* is that aspect of the Divine Being which is represented in historical terms by Christ the Son of God, the *Logos* or Word become flesh. Since Christ participated in our humanity in His incarnation, this imparts to man a special relationship with the *Logos* which underlies all created being. Knowledge of the world of creation thus becomes religious knowledge and man is uniquely positioned to acquire it. In an essay in *The Friend*, first published in 1809, Coleridge summed up his position:

the material world must have been made for the sake of man, at once the high priest and representative of the Creator, as far as he partakes of . . . reason . . . I speak of man in his idea, and as subsumed in the divine humanity, in whom alone God loved the world.[28]

Scientific discoveries about the material world could hold no terrors for the faithful if this position was adopted: Kingsley the disciple of Coleridge took pride in the scientific advances of his age and in popular lectures and children's books as well as in *The Water-Babies* he helped to popularize the new geology and marine biology. Indeed scientific discovery becomes identified with the Christian manly quest at one point in *The Water-Babies*, as it will appear.

Coleridge's religious understanding of man requires man to be energetically moral and a scientific interpreter of God's world. He must also be truly humane, responding to the challenge implied in the fact that he is 'subsumed in the divine humanity'. From his earliest days as a radical critic of corrupt institutions to his latest phase as conservative apologist in *On the Constitution of Church and State* Coleridge insisted on the dignity of the individual, however humble, and on his just claims on his fellow man's humanity and charity. As he wrote in a letter of 1826, 'In vain the informing Reason ... [without] the right appreciation ... of all that man can do for Man!'[29] Both Church and State should seek to give institutional expression to this ethical imperative. Unfortunately the Church often neglected man and the things of this world. Even in the early days of the Church the New Testament command to Christians to keep themselves 'unspotted from the World' was misinterpreted under pagan, Gnostic influences as a call to detached otherworldliness rather than a stern warning not to acquiesce in the social and moral enormities which made the World 'a contradistinction to the kingdom of God'.[30] The practice of fasting could be regarded as a special case of this general, mistaken tendency to divide the things of the world and the flesh from the things of the Church and the spirit to the moral and religious detriment of the former. The State also tended to neglect its responsibility to ordinary men. Coleridge's indignation boiled over when the Government of the day decreed a national fast-day in 1795, apparently hoping to enlist the Almighty's support in the long-drawn-out war against France. This was a mere mockery, he felt,

Prayers of hate to the God of Love – and after these, a Turbot feast for the rich, and their usual scanty Morsel to the poor, if indeed debarred from their usual labour they can procure even this.[31]

The class-division and lack of social concern as well as the near-blasphemy of the fast-day as Coleridge perceived it touched off a humanistic indignation and a sense of the importance of social harmony which finally issued in *On the Constitution of Church and State* thirty-five years later. Whether in science or in politics, the 'mechanico-corpuscular' theories of the Enlightenment took no account of the fundamental cohesion of all created nature and the vital interrelatedness of all men who both locally and nationally participated in society through which their very being acquired meaning and significance. Unfortunately the political and social history of England for the last century and a half had tended to deny this, as a result of which the country was saddled with a stumbling, myopic pragmatism in politics and a dehumanizing economic system which fostered the miseries and brutalities of the Industrial Revolution.

Unlike the Whig historians such as Hallam and Macaulay who claimed that English liberties were affirmed and secured by the revolution of 1688 and had blossomed ever since,[32] Coleridge maintained that true freedom and political idealism of the kind represented by Algernon Sidney, Whig martyr and republican theorist, had actually languished from that date.[33] Like his brother-in-law Southey, who attracted the progressive Macaulay's wrath for his attack on the modern industrial system in 1829,[34] Coleridge was sure that recent material advances had damaged rather than fostered the welfare of the country as a whole. The majority suffered to procure the benefit of a plutocratic minority and the very idea of the nation as an integrated commonwealth of interests was destroyed. This vision of society as an organic unity, however damaged, prepared the way for the Christian socialism of his disciples Kingsley and Hughes in the next generation.

At an early stage of his career Coleridge had proposed patriot-heroes as Redeemers of a sick society, an Elect of moral and spiritual heroes who had made a full response to the call of Duty as indicated by the Divine Will.[35] But by 1830 the lonely and glittering heroes of his earlier, more romantic conception had donned black coats and grouped themselves together as the 'Clerisy'. This was an institutionalized cultural and moral élite representing the third estate in the realm, a reinvigorated national church (which Coleridge saw as a secular agency, the church in its social aspect, distinguished from the church in its spiritual aspect) presiding over the other two estates or interests of permanence and progress which together made up the nation.

Coleridge's clerisy was made up of 'clerks' in the old mediaeval sense, learned and devoted men like Chaucer's Clerk of Oxenford, who were to be distributed over the whole country through the network of parishes already maintained by the Church of England. They actually represented the ideal secular functions of the clergymen of the Established Church: the members of the clerisy would maintain a germ of 'Culture' in every corner of the land and assume responsibility for education and welfare, 'to secure to the subjects of the realm generally, the hope, the chance, of bettering their own or their children's condition'.[36] The responsibility of this national church, through the clerisy, was to develop in every potential citizen of the realm the faculties and the knowledge which would make him 'the free subject of a civilized realm'.[37] In fact, the clerisy would operate very much like the manly socially committed heroes of Kingsley's novels: Tom Thurnall, the doctor-hero of *Two Years Ago*, is a clever man who puts his knowledge of disease and bad housing as a cause of disease at the disposal of a remote village community. In *Alton Locke* Sandy Mackaye communicates a more overtly political sense of responsibility to society to the gifted poet Alton Locke whose muse has hitherto been devoted to remote and exotic subjects. When Tom Brown leaves Rugby with a good education the second instalment of his adventures, *Tom Brown at Oxford*, is really the story of how he puts his education and talents to satisfactory use in the larger communities of Oxford and London.

Like Kingsley, whose vigorous educational and welfare work in his Eversley parish makes him a model member of the clerisy, Coleridge thought of social improvement not on a broad international front but very much in protestant national terms. The immediate occasion of *On the Constitution of Church and State* was the debates about Catholic emancipation in 1829, and this led Coleridge to insist that the Roman Catholic clergy could never form part of the clerisy because they owed their allegiance not to the nation but to a foreign power, the Pope in Rome. Clerical celibacy was a requirement of the Roman Church not on spiritual but political grounds, to ensure that priests had no families and therefore no really fundamental involvement in the national life of which the family was the smallest unit. Lacking this involvement, priests were the more easily confirmed in their allegiance to Rome.[38] The conditions of mid-Victorian anti-Catholicism and national pride were rather different, but Kingsley shared Coleridge's suspicion of a celibate priesthood and was sceptical about the usefulness of the celibate ascetic in the national life or indeed in any aspect of the Christian life.

Personal circumstances gave Kingsley reasons to distrust celibacy which Coleridge did not have, as the previous chapter has indicated. By temperament both Kingsley and Hughes were much more physically active and practical men, and their vigorous, patriotic, socially committed Christianity interacted with different historical circumstances. Yet despite all these differences Coleridge's religious understanding of man as moral, scientifically enquiring, fundamentally social and so socially committed being had a profound influence on the shaping of manly Christian idealism. By bringing his earlier patriot-heroes into a closer if more prosaic working relationship with everyday society in the idea of the clerisy Coleridge initiated the domestication of the romantic hero which culminated in Elizabeth Barrett Browning's assurance that 'all men [are] possible heroes'[39] and in the gospel of Christian manliness as a generally applicable ideal of conduct.

MAURICE

Unlike Coleridge, his disciple F. D. Maurice was a contemporary and close personal friend of both Kingsley and Hughes. A devout and saintly man with a rather endearing lack of practical capacity, he seems if anything an even more improbable inspiration for the robust and intensely practical Christianity of Kingsley and Hughes. He was distinctly alarmed when Hughes proposed to teach boxing at the Working Men's College[40] and was afraid that the fighting in *Tom Brown's Schooldays* might be used to justify the brutalities of professional prize-fighting, in particular the prolonged Anglo-American championship fight between Heenan and Sayers which was eventually stopped by the police.[41] But it is to his credit that he accepted Hughes' argument that education should be of the whole man and that boxing could improve round shoulders and narrow chests. Unlike many of *Tom Brown*'s readers he accepted that the novel did not advocate indiscriminate violence but only what Hughes called 'fighting rightly understood', fighting for a good cause, sanctified by chivalrous concern. In a moral if not physical sense Maurice was a fighter himself.

Paradoxically this man of peace was involved in many battles. He loathed religious dissension and was so determined to do justice to the opinions of others that it was often difficult to disentangle what he thought himself. This reflected his sorrow at the bitter religious differences which had arisen in his own family, kept together only by the love and the determination of his mother.[42] But love and determination could provoke hostility: Maurice's conviction, affirmed in his *Theological Essays* (1853), that a God of love could not condemn man to everlasting punishment provoked a storm of controversy; his belief that that same loving God must be just in ways mankind recognized as just led him into dispute with Henry Mansel who claimed a total separation of human and divine justice. Christ himself, the supreme Love, intervened in the affairs of mankind, as Maurice told Kingsley, and that was 'the one protection of nations and men against sloth, effeminacy, baseness and tyranny'.[43] This combative Mauricean Christ, champion (by implication) of energy, manliness, nobility and freedom in men and nations, is the inspiration of the robust and active Christianity of Kingsley and Hughes and others involved in the Christian socialist movement and the Working Men's College even though Maurice often found himself rather overwhelmed by the vigorous energy of his disciples. The moral courage which caused him to resign from King's College on the eternal punishment question and sustained him in later controversy passed on to later generations in the more practical form of high-principled military manliness. Both his eldest son and his grandson rose to the rank of major-general in the British Army. The latter, Sir Frederick Maurice, sacrificed his military career on a point of principle during the first world war, publicly challenging Lloyd George on a politically sensitive question of military statistics. As if to sustain this fidelity to the noble altruism of his grandfather he took over as principal of the Working Men's College which F. D. Maurice and Hughes had established more than half a century before.[44]

The Working Men's College, still active in NW 1, is perhaps the most enduring memorial to Maurice and the Christian socialist enterprise. But Maurice's 'prophetic' influence extended in many other directions. He dedicated his *Theological Essays* to Tennyson, who had asked him to be godfather to his eldest son in 1852. At the height of the King's College row the poet laureate addressed a poem to him inviting him to stay and paying tribute to him as a friend of the poor and exemplar of valour and charity.[45] It was these qualities which attracted Hughes to Maurice: their first encounter at Lincoln's Inn arose through a discussion of whether to take a chapel collection for the distressed in the Irish famine, and it was not long before Hughes was helping out at Maurice's night-school for the poor of the neighbourhood in Little Ormond Street.[46] So great was Maurice's influence on *Tom Brown's Schooldays*, some of which was submitted to him in draft with a request for help in religious matters, that Macmillan's reader observed that Dr Arnold was presented preaching Mauricean doctrines which he might have paved the way for but which he did not actually profess.[47]

Unlike Hughes, Kingsley first encountered Maurice through his writings, claiming in his first letter to him that *The Kingdom of Christ*, like Coleridge's *Aids to Reflection*, came to his rescue at a time of great religious difficulty and provided him with

the foundation of any coherent view of the word of God, the meaning of the
Church of England, and the spiritual phenomena of the present and past
ages.[48]

They corresponded on clerical and parish matters and in 1848
became colleagues on the staff of the newly-founded Queen's
College, London. Kingsley always saw himself very much as
Maurice's pupil, describing his own sermons self-deprecatingly as
'accompanying your angel's trump on my private penny-whistle'.[49]
But what tune did Maurice play on his angel's trump? Apart from
the general moral and spiritual uplift diffused by his extraordinarily
magnetic personality he imparted to his manly Christian disciples a
high and hopeful doctrine of man, partly derived from Coleridge, a
view of human society as the kingdom of Christ upon earth, and an
urgent sense of social and moral purpose deriving from this insight.

Like Coleridge and Southey, and like Kingsley after him,
Maurice had nothing but contempt for the ascetic, dualistic
approach to Christianity which devalued man in his ordinary
human nature and activity in the perspective of a heavenly
kingdom. Again like Coleridge and Southey he saw this as a pagan
contamination of Christian teaching and stigmatized it as
'Manichaeism',[50] a term taken over in a much more polemical vein
by Kingsley himself, as has already been discussed. He founded his
own beliefs as Coleridge had done on the idea of the *Logos* or eternal
Word of God as it is set out at the beginning of St John's gospel.
Because the Word became flesh, because God Himself came to
participate in human nature through the Incarnation, this confirmed that mankind, 'standing in that divine Word', was still made
in the image of God and every aspect of the human body and the
human soul was good and holy in God's sight.[51] Roman Catholicism
and extreme Protestantism might have degraded and secularized
common life by an excess of heavenly-mindedness, but the Bible and
the Reformation together proclaimed otherwise. In his book *The
Church a Family*, published in 1850, Maurice clears the ground
theologically for the full-blooded Elizabethan adventure of
Kingsley's *Westward Ho!* (1855) by suggesting that the Protestant
Reformers' recovered sense of the profoundly human significance of
the Incarnation made possible 'A vigour and energy in the pursuits
and vocations of civil life, such as characterized our own Elizabethan period'.[52] Like Coleridge in his discussion of the communicable
light of reason linking God and man, Maurice felt that true self-
realization and human dignity depended on an acknowledging of a

special relationship between man and God which already existed in some sense because God became man in Christ. Christ as the light of the world was already present in man waiting to reveal the world and the self in their completeness if only the individual would 'Turn and confess His presence. You have always had it with you. You have been unmindful of it.'[53] This acceptance of Christ involved accepting the fact of human solidarity with Christ: in a sense all men were sons of God as He was, so all men were brothers in Christ and Christ himself could be regarded as the elder brother of the human race.

This perception lay at the heart of Maurice's social teaching, first developed in *The Kingdom of Christ* (1838). The language of family which he so often employed reflected the emotional security he had drawn from his own close-knit family as a child despite the potential disruptions of religious difference. As he wrote to Kingsley, who shared his view of the religious importance of the family as fact and metaphor, 'the only corrective of the error of the Middle Ages lies in more closely connecting human relationships with divine'.[54] His sense of universal sonship under God and universal brotherhood in Christ might seem sentimentally benign to the point of naïveté, piously oblivious of the existence of human dissension and evil inside and outside the family. But Maurice was not so foolish. He acknowledged and defined human iniquity as failure, lack of self-realization, in terms of relationship. A bad father, for instance – one who ill-treated his children, perhaps – was a failure in the function of fatherhood and to that extent inconsistent with his own definition.[55] Since all men could be regarded as participants in actual if unacknowledged relationships, sons of God and brothers to each other, offences against God and man, selfish aggression, tyranny, uncharity, could be regarded as unworthiness as sons or brothers, failure to acknowledge and act out the implications of sonship and brotherhood. Such failures might invite retribution in the hereafter according to the lurid hellfire theology which still enjoyed an emotional and imaginative ascendancy in Maurice's day,[56] but for Maurice the consequences were more immediate. Failure to repent, failure to acknowledge inadequacy in relationship, involved appalling and unnecessary isolation and loneliness in the world: man considered in himself, independent of his relationship with Christ and therefore with God and man, was an empty shell, an image without an archetype, miserable and accursed.[57]

This emphasis on the present world as the arena of divine activity and judgement reflects Maurice's contact with millenarian views on prophecy. As a young man he had stayed with the Rector of Lympsham, J. A. Stephenson, and under his influence came to believe that

the hills and valleys of this earth, redeemed, purified and regenerated, were to be the scene of the felicity of the ransomed children of God.[58]

If the new Jerusalem was to come about in the present world it must be through the complete realization of the universal fellowship among men already provided for in the fact of their brotherhood in the incarnate Christ. This process of realization, which would inaugurate the kingdom of Christ or universal spiritual society upon earth, would involve more and more co-operation between man and man of an increasingly fraternal kind. This provided the Christian socialist disciples of Maurice with the theological basis of their endeavours. One of their first moves was to set up Working Men's Associations, co-operative bodies of tailors, shoemakers and the like, privately funded in the first instance but with the aim of reorganiz-ing the traditional relations between labour and capital so that these working men would collectively own the capital which funded their work and share the profits among themselves. Maurice and his friends were aware that this had been tried before, by Robert Owen in particular. But for all its virtues Owen's New Lanark project was vitiated by an arid worldliness, a disabling conviction that man was merely the creature of external circumstances rather than a voluntary spiritual being whose dignity and importance derived from his membership, acknowledged or not, of the kingdom of Christ as a present reality.[59] Charles Kingsley, a much more combative Christian socialist than Maurice himself, published a series of extracts from Southey, critical of Owen, which drew attention to the more specifically religious perspective of the traditionalist-radical school of thought to which he and Southey and Maurice himself belonged.[60]

While some of the Christian socialists such as J. M. Ludlow had first-hand experience of French socialist activity[61] and saw the movement in aggressively activist terms, Maurice and most of his associates were radical in their religious and social insight rather than in their behaviour. It is unfair and inaccurate to dismiss Christian socialism as only 'the holy water with which the church sanctifies the heart-burnings of the aristocrat', as the Communist Manifesto alleged,[62] but it is equally misleading to seek to identify it too closely with any of the different strands of socialism which came together at the end of the century to provide an ideological basis for the emerging Labour Party. Maurice and Kingsley were Anglican clergymen who felt on Coleridgean grounds that their Church, allegedly the national church, should be more fundamentally concerned about social injustice in the nation, but neither had any desire to found or lead a political party, to engage in the politics of disruption or seek in any partisan spirit to 'Christian-Socialize the universe'.[63] In Maurice's only novel *Eustace Conway* (1834), a rather tedious performance, the hero burns with vague but passionate indignation against the present organization of the world, rather like Lancelot Smith in Kingsley's *Yeast*, but like Maurice himself he shrinks from the crudities of political agitation and the sycophantic rhetoric often associated with urban radicalism, observing

I have a great aversion to eat the words in which I affirm, that their [the workers'] rulers deserve to be hanged for not enlightening them by declaring, that they are thoroughly enlightened already.[64]

This early distrust of populist politics remained with Maurice throughout his life. He admired Abraham Lincoln but would not have him a drum-beating democrat: the franchise which Lincoln had hoped to broaden was not a licence to wield unlimited political power, he claimed, but a qualification for ministry and obligation in society.[65] Though he distrusted Carlyle's ultimately amoral cult of the hero as political deliverer he shared his fierce conviction that God and not *Demos*, the rabble at the hustings, should be the basis of all government and politics.[66] The acknowledgement and service of one's brothers in Christ, rather than inflammatory declamation from the barricades, was what God required of man in society. Implicitly following Maurice's example, Tom Brown and Kingsley's fictional heroes seek to overcome self in the service of others: they do not go into politics.

Maurice's notoriously controversial views on eternal punishment must be understood in this context of universal brotherhood in Christ. Since the present world was the setting for the realization of the Kingdom of Christ the concept of another, eternal world of everlasting bliss or everlasting torment to which one departed at death called for reappraisal. For Maurice eternal life was knowing God, as St John put it, the quality of life which began the moment Christ was acknowledged within as friend and brother and one began to act out the implications of that brotherhood in one's work in the world.[67] Death did not interrupt this transformed quality of life which had already begun. Attempts to see the New Testament word translated 'eternal' as relating not to quality but only to quantity, to infinitely prolonged duration whether in heaven or in hell, Maurice dismissed as a crudely materialistic conception traceable to the influence of Locke who for Maurice as for Coleridge represented something of a philosophical *bête noire*.[68] Locke had been one of the mainstays of Coleridge's abhorred 'mechanico-corpuscular' theory.[69] In place of popular notions of unquenchable hellfire, and eternal punishment, convenient as an instrument of moral coercion but arguably unbiblical,[70] Maurice saw hell as a terminable state in which one refused to acknowledge Christ, a self-imposed, self-annihilating exile from the vital principle of one's being, a life which was as miserable and impoverished in quality as the life which did acknowledge him was rich and fulfilled. Death in itself made no fundamental difference to either quality of life. There was in man a principle or organic continuity which survived death, so that the Christian 'shall not cease to see the Lord, even the Lord in the land of the living; no, nor man with the inhabitants of the world. A new and mysterious attraction holds him to both.'[71]

While this liberal theology deprived his disciples Kingsley and Hughes of the literary opportunity to indulge in the conventional melodrama of the squalor of sin and the terrors of death and hell balanced against the remote splendours of heavenly glory it released other imaginative possibilities. *Tom Brown's Schooldays, Alton Locke* and *The Water-Babies* all contain dream-visions of what might be described as eternal manliness, purposeful work in the world which continues irrespective of the everyday constraints of time and mortality. As Kingsley's Alton Locke observes, this 'would seem to give my namesake's philosophy the lie'.[72] Hughes even more than Kingsley was profoundly grateful to Maurice for the consoling insight that death involved no fundamental interruption, no sting of final separation in the perspective of eternal life. This had helped him to recover from the grief of his little daughter Evie's death as he was writing the later chapters of *Tom Brown's Schooldays*.[73] Arthur's dream of the river and the people working on either side of it in chapter 6 of Part II is a kind of Mauricean parable of manly work continuing on either side of the river of death. The landscape and the river derive from *Pilgrim's Progress*, a favourite of Dr Arnold's,[74] but their significance in this context comes from Maurice's *Theological Essays*.

The Mauricean vision of eternal work in the world to realize the kingdom of Christ is eloquently summed up in one of his best sermons, 'The Word of God Conquering by Sacrifice'. Maurice's text came from the Book of Revelation, from the description of apocalyptic battle where the forces of righteousness were led by the one called Faithful and True, identifiable as Christ Himself. For Maurice this battle was not to be postponed to the end of the world: it was the present and perpetual struggle against falsehood and unrighteousness and all that thwarted the coming of the kingdom of Christ and the realization of universal brotherhood in Christ.[75] Christ as military leader in this struggle was easily assimilated to the literary tradition of Christ as hero-knight with its chivalric over-tones,[76] and his followers then assumed the mantle of nobly embattled Christian manliness, committed to 'fighting rightly understood' as Hughes was to describe it in *Tom Brown's Schooldays*. This sermon inspired the only hymn which Hughes ever wrote, a near-paraphrase of Maurice's words which demonstrates convinc-ingly the link between the shy theologian who was worried about boxing and the boisterous manliness of Thomas Hughes and Charles Kingsley. Tom Brown, like Amyas Leigh and Lancelot Smith and Kingsley's other manly heroes, must learn self-mastery before he can serve Christ and his fellow men in just causes. Hughes' Mauricean hymn concludes:

> We fight for truth! we fight for God!
>   Poor slaves of lies and sin;
> He who would fight for thee on earth
>   Must first be true within.[77]

CARLYLE

Maurice did not feel altogether happy about aspects of Carlyle's teaching, but we have seen that he shared his conviction of God's fundamental and vital presence in the conduct of the present world. Maurice's vision of a continuing heroic battle for righteousness also strikes a Carlylean note, for Carlyle's Cromwell and many of his other heroes tend to be represented as embroiled in the same unending struggle. Like Maurice, Kingsley and Hughes could not swallow the vague theistic gospel of Carlyle entire, but it made a profound impression upon them. The angry Old Testament rhetoric of Carlyle's social criticism, particularly in *Past and Present* (1843), was a brutally direct stimulus to social action and interven-tion, the precise theological rationale of which could be derived from elsewhere, especially from the teaching of Maurice. A continental observer, the Prussian Ambassador Baron Bunsen, anticipated Ford Madox Brown in *Work* by grouping Carlyle and Maurice together, seeing them both as exemplars of 'the same national instinct to consider real life and action as the final object of man'.[78] Carlyle, even more than Maurice, inspired Kingsley and Hughes with moral energy, with a vivid sense of the presence of God in nature and in History, and with an imaginative affirmation of the value of heroes and hero-worship. For Kingsley at least Carlyle also served as a means of access to German romantic thought.

Carlyle first came to the attention of Kingsley and Hughes amidst the discontent and want of the 'hungry forties' when both were alert and impressionable young men: Hughes was still an undergraduate at Oriel and Kingsley a fledgling curate in Dorset when *Past and Present* was published. Both had already had some direct experience of the social and political disquiets which had shaken the country at intervals ever since the end of the Napoleonic Wars, just before they were born. At school in Clifton in 1831, Kingsley witnessed the Bristol Riots sparked off by the refusal of the Lords to pass the second Reform Bill.[79] Less than a year previously, in November 1830, Thomas Hughes, then aged eight, would have heard about the agricultural riots in the Vale of the White Horse in Berkshire, including one at Baulking, less than two miles from his home.[80] The scenes of mob violence in Kingsley's novels, such as the riot in *Alton Locke* and the murder of Hypatia, derive their anarchic vigour from this early experience, while the background of rioting and physical-force Chartism in *Tom Brown at Oxford* clearly draws, anachronistically, on Hughes's childhood memories. Carlyle had gloomily observed these and other terrors and had written his *The French Revolution* (1837) as a moral and political warning to his countrymen in their own country and in their own time as well as a history of social disintegration and violent disruption abroad. By the 1840s matters had got worse, as *Past and Present* testified. Despite the new wealth generated by manufacturing industry people were actually dying of starvation in the mean streets and filthy cellars of the great new industrial cities. Corn Laws which favoured landowners by taxing grain imports inflated the price of bread with disastrous consequences for the poor. There had been an attempt to reform the inefficient old Poor Law in 1834. But this had only the effect of almost starving people by schedule in the dehumanizing work-houses which Carlyle called 'Bastilles' to reinforce the French parallel and dramatize the ominous condition of the country. The government policy of non-intervention buttressed by a heartless *laissez-faire* economics had a lot to answer for. Carlyle's attack on contemporary economic theory, the 'dismal science' as he later called it,[81] is his version of Coleridge's attack on the 'mechanico-corpuscular theory'. This critique of contemporary society had far-reaching consequences. Both Hughes and Kingsley had inherited staunchly conservative political views which their childhood experience of civil disturbance seemed to have confirmed. Kingsley observed that

> What I saw made me for years the veriest aristocrat, full of hatred and contempt for those dangerous classes, whose existence I had for the first time discovered.[82]

But the distresses of the 1840s and Carlyle's prophetic denunciation of them changed all that. After an undergraduate tour of Lancashire and Scotland where Hughes had listened to anti-Corn-Law talk he abandoned for ever the Tory protectionism denounced by Carlyle but espoused by his father Squire Hughes.[83] Kingsley at this time was witnessing the effects of agricultural depression and greedy landlords in Pimperne in Dorset where he had a curacy. His indignation was aroused in the first instance by a neighbouring clergyman, the Revd Lord Sidney Godolphin Osborne, brother-in-law of his future wife, who as 'SGO' wrote scathing letters to *The Times* on the state of the labouring poor in the country.[84] But *Past and Present*, with its apocalyptic account of wretchedness throughout the land, allowed him to generalize from what he could see in his own area and opened up a lurid vision of an unrighteous society in the very jaws of hell which made a much deeper impression than SGO's practical but often rather superficial critique of the *status quo*. The combination of Carlyle and the state of Dorset and Lancashire started Kingsley and Hughes on the road which was to lead to Christian socialism some years later. Carlyle's angry rhetoric is actually reproduced on the lips of Sandy Mackaye, Scottish bookseller and social observer, in Kingsley's early novel of social protest *Alton Locke*. Carlyle could not resist the compliment: he thought Mackaye was the best feature of the book and paid tribute to its insight and poetic descriptions and 'headlong impetuosity of determination towards the manful side of all manner of questions'.[85] Considering that Carlyle did not usually like novels at all this was praise indeed.

Carlyle stimulated Kingsley and Hughes to rush to the manful side of things in personal as well as in social matters. His early book *Sartor Resartus* (1834), a bizarre mixture of quasi-autobiographical narrative, fantastic parody and semi-serious philosophical discussion, recounts among many other things how the protagonist Professor Teufelsdröckh finds himself spiritually and metaphysically marooned in the 'Centre of Indifference'.[86] His plight reflects Carlyle's own lost sense of direction as a young man at Edinburgh University disillusioned with the dry rationalism of his studies and no longer certain of his vocation for the Presbyterian ministry. It also provides a model for the agonies of several generations of honest doubters, at least in literature: Carlyle's disciple J. A. Froude (later Kingsley's brother-in-law) in *The Nemesis of Faith* (1849) and Mrs Humphry Ward in *Robert Elsmere* (1888) seem to have had the Professor at least partly in mind. A residually Christian belief that man is 'a Spirit, and unutterable Mystery of Mysteries' mingles with a simplified version of the German Idealist philosopher Fichte's conception of the possible relations of the self (*Ich*) to the infinite in an apparently alien universe (*Nicht-Ich*), and a certain amount of gruff Scottish common sense, to deliver the Professor from intellectual and moral paralysis. Meaning and purpose are recoverable in the depths of one's own being, but only in relation to the practical duties and opportunities which press upon one. Instead of the Delphic and romantic precept 'Know thyself' Carlyle proposes 'this partially possible one, *Know what thou canst work at*'. No human situation is without its manifest Duty, and only by working away at one's Duty is it possible to 'believe, live, be free'.[87]

This stern but liberating doctrine, effectively jettisoning the vexed questions of theology in return for sturdy practicality and a romantic-intuitive assurance that all was well which could be dignified by religious language, was a very present help in time of trouble. With characteristic exaggeration, dramatizing himself as a reclaimed reprobate, Kingsley glossed over the influence of Coleridge already discussed to express his gratitude:

At a time when I was drowned in sloth and wickedness, your works awoke in me the idea of Duty; the belief in a living righteous God . . .[88]

The Duty both Kingsley and Hughes found lying to hand was the service of the poor in town and country, through education, through co-operation, and through the propaganda campaigns of Christian socialism. But for both men as for the older Tom Brown at Oxford and Lancelot Smith in *Yeast* all this manly work in the world and the combative indignation which fuelled it were modes of deliverance from self-doubt and the guilt associated with a sense of educational and social privilege. They were grateful to Carlyle for pointing them in the right direction even in later years when Kingsley grew exasperated with the relentless ferocity and 'raving cynicism' of the gloomy sage and Hughes parted company with him over the Governor Eyre issue.[89]

Kingsley also acknowledged that Carlyle had helped him to a belief in a living righteous God both in the world of nature and in history. Like the young Wordsworth, Kingsley was a passionate nature-worshipper from an early age. While the *Logos*-centred theology of Wordsworth's friend Coleridge permitted some kind of religious accommodation, Maurice was always worried that Kingsley's 'sympathy with what is beautiful in nature' would make him too tolerant of the world as it was.[90] No-one was ever less tolerant of anything than Carlyle, but Kingsley could still find religious sanction for his love of nature in his writings. This was possible only because Carlyle was frankly inconsistent. The things of the material world and the things of the spirit are the two poles about which his rhetoric swirls, but depending on the argumentative requirements of the moment he links these elements or shows them in stark contrast. To the man of prophetic vision and bad digestion the whole material world can seem appallingly insubstantial in relation to the underlying spiritual realities which obsess his imagination, unobserved but inexorable. This was Carlyle's experience while working on *The French Revolution*, according to his biographer,[91] and it is one reason why he alludes frequently to Prospero's lines in *The Tempest*, 'We are such stuff / As dreams are made on', as if to suggest that the world itself is an airy nothing, a flimsy veil cast over the infinite abysses.[92] On the other hand, in happier moments he found it convenient to be more conciliatory. Nature and the whole rush of activity in the natural world can be regarded as manifestations of Spirit. In *Sartor Resartus* Carlyle loosely translates the song of the Earth-Spirit at the end of the first act of Goethe's *Faust* to suggest that the world of action and appearance can 'weave for God the Garment thou seest Him by'.[93] Like Wordsworth, whom the 'meanest flower that blows' could inspire with intuitions into the mystery of things, Carlyle claimed 'no meanest object is insignificant' to the philosophic eye which would look through it into 'Infinitude itself'. Matter, however despicable, was Spirit and the manifestation of Spirit.[94] Kingsley selected this perception out of the confused and confusing torrent of Carlyle's utterance and used it to justify to himself not only his emotional and aesthetic delight in nature but also his scientific curiosity. In a lecture on 'Science' delivered at the Royal Institution he paid tribute to Carlyle as the idealogue of scientific manliness, giving men 'moral and intellectual courage, – to face boldly, while they confess the divineness of facts'.[95] In *The Water-Babies* and in the person of the scientific doctor Tom Thurnall in *Two Years Ago* the manliness of science was presented in more dramatic form.

Thomas Hughes had less need of Carlyle in this respect because he did not share Kingsley's intense scientific curiosity and delight in nature, or at least not to the extent of worrying about them. He loved the countryside of his native Berkshire, but less for its natural history than for its local traditions and human history. Alfred defeated the Danes at Ethandun in the neighbouring county of Wiltshire, which may have been why Hughes was persuaded to contribute a rather thin biography to Macmillan's eminently Victorian Sunday Library in 1869. The Preface acknowledges the paramount influence of Carlyle's teaching upon 'the hearts of this generation' and enlists his support in a discussion of the need for hero-kings in the crises of history.[96] The category of hero-king invented by Carlyle is taken over by Hughes as the framework of his account of Alfred. The 'Heroic in History', sub-title of Carlyle's *Heroes and Hero-Worship*, is only one aspect of Carlyle's profoundly theocratic historical vision which deeply impressed both Hughes and Kingsley.

At times it almost seems that the Devil looms larger in Carlyle's historical imagination than the God of righteousness. Unexpectedly, Kingsley claimed that it was possible to see in Carlyle 'not a dark but a bright view of life', but this was only when his teaching was 'translated and explained by the great truths of Christianity' which were available to Kingsley from other sources.[97] The religion of hope and love was perhaps too amiable to sit comfortably alongside Carlyle's lurid rhetoric of cataclysm and disaster. Kingsley was surely poking fun at him as well as at his American visitor R. W. Emerson when he described how in an unsuccessful attempt to shake Emerson's serene optimism Carlyle took him to the most squalid parts of London and then, as a last resort, to the House of Commons, asking 'd'ye believe in the devil noo?'[98] But the devil who stalked the earth like a raging lion had his opportunity in the past and present only when the God of righteousness was flouted and ignored by a wicked and unjust society. The heedless frivolity of French aristo-cratic society in the 1770s represented a case in point:

Ye and your fathers have sown the wind, ye shall reap the whirlwind. Was it not, from of old, written: *The wages of sin is death*?[99]

This pattern of moral judgement, expressed in the language of the Kirk, coexists with a precarious balance between chaos and order, darkness and deliverance in Carlyle's historical and social writing. The archetypal imagery of fire, instrument of judgement and destruction but also of purification and rebirth, Phoenix-like, from the ashes, helps to articulate this complex of ideas. The end of the *ancien régime* is presented in this light: 'skyward lashes the funeral flames, enveloping all things: it is the Death-Birth of a World'.[100]

The dialectic of God and the Devil, Anarchy and Authority, recurs eternally in Carlyle. It is present in twelfth-century England as well as in the 1840s in *Past and Present*. Its most dramatic manifestation is in the English Civil War, when God was ranged against 'very many visible Devils, on Earth and Elsewhere'.[101] Irrespective of the precise historical circumstances, which Carlyle tended to see as symptoms rather than as causes, the problem and the solution were much the same. No time need have gone to ruin could it have found a great man as deliverer.[102] Consultative democracy, parliamentary action, extending the franchise, conced-ing the demands of the Chartists, were hopelessly superficial responses to threatening chaos and disaster. Heroes were needed:

Hero-kings and a whole world not unheroic, – there lies the port and happy haven, towards which, through all these stormtost seas, French revolutions, Chartisms, Manchester Insurrections, that make the heart sick in these bad days, the Supreme Powers are driving us.[103]

The story of Abbot Sampson of St Edmundsbury is rescued from the obscurity of a mediaeval chronicle as a parable: a strong and resolute hero-figure can emerge in the midst of chaos and disorder and restore order and harmony by sheer force of personality and an intuitive sense of what needs to be done. This inner conviction can be assimilated to the Divine Idea to which the elect band of the initiate have privileged access in Fichte's philosophy as Carlyle understood it.[104] While Justice, Valour and Pity are the ostensible characteristics of the Carlylean saviour-hero his embodiment of the Divine Idea and the purposes of God makes him alarmingly independent of ordinary moral and social restraints, provided only that he is manifestly in earnest. Perhaps conscious of himself as a wild outsider uttering lurid prophecies in broad Scots to London audiences, Carlyle goes out of his way to emphasize the vaguely Germanic uncouth vigour of his heroes, charged with a message and a majestic purpose which almost defies the glib orderliness of articulate speech. Odin the god and Mirabeau hero of *The French Revolution* turned out to have unexpected affinities with Mohammed as beings who were all wild, earnest, profound, with a great soul 'struggling vehemently to utter itself in words'.[105]

Oliver Cromwell, rescued from the contempt or neglect of earlier historians, was the greatest and the most vividly imagined of all Carlyle's strong and almost silent heroes. This great 'inarticulate prophet' whose silences and unconscious instincts as Carlyle deciphered them demonstrated his spiritual profundity was the supreme deliverer of the age.[106] He rescued his countrymen from the deadness of well-worn clichés in religion and politics, 'formulae' which for too long had masked injustice and wrong. As statesman and as warrior he was supreme among the Puritan heroes who fought for righteousness on God's side, representing 'the essence of all Heroisms and Veracities that have been, or that will be'.[107]

Carlyle's Puritans, imagined as latter-day Children of Israel on the march to the promised land,[108] can easily be assimilated to the manly Christian heroes engaged in the battle for truth and right and social justice as Maurice and Kingsley and Hughes envisaged it. But the relationship between Carlylean heroes and Christian manliness is complex. Kingsley and Hughes wanted all men to be brothers in Christ and manly Christian heroes where Carlyle would have been content to have them hero-worshippers. Both Kingsley and Hughes were inclined to hero-worship themselves, like many of their generation, and both wrote about heroic individuals in the world around them as well as in their novels. But these heroes were for emulation rather than adulation. They tended to be both less romantic and more accessible and domestic than Carlyle's remote quasi-mythical figures: Florence Nightingale and David Livingstone rather than Mohammed and Napoleon.[109] The Carlylean saviour-hero instinct with the Divine Idea and privy to the eternal purposes of God is a vaguely heretical notion which challenges the uniqueness of Christ the Saviour, the Word of God in human form. Victorian paintings of Carlyle's supreme hero Cromwell unconsciously draw attention to this: Augustus Egg's *Cromwell Before Naseby*

2   Augustus Egg, *Cromwell Before Naseby* (1859)

(illustration 2) depicts an earnest hero at prayer very much in the
tradition of paintings of Christ at prayer in Gethsemane.[110] The
Carlylean cult of the hero could be sanctified (as it was by Kingsley
and Hughes) only if it was simultaneously concentrated upon the
person of Christ and democratically diffused so that all men who
followed Christ could be not merely possible but actual heroes.
Carlyle's celebration of the hitherto derided Cromwell and his
down-to-earth Puritan followers helped to broaden the romantic
conception of the saviour-hero just as Coleridge's notion of the
clerisy had done, but it took the Mauricean ideal of brotherhood in
Christ to complete the domestication of the hero into the manly
Christian.

   Carlyle himself anticipated this consummation in *Past and Present*
by appealing to all men to enlist in the army of righteousness to be
led by the great Captains of Industry so that by heroic endeavour

the nation could be rescued from disaster, but for the most part his heroes are a very select company. As he grew older these heroes became more and more authoritarian and unpleasant: the Drill Sergeant, the bully, the tyrant, Governor Eyre and, worst of all, Frederick the Great of Prussia. Thomas Hughes resisted Eyre and Carlyle's more tyrannical heroes without difficulty, but Kingsley's attitude was more equivocal. It was unfair to complain that he was as much a might-worshipper as Carlyle,[111] but he joined him in defence of Governor Eyre. In his Cambridge lectures on history and in his indulgent presentation of vigorous but brutal and amoral Teutonic manliness in *Hypatia* and *Hereward the Wake* he too readily accepted that the great men who made history and the heroes of past ages could be admired uncritically provided they were strong and in earnest and broadly speaking in the right. Carlyle intermittently seduced him from his own conviction that only self-mastery, unselfishness and moral discipline could make one a manly Christian.

The Mauricean dream-visions of manliness in *Alton Locke* and *The Water-Babies* through which Kingsley expresses the ideal of moral strenuousness corrupted by Carlyle actually owe something to Carlyle, though only indirectly. Kingsley was interested in Carlyle's early articles on German literature. He was worried by the pantheistic tendency which could be detected in Fichte and in Schiller and condemned it under the general label of 'Anythingarianism',[112] but he was fascinated by the account of 'Novalis' and contemplated a translation of his writings. In Novalis's 'Hymns to Night' Sophie von Kühn, a cherished friend who died young, is imaginatively transformed into a spiritualized female principle leading man to the loftiest conception of earthly existence.[113] The veiled prophetess-figure in Alton Locke's dream, actually his beloved Eleanor, serves a similar function: she stands outside time and unfolds the destiny and the moral history of mankind. In *The Water-Babies* there is a visionary fusion of different aspects of the female principle as Novalis had envisaged it in the final scene of the book when the inexorable Mrs Bedonebyasyoudid, the kindly Mrs Doasyouwouldbedoneby, the friendly Irishwoman and the sailors' myth-figure Mother Cary all merge into a single dazzling figure who turns out to have encouraged and rewarded Tom's progress to a better life from the beginning.[114]

Christian manliness benefited selectively from Carlyle's teaching. Perhaps his most valuable contribution was to provide a *rationale* for hero-worship and so help to reinvigorate the tradition of Christian heroism and moral manliness discussed in an earlier chapter. One of the great moral heroes of the nineteenth-century imagination was Arnold of Rugby, particularly as he appeared to hero-worshipping schoolboys in the pages of *Tom Brown's Schooldays*. A patronizing reviewer of the novel tried to dismiss Arnold as an impatient fanatic, but this stung Matthew Arnold into paying tribute to his father as a Carlylean hero, a strong soul at one with the noblest heroes of past generations, 'Helpers and friends of mankind'.[115]

ARNOLD

The heroic Dr Arnold influenced Thomas Hughes more directly than Kingsley. But because Hughes was neither outstandingly gifted nor outstandingly pious at school, unlike the true Arnoldians A. H. Clough the poet and A. P. Stanley, Arnold's biographer, it has been suggested that even he had little real contact with the Doctor and did not come much under his direct influence.[116] In fact Arnold had more impact on both Hughes and Kingsley, and more to do with mid-Victorian Christian manliness, than it might at first appear. Tom Hughes admitted that he left Rugby with 'dreadfully bad scholarship' but he was neither a Philistine nor a fool, and his enthusiasm for historical study and modern literature commended him to the Doctor even if his Latin and Greek did not. There were family connections as well: Squire Hughes had been Arnold's friend and contemporary at Oriel, and George, Tom's eldest brother, had been at Rugby before him. Expelled for failing to support the Doctor's authority in a disciplinary crisis, George was magnanimously invited to spend the Christmas of 1839 with Arnold and his sons at Fox Howe, their lakeland home.[117] Even if Tom Hughes was not quite in the inner circle, he must have come more under the Doctor's eye than many of his school-fellows. Like every other boy at the school he had worshipped regularly in Chapel, where the Doctor's majestic presence in the pulpit, his aura of terrible righteousness, would have made a deep impression, to be confirmed later on by reading Stanley's famous biography.[118] The Arnold posthumously rediscovered in Stanley's pages was not only a great schoolmaster famous for his moral strenuousness: outside the world of school he was also a distinguished scholar, Professor of Modern History at Oxford and an advocate of ecclesiastical and social reform, though these aspects of his achievement might not have been fully understood at the time by his pupils at Rugby.

Charles Kingsley never went to Rugby, to his lasting regret. His

parents considered sending him there but decided against it because
the Doctor's well-known political and religious liberalism offended
their staunchly Tory and Evangelical principles.[119] In later years,
reacting against the views of his parents under the combined shock
of social unrest and Carlyle, Kingsley was attracted precisely by this
liberalism as Stanley had recently described it and identified himself
with the 'Arnoldite spirit', resolving to 'devote body and soul to get
together an Arnoldite party'.[120] One hears no more of this party as
such. It seems it was intended to co-ordinate social concern and
moral indignation against political complacency and Evangelical
and Tractarian otherworldliness. In a sense this was achieved in the
Christian socialist movement a few years later. Arnold's own social
concern and moral indignation, directed to establishing a more
Christian society, can be seen as an influence on the ideology of
Christian socialism and Christian manliness. Thomas Hughes
probably exaggerated when he claimed that only Lord Shaftesbury
and Maurice himself made more positive contributions to social
regeneration in the 'condition of England' crisis of the 1840s.[121] The
rhetoric of Carlyle had surely more effect on the social conscience of
the nation, and the theology of Coleridge and Maurice did more to
sanctify the manly Christian effort to fight iniquity and restore social
justice. But Arnold's influence as schoolmaster, social critic and
historian must be carefully considered.

Arnold's varied activities are unified by his uncompromising
moral severity and his sense of the dramatic. A permanent sense of
crisis made his preaching and his conduct of school discipline an
impressive and exciting affair and animated the intermingled
moral, social and historical commentary in his writings. It is one of
the ironies of history, as Lytton Strachey observed, that this
vehemently earnest moralist should have been misrepresented by
posterity as the founder of the worship of athletics and good form.[122]
Arnold certainly gave a new dignity to schoolmastering as a
profession and enhanced the status of public school education. This
had its effect on the great mid-Victorian expansion of the public-
school system which took place just after his death, but Arnold
cannot be held responsible for all that came after him. The emphasis
on games and good form developed in many of the newer schools
had nothing to do with Arnold himself and only a little to do with the
presentation of games and the conventions of boy-society at
Arnold's Rugby in *Tom Brown's Schooldays*. Harry East takes Tom
Brown to task on his first day at school for not wearing the right sort

of hat,[123] but this trivial example of bad form is in breach not of official school rules laid down by the Doctor but the informal code of behaviour current among the boys themselves. The Homeric football games of the novel are non-compulsory and informal, organised by the boys themselves. Arnold used to take the trouble to come and watch, with 'unaffected enthusiasm', but he remained on the touchline, unlike later sporting headmasters such as Thring of Uppingham or H. H. Almond of Loretto. At a theoretical level Arnold held to the Platonic educational ideal of a blend of 'music' and 'gymnastic',[124] scholarship and sport, but he did little more than tolerate the latter. He could pay lip-service to the rugged British tradition of physical hardihood in a whimsical note on the surprising use of cushions by tender-skinned Athenian oarsmen,[125] but he was appalled by the 'lawless tyranny of physical strength' at school and complained rather priggishly about the unregenerate exuberance of schoolboy life:

when the spring and activity of youth is altogether unsanctified by any thing pure and elevated in its desires, it becomes a spectacle that is as dizzying and almost more morally distressing than the shouts and gambols of a set of lunatics.[126]

Arnold proposed a rather austere Christian manliness as his educational objective: not the physically vigorous manliness of Tom Brown and Tom Hughes but a self-reliant moral maturity which recalls the Coleridgean ideal of self-superintendent virtue.[127] His pupils were given a fair degree of moral and intellectual independence. Discipline was administered by the boys themselves through a system of 'praepostors' or prefects imported from Winchester, Arnold's old school. The view that Arnold was a savage flogging headmaster cannot be sustained. He had comparatively liberal views on corporal punishment and in general boys were treated as much as possible with the courtesy and consideration due to reasonable adults: hence the famous dictum that it was no good telling lies to the Doctor as he always believed you.[128] General reading and individual interests such as geology were encouraged at a time when most schools insisted on the classics to the exclusion of everything else. To stimulate private initiative Arnold seldom offered much actual information as a teacher except as a reward for an intelligent answer.[129] Perhaps this was expecting too much of mere boys: Arnold's denunciations from the pulpit of 'a prevailing spirit of combination in evil', 'general idleness', 'systematic practice of falsehood' suggest that most of the boys disappointed him most of the time, and those who did not may have gratified him at the cost of moral and intellectual overstrain.[130] Lytton Strachey offers a caricature of this possibility in his picture of Clough degenerating by degrees from Arnoldian earnestness into bewildered agnosticism and tying up parcels for Florence Nightingale.[131] Even before he took up his appointment at Rugby Arnold grimly noted the contemporary observation that 'Public schools are very seats and nurseries of vice.'[132] If this was true any attempt to cultivate an earnest moral maturity in such an atmosphere was bound to involve a battle of heroic proportions, a battle which appealed strongly to Arnold's sense of dramatic confrontation and his vigorously combative nature. One cannot help feeling that he exaggerated his expectations and his disappointments, both publicly proclaimed, to secure maximum attention and, if possible, to stir up feelings of guilt and remorse among the boys. The sheer obduracy of boy-nature, which he could never accept on its own terms, was his biggest obstacle as a moral and educational reformer with high hopes of training Christian gentlemen: emotional shock tactics were one of the few weapons to hand, and when one master and seven boys died in a single year (1841) he rather shamelessly exploited the situation in his preaching: given these terrible indications of the uncertainty of life, despite youth and health, 'it does seem a fearful risk to be living unredeemed'.[133] Hughes was still at Rugby in 1841, and it was probably these deaths and the doctor's response that provided him with the setting for Tom Brown's moral reformation which is secured when Thompson dies a Christian death after fever in the school and Arthur almost follows him.

There were more indirect ways of countering the evils of boy-society at school. Though the boys enjoyed a far greater degree of independence than in the later public school, working and playing games with relatively little supervision, the closed, conservative boy-society which this encouraged was not completely impervious to reform and wholesome moral influence, whatever Arnold's pulpit rhetoric might suggest. The fagging system which placed small boys at the service of their seniors was capable of gross abuse, but at its best, Arnold maintained, it could secure quasi-feudal patronage and protection against bullying for otherwise defenceless young-sters.[134] Some of the worst brutalities of school life could thus be kept in check, and superior strength and seniority could be ennobled as chivalric manliness. Evil companions could ruin the character of a schoolboy, but friendship of the right kind could be a source of moral benefit and a stimulus to moral courage. The friendship between Tom Brown and young Arthur, protective on Tom's part, improving on Arthur's, is carefully engineered by the Doctor. In effect it illustrates his sense of the value of friendship in the Christian life at school: one need not be alone in the struggle against the polluted stream of school opinion. The same can be said of the relationship between Tom Brown and Harry East, at first a cheerfully lawless partnership. Even if he had not remembered the Doctor saying so at school, Hughes could have read in his published sermons how

God approves of your being drawn to one another; . . . He knows that the mind's and soul's growth never expands so healthfully as in the society of equals: that no example of good is half so striking as that given by one whose temptations and whose strength are altogether the same as our own.[135]

The Doctor's optimistic plans for the fostering of manliness and moral maturity depended on trusting the boys, encouraging self-regulation through the system of praepostors, emotional appeals from the pulpit, the fagging system and wholesome friendships. It was left to Tom Hughes to add in the one tactic which one feels might have had some chance of success: the appeal by way of the values of the boy-culture itself. Old Brooke is an idealized Christian manly hero, but he is also a sporting hero, a type for which the Doctor had no special enthusiasm, and it is this which makes him popular among the boys. He makes use of this popularity and deploys the rather Philistine rhetoric of school and sporting loyalties in an attempt to promote the Doctor's reforms.[136] By celebrating school games and their heroes before trying to turn them to moral advantage Hughes comes closer to the spirit of boyhood than Arnold ever did, but boyish fun and manly morality, the cheerfulness of Tom Hughes and the seriousness of Thomas Arnold, somehow jar with each other in the novel.

Arnold's seriousness extended to the affairs of Church and State outside the school and gave a sombre tone to his historical writing. One encounters the same grave dissatisfaction with human nature and the existing state of things and the same liberal confidence in the possibilities of improvement and reform against the odds. 'The Church, as it now stands, no human power can save' he exclaimed,[137] but he had hopes that Church and State could be brought into a closer relationship of the kind envisaged by Coleridge so that the welfare of the nation as a whole could be served by a comprehensive and genuinely national church embracing dissenters as well as Anglicans. Like his friend John Renn Hampden, *bête noire*

of the Tractarians, he was in favour of relaxing the religious tests still
in force at Oxford. This led him into open war with the Tractarians
in the pages of the *Edinburgh Review*.[138] Unlike Newman and his
colleagues, Arnold welcomed the rising tide of liberalism in the
country and had no objection in principle to state interference in
Church matters: he insisted that there could be no real conflict
between Church and State, sacred and secular, for 'nothing was too
secular to claim exemption from the enforcement of Christian
duty'.[139] This neatly summed up the attitude of Charles Kingsley to
good and manly work in the world, but it annoyed the aggressively
Evangelical organ *The Record* which turned a deaf ear to the moral
denunciations of Arnold's sermons and claimed he had a heretically
optimistic view of human nature and the proper scope of religious
endeavour.[140]

It was not that Arnold was a worldly reformist cleric who was
happy to co-operate with existing secular movements for social
improvement. He founded the short-lived *Englishman's Register* to
publish information on the 'condition of England' question in a
more Christian manner than Cobbet's *Political Register*. He insisted
on a moralized and Christianized politics and had no sympathy for
the working-class radical movements of his time so affectionately
surveyed by the historian E. P. Thompson. Like F. D. Maurice after
him he thought as a Churchman rather than as a politician. If like
many progressives in the aftermath of the French Revolution he
found aristocratic government indefensible he was equally hostile to
Jacobinism and egalitarian democracy. Both involved the moral
degradation of the people, through tyranny or license. While
extreme inequality was obviously wicked and sinful 'Equality is the
dream of a madman, or the passion of a fiend.'[141] He had the
authority of Napoleon himself for the view that the French like the
ancient Romans had pursued equality at the cost of liberty and the
political welfare of the whole state.[142] Human nature would always
tend to let the side down. His historical studies confirmed his distrust
of aristocratic oligarchies like the Athenian Four Hundred in 411 BC
and democratic political movements such as the Roman popular
party in the time of Tiberius Gracchus.[143] The only sound basis for
political liberty and social improvement in the ancient or the
modern world was educated and enlightened citizens. Moderation,
self-restraint, cool judgement and sturdy self-reliance emerge as the
qualities of the free citizen and progressive, easily identified with the
Christian gentleman Arnold was hoping to train at Rugby.

Education alone could reform the citizen and the state: in contemporary England it had the power to bring about much-needed improvements in the physical condition of the people. But like the Christian socialists, also strongly committed to education, Arnold could see the vicious circle: until there was an improvement in physical conditions there was no hope of education making much headway. Both must proceed together. The complementary tasks of education and social improvement were the plain duty of the church of Christ in the present circumstances.[144]

This vigorous activism provided a model for the manly Christians of the next generation. Like Kingsley, Arnold was to claim the support of Bacon for his endeavours: had not Bacon insisted that 'In this world, God only and the angels may be spectators'?[145] If such manly work in the world involved controversy with school governors or *The Record* or the Tractarians so be it: the battles of righteousness were never won any other way. This fighting spirit appealed strongly to both Kingsley and Hughes. While individual temperament and the stimulus of Carlyle and Maurice had a great deal to do with the combative righteous indignation of their manly Christianity Hughes gave Arnold the credit in his case, recalling his schooldays at Rugby as

training . . . for the *big* fight to which we had all been pledged at our baptism, 'manfully to fight under Christ's banner against sin, the world, and the devil, and to continue His faithful soldiers and servants unto our life's end'.

Hughes was echoing a prayer he would often have heard at school, the prayer Arnold always used after confirmation and communion.[146]

The big fight was not merely lifelong: it continued throughout history. Arnold imported his social, moral and religious preoccupations into his historical scholarship. Following the example of the great German historian Barthold Niebuhr, whose researches on Roman history provided the basis of his own work, he constantly drew analogies between ancient and modern problems and institutions.[147] He linked the early Trade Unions with the subversive *hetairiai* or political clubs of ancient Athens.[148] Discussing the unhealthy reputation of the Roman Campagna in a practical spirit which would have appealed to Kingsley he drew on modern medical evidence and the disastrous experience of British troops in the disease-ridden Walcheren campaign of 1809.[149] The epigraphs which head the chapters of his unfinished *History of Rome* come from commentators on Greek history and the modern history of England, Europe and America, implying with Carlyle that there were fundamental continuities between past and present and that all history could be understood in terms of the same patterns and principles. Supreme among these was Divine Providence, which became dramatically manifest at moments of crisis. For Arnold the two most important battles in the history of the world were Charles Martel's defeat of the Moors at Poitiers in 732, which providentially preserved Europe from the infidel, and the German Arminius' (or Hermann's) defeat of Varus and three Roman legions in AD 9 which confined the Romans to the west of the Rhine and 'preserved the Teutonic nation, – the regenerating element in modern Europe, – safe and free'.[150] This romantic Teutonism was to be reproduced in Kingsley's historical lectures on *The Roman and the Teuton* and in some of his historical novels as historical and racial underpinning for the ideal of sturdy Protestant manliness. After all, Germany had been the cradle of the Reformation and the Anglo-Saxons were one of the Germanic peoples. Like Kingsley, Arnold was intensely English and intensely patriotic, but again like Kingsley he gave God his due: the final defeat of Napoleon's apparently invincible armies brought about the deliverance of Europe, but this was 'effected neither by Russia, nor by Germany, nor by England, but by the hand of God alone.'[151] The hand of God reached out even to unbelievers: when the Carthaginian armies laid siege to Syracuse in 396 BC and imperilled the Greek presence in Sicily this also threatened the 'yet unripened strength of Rome' so that 'the fate of the world' depended on the outcome. Fortunately

Dionysius was inspired with resolution to abide the storm, that so he might fulfil that purpose of God's providence which designed the Greek power in Sicily to stand as a breakwater against the advances of Carthage.[152]

Thomas Arnold gave both Kingsley and Hughes a moral and religious interpretation of history which served to confirm from an unimpeachably Christian source the Carlylean vision of history as the drama of righteousness. As schoolmaster, churchman and campaigner for social reform, seeking to train Christian gentlemen for a Christianized state, he had a powerful influence on the personal and social dimensions of manly Christianity. But despite his dramatic flair and his towering personality Arnold remains a rather severe and humourless figure. One sometimes feels that his indictment of the later Roman Empire for 'social helplessness and intellectual frivolity'[153] applied to the rest of mankind as well. It took the novelist's sympathy with human nature, and particularly boy-nature, to transform Arnoldian earnestness into imaginatively compelling Christian manliness.

4

Kingsleyan manliness (I): its life and times

Kingsley acquired his theology of man, nature and society chiefly from Coleridge and Maurice. He had the benefit of historical and rhetorical stimulus from Carlyle and Arnold, and of a good deal of creative exasperation from the preaching and practice of Evangelicals and Tractarians. But he was too hasty and too much a man of action to be a serious theologian himself. He saw himself more as a 'sporting wild man of the woods' whose temperament and training and such theology as he had equipped him to fight manfully for noble causes and to preach a correspondingly manly Christianity.[1]

After a decade of popular preaching and novel-writing he could sum up his message as the vindication of Esau, a wild man like himself but a good man at bottom. Esau the rough man of the fields, tricked out of his birthright by the smoothly plausible Jacob, is the type of Kingsley's manly Christian heroes from Alton Locke to Hereward the Wake. These latter-day Esaus, often scorned or rejected by the Jacobs of the social and religious establishment, turn out to be splendid fellows with an unacknowledged capacity for gallant service in the battles of righteousness.[2]

But if Esau is an eternally recurring type and part of the eternal purposes of God as Kingsley sees them, he also operates in particular historical and social circumstances. Esau's adventures can in a sense be reduced to pattern, for the Christianity in Kingsley's Christian manliness is a constant. But this does not make his fiction monotonous. Eternal truth mingles in different patterns in different novels with strong personal obsessions, imaginative responses to contemporary events and an awareness of the current cultural and literary atmosphere. One occasionally suspects that Kingsley had read all the popular books of his time, particularly the bad ones. Not surprisingly, form and structure often buckle under the pressure. *The Water-Babies*, for example, is a Mauricean parable of eternal manliness, a novel about cleanliness and climbing-boys, and a satire on Victorian scientists and Victorian children's books. It is also an

78

anarchic fantasy of Rabelaisian extravagance.[3] Formal anarchy
and imaginative extravagance are as characteristic of Kingsley's art
as the brilliant descriptive passages or the scenes of furious dramatic
action. His method of writing accounts for the disorganized vigour of
his narrative: he would compose isolated fragments in his head, 'a
bit here and a bit there', working himself into a frenzy of excitement
as he stormed round his garden before dashing into the study to
commit it all to paper. Descriptions and episodes would be shuffled
into sequence at a later stage; even then the sequence might alter
between serial publication and the finished book.[4] For this reason
the Christian manliness which animates his novels tends to be
disclosed in vivid scraps of dialogue and action and sudden twists of
plot rather than through the gradual unfolding of complex overall
structures. Discussion of it must therefore involve a rather piecemeal
approach to the texts. It might be helpful to begin by reviewing the
background against which each novel was written. Between 1848
and 1866 Kingsley wrote and published seven novels. If they are
considered in chronological order they provide the reader with an
intellectual biography of a prominent Victorian from his twenty-
ninth to his forty-seventh year and an idiosyncratic informal history
of the middle years of the nineteenth century.

Yeast was Kingsley's first novel, published in serial form in *Fraser's
Magazine* between July and December 1848, though not appearing
in book-form until 1851 after the success of *Alton Locke* (1850). The
book conveys the yeasty ferment of ideas and anxieties in Kingsley's
own mind and in the country as a whole. The wooing of the Anglo-
Catholic Argemone by the uncouth but energetic and intelligent
Lancelot Smith reflects the anxious wooing of Fanny Grenfell by the
wild young Charles Kingsley eight years before. Smith's extravagant nature-worship, expressed in the blithe accents of the American philosopher R. W. Emerson, mocks Kingsley's early fascination
with the natural world which never entirely left him. It seeks to
discredit the pagan and pantheistic tendency of an excessive love of
nature by ridiculing Emerson's more ecstatic pronouncements. To
Kingsley's dismay London audiences had been flocking to
Emerson's lectures in the West End as he was at work on the novel in
June 1848: Lancelot Smith would have been particularly interested
in the second lecture on 'The Relation of Intellect to Natural
Science'.[5]

Smith is an unhappy and unsettled man. His emotional and

intellectual disorientation is rather self-consciously literary, a romantic divine discontent culled from Byron's *Manfred* and Goethe's *Werter* with a spice of Bulwer Lytton's *Ernest Maltravers*, one of Kingsley's favourite novels. But Carlyle's *Sartor Resartus* had passed beyond the sorrows of Werter to proffer duty and practical common sense as a route out of the slough of despond, a route which the younger Kingsley had taken and which Lancelot Smith has resolved to take by the end of the novel. Lancelot Smith is a sportsman and a gentleman. This attracts some of the best writing in the novel in the description of the hunt in the opening chapter. Kingsley was a hunting parson and the son of a New Forest squire turned clergyman, so he could identify with Smith as sportsman as well as Smith as romantic pessimist. But the literature of sporting manliness, well-represented by Charles Lever's Irish novels of reckless adventure on horseback, stood in some need of sanctification. One of Kingsley's objects in *Yeast* was to justify the sturdy manliness he loved by linking it with moral manliness. He felt that he had a model before him in the fiction of Captain Marryat for novels such as *Masterman Ready* (1841) had moralized the secular excitements of the sea-story. In later novels Kingsley tried to take in a much wider range of secular concerns but he kept the example of Marryat at the back of his mind and modelled Captain Willis in *Two Years Ago* on Masterman Ready.[6]

Yeast is a story of love, nature-worship, despair, deliverance and sporting manliness. It is also, perhaps more importantly, a novel about the 'condition of England' question which Kingsley had begun to worry about five years before in his Dorset curacy. Carlyle and further experience of rural distress in his Eversley parish in Hampshire increased his sense of urgency which came to a climax when he rushed up to London at the time of the last great Christian demonstration in April 1848. At the time it looked as if there might be violence, perhaps even the beginnings of a revolution. In the event it rained heavily on the day and the demonstration was not only peaceful but miserably ineffective. But it showed that it could be dangerous to ignore the popular indignation and the pressure for urgent constitutional reform which Chartism represented. Kingsley was profoundly impressed and declared that 'my only quarrel with the Charter is, *that it does not go far enough*'.[7] He became a founder-member of the Christian socialist movement which sought to circumvent the extremes of 'physical force' Chartism by involving church and people in the common cause of social improvement in town and country. Information about particularly distressed areas was available to the Christian socialists in Government reports, which were useful to Kingsley for the writing of *Yeast*.[8] So much has been written about *Yeast* and *Alton Locke* as Christian socialist fiction[9] that it will be enough to observe here that Christian socialism was the first and most important social expression of the manly Christianity Kingsley preached in his novels and tried to put into practice.

As the instalments of *Yeast* were appearing in *Fraser's Magazine* Kingsley was frantically busy as parson, man of letters and Christian socialist, with his parish in Eversley, his weekly lecture as Professor of English at the newly-founded Queen's College, London, articles over the signature of 'Parson Lot' for the Christian socialist organ *Politics for the People* and constant meetings with F. D. Maurice, Thomas Hughes, J. M. Ludlow and the other Christian socialist pioneers. Something of this frenzy of excited activity transfers to the novel: both author and narrative gallop faster and faster, one feels, leaping wildly from personal concerns to rural distress and bad landlords to religious questions to London life and finally collapsing from sheer exhaustion. Kingsley had a physical breakdown in the autumn of 1848; the novel ends in disarray when the conventions of realistic narrative are abruptly suspended and Lancelot Smith follows the strange prophet-figure Barnakill into a mysterious otherworld of fully-fledged Christian socialism. Disraeli's 'Young England' novels *Coningsby* (1844) and *Sybil* (1845) were the most recent literary treatments of Kingsley's theme of social crisis and possible renewal. It is not clear whether Kingsley had actually read Disraeli at this date but he had certainly heard of his work. The feudal paternalism of Young Englandism of Lord Vieuxbois in *Yeast* is demonstrated to be an inadequate response to the ferment of distress which only manly Cristianity can cure.

Many of the same obsessions, external circumstances and literary models recur in *Alton Locke*. But the hero is no longer based on Kingsley himself. As the French critic Louis Cazamian demonstrated,[10] Alton Locke the London Chartist and tailor-poet derives from Thomas Cooper the Leicester Chartist and shoemaker-poet, imprisoned for sedition in 1843–4 and when Kingsley first knew him a proselytizing freethinker among working men. Alton Locke was reclaimed for Christianity sooner than his prototype: it was not until 1856 or so, after long correspondence with Kingsley, that Cooper was reconciled to the faith. It was from the earlier part of this correspondence, and perhaps from the published version of Cooper's lengthy autobiographical *Address to the Jury* when he stood trial at Stafford Assizes,[11] that Kingsley got to know about Chartism from the point of view of the working man. Carlyle's idiosyncratic growlings in *Chartism* (1839) and the great Chartist demonstration of April 1848 which had brought Kingsley rushing up to London had hardly given him a full picture of the movement. Other developments served to add depth and substance to the novel's account of the Chartist fiasco of 1848, a year of revolutions in Europe though not, as it happened, in England. In October 1848 Asiatic cholera began to take its toll in London and country districts, and this continued for more than a year. Kingsley spent the last months of 1848 and a good part of 1849 in the west country planning *Alton Locke* and recovering from the exhaustion of the previous autumn so he missed the earlier stages of the epidemic. But he rushed back to Eversley in September 'panic-struck at the increased ill-health of the parish'.[12] Where 'Manichee' Evangelicals such as William Carus Wilson regarded cholera as a divine visitation and did little about it Kingsley set to and declared war on the bad drainage and polluted water-supplies which harboured the disease. From the pulpit he urged preventive measures rather than passive resignation. He had suffered from intestinal cholera, a milder form of the disease, as a child, and this gave a personal urgency to his message.[13] When the *Morning Chronicle* published a graphic account of the cholera districts of Bermondsey he went to look for himself: this experience provided the background for the descriptions of appalling housing and disease towards the end of *Alton Locke*.[14] The *Morning Chronicle*'s brilliant investigative journalist Henry Mayhew began his series of reports on 'London Labour and the London Poor' in October 1849. These included accounts of sweated labour, particularly in the tailoring trade, which gave Kingsley material for his Christian socialist pamphlet *Cheap Clothes and Nasty* published at the beginning of 1850. Out of this evolved Alton Locke's first-person account of his wretched life as a working tailor which helped to drive him into Chartism.[15]

For the rest, the novel is almost bewilderingly eclectic in its range of reference and allusion.[16] This is appropriate enough in a tale supposedly recounted by an earnest autodidact instructed from time to time by Sandy Mackaye the pedantically learned Scotsman. But it also reflects the chaotic variety of Kingsley's own interests and concerns at the time. Emerson is mocked at much greater length than in *Yeast* in the person of Professor Windrush. Kingsley's own fascination with nature and natural history is attributed to Alton Locke and linked with the philosophy of Bacon. Lamarckian biology, ancient and modern history, theories of racial migration, Shelley and Shakespeare, Byron and Burns, St Augustine and the *Arabian Nights* contribute a sense of intellectual as well as of social and political turmoil. Kingsley pays tribute to the Evangelical Lord Shaftesbury, Lord Ashley as he then was, President of the Board of Health throughout the cholera epidemic. But he is severely critical of the otherworldly Calvinist Evangelicalism of Alton Locke's mother. He makes her a Baptist, perhaps reflecting his exasperation with the well-established Eversley Baptists whom he thought a bad influence in his parish.[17] But the established church fares little better: Alton Locke's cousin George becomes a clergyman of Tractarian leanings, but more out of a self-interested desire to fill a fashionable pulpit than to proselytize for Pusey or to serve the people of God who suffer and die all around him. Dean Winstanley is a good man and a naturalist but theologically a hidebound conservative who cannot meet Alton Locke's enthusiasms with an appropriately comprehensive and manly Christianity.

Like *Yeast*, like most of Kingsley's novels, *Alton Locke* is several books in one. It is a novel about urban squalor which describes the disease-ridden area of London where Dickens's Bill Sykes the burglar met his death in *Oliver Twist* (1838). It is a novel about working-class protest like Disraeli's *Sybil* or Mrs Gaskell's recently published *Mary Barton* (1848). Ludlow actually called it 'a man's *Mary Barton*'.[18] But by making its central character a self-taught poet and naturalist Kingsley brings it much closer than its predecessors to the atmosphere of politically alert working-class culture of the kind demonstrated in Ebenezer Elliott's *Corn-Law Rhymes* (1828), subject of an essay by Carlyle and mentioned by Alton Locke himself.[19] Like *Yeast*, Alton Locke is partly concerned with rural distress, drawing again on Kingsley's parish experiences and on SGO's letters to *The Times*. The conventions of picaresque narrative inherited from the eighteenth century and successfully modernized by Dickens in *Oliver Twist* permit an episodic plot which takes the hero to Cambridge and into great houses as well as sweaters' dens. This gives Alton Locke opportunities to disclose his own and other people's snobbery rather in the manner of Thackeray's 'Yellowplush' sketches (1837–1846). It also allows him to present the good and the bad at all levels of society. Lancelot Smith learnt his destiny from contact with both

rich and poor and so does Alton Locke, though Sandy Mackaye
warns him not to be corrupted by fashionable success like the foolish
poet Castruccio Cesarini in Bulwer Lytton's *Ernest Maltravers*
(1837).

Bulwer Lytton's much better-known *Last Days of Pompeii* (1834)
probably gave Kingsley background and atmosphere for his next
novel, *Hypatia* (1853) Both novelists exploit the romantic possibilities of bizarre religious practices in the ancient world and both
explore an imaginatively recreated territory, vivid and brilliant in
the southern sun, which is more violent and licentious and
altogether more exciting than sober mid-Victorian Britain. But
there the resemblance ends, for where Bulwer Lytton offered simple
entertainment Kingsley had complex designs on the past. He rightly
insisted that *Hypatia* was not an allegory of the contemporary scene,
but at one point in it he describes Alexandria as 'the workshop of the
world', Disraeli's phrase for industrial England.[20] Kingsley hoped to
give historical substance to his constant argument in the Christian
socialist *Politics for the People*, that Christianity was not, or should not
be, an exclusive religion but 'the only true gospel for the people',[21]
unlike the esoteric and aristocratic philosophy of fashionable
teachers. The point is made negatively rather than positively. The
sub-title is 'New Foes with an Old Face', Kingsley's admission that
there is a link between his adversaries of the 1850s, specifically, the
Tractarians and Emersonian philosophy, and the churchmen and
the neo-Platonist philosophers of fifth-century Alexandria. The
church of the first five centuries provided the Tractarians with a
model of the Catholic Church which they were hoping to restore
within the Church of England. Christianity had survived persecution to become the official religion of the Roman Empire in the
fourth century, and the fifth century was the epoch of great teachers
such as St Augustine and of austere spirituality such as that of the
monastic communities in the Egyptian desert. But the embattled
Tractarians took a stand on matters of ecclesiastical politics as well
as of doctrine and spirituality. The fifth century was also the era of
Cyril of Alexandria, a formidable churchman well able to establish
political ascendancy over a decadent and enfeebled secular state.
Newman and Pusey must occasionally have longed for another
Cyril to resist the rising tide of liberalism and state-intervention in
church affairs, but the liberal Dr Arnold and Kingsley after him saw
the seeds of corruption in all manifestations of an autocratic church
acting over against the secular state.[22] When Cyril's monks

murdered the philosopher Hypatia and the civil authorities were powerless to stop it this was a black day for church and state and a golden opportunity for the historian Gibbon to renew his gibes against Christianity.[23] Kingsley's novel took its cue from Gibbon, for the Christianity of Cyril's Alexandria was an extreme and degenerate version of the 'Manichee' religion espoused by the Tractarians against which true and manly Christianity had to contend.

Manly Christianity also resisted the soothing vagueness and seductive pantheism of Emerson's transcendentalism, which Kingsley had already attacked in *Alton Locke* and *Yeast* and which he now recklessly assimilated to the neo-Platonism in which Emerson had dabbled. In his Socratic dialogue *Phaethon*, published the year before *Hypatia*, Kingsley attempted a systematic refutation of Emerson's doctrines. This vendetta against Emerson seems curious in retrospect: English thinkers had more influence on Emerson than he upon them. Englishmen were mildly interested in what Emerson had to say, but there was never a formidable school of Emersonians as there was of Darwinians or Marxists later in the century. Kingsley's sustained hostility to Emerson had personal origins. Emerson was inspired among other things by a love of nature, by Coleridge and Carlyle and by neo-Platonism. So was Kingsley. Emerson was the man Kingsley might have been if he had not been saved for the Church of England and a career of social action by his wife and F. D. Maurice. Maurice had warned Kingsley of the danger of tolerating and accepting the moral and physical world as he found it,[24] and Emerson's bland confidence in the goodness of man and nature represented that danger in concentrated form. As long as Emerson's gospel was heard Kingsley felt he and his generation might be seduced from manly moral activism and lulled into lofty dreams and an unwise passiveness. Coleridge had read widely in neo-Platonism, and Coleridge's schoolmaster son Derwent had been surprised and pleased to find his pupil Charles Kingsley poring over neo-Platonic lore in his library.[25] In Iamblichus and Porphyry Kingsley could find a spiritualized view of nature. Hypatia's meditations in this vein, frankly inconsistent with the general tenor of the austere and otherworldly teaching which Kingsley attributes to her, are quite sympathetically presented in the novel. Perhaps such meditations had once been Kingsley's own.

Against this background the sturdy young Philammon, educated by the monks, and the much more interesting cosmopolitan intellectual Raphael Aben Ezra, modelled on the restlessly brilliant Jewish barrister A. H. Louis whom Kingsley had just confirmed,[26] have to discover true religion. This is not easy. Surrounded by religious and philosophical foemen, manly Christianity is left rather short of friends, except for the amiably lawless Goths who make a rather unhistorical appearance. They are the heralds of a brighter and more manly future which was to culminate in the German Reformation and Anglo-German protestantism, a theme Kingsley later elaborated in his lectures on *The Roman and the Teuton*. The citizens of Roman Alexandria and Orestes the Roman prefect, on the other hand, represent the effete and degenerate Roman civilization which was already crumbling before the northern invader.

The contrast between manly Goth and effeminate Roman, at least as old as Tacitus, had presented itself vividly to Kingsley on a recent holiday in Germany. He liked what he saw of modern Germany, but he shuddered when he saw the ruins of the Roman amphitheatre at Trier, symbol of the decadence and iniquity of the later Roman Empire which had collapsed in the west in the face of the emerging vigour and virtue of the Gothic or Germanic peoples.[27] This enthusiasm for Goths and Germans was almost a kind of patriotism: it was always easy to include England with its Anglo-Saxon heritage among the Germanic peoples, particularly when the Royal Family was more or less German and Carlyle had established a fashion for Teutonic heroes. Like many British intellectuals of the period Kingsley had German friends, and in a letter to one of them he eagerly sought confirmation for his theory that the Goths had invented the violin, liking to think that that supremely civilized instrument was unknown to the Romans until the 'barbarians' invaded them.[28]

Kingsley's sturdy and perhaps not so very uncivilized Goths represent Victorian Christian manliness at an earlier stage of development. So do the Elizabethan sea-dogs of his next novel, *Westward Ho!* (1855). He dedicated it to two aggressively manly Christians of his own day, Rajah Brooke of Sarawak, whose bloodthirsty exploits Kingsley was always eager to defend, and George Selwyn the energetic and warlike Bishop of New Zealand, as if to suggest that the spirit of Drake lived on. Kingsley's fascination with the sailor-heroes of Elizabethan England went back a long way, probably to his west-country boyhood, for he emphasizes that Drake and Grenvile and his own hero Amyas Leigh were men of

Devon and works in references to Clovelly of which his father was rector from 1831 to 1835. But his interest was reawakened by the historian J. A. Froude, his brother-in-law and a close friend despite or perhaps because of the offence given to the religious establishment by his agnostic novel *The Nemesis of Faith* (1849). Froude's articles on 'England's Forgotten Worthies' (1852) and 'The Morals of Queen Elizabeth' (1853), precursors of his massive *History of England from the Fall of Wolsey to the Defeat of the Spanish Armada* (1856–70), inspired Kingsley with the sea-going patriotism and the chivalrous loyalty to the much-maligned Queen Elizabeth which animate *Westward Ho!* To recapture the atmosphere he went back to Drake's Devon and stayed at the little port of Bideford while working on the book. Another close friend, Charles Mansfield, had recently returned from travels in Brazil and Paraguay: his experiences helped to enliven Amyas Leigh's South American adventures against the Spaniards.[29]

The Elizabethan conflict with Catholic Spain was often regarded in the light of a Protestant crusade. The circumstances of the early 1850s made this a particularly timely theme. Unashamedly anxious to write a best-seller to improve his threadbare finances, Kingsley wrote to his publisher about the book in February 1853, observing that 'considering these times of The Pope & the French Invasion, it may make a hit, & do good'.[30] Once again, as in Elizabeth's reign, Pope and politics were closely, even dangerously intertwined. Victorian anti-Catholicism had taken on a new lease of life in 1850 when the long-defunct Roman Catholic hierarchy was restored in England to the accompaniment of some magniloquent bluster from Cardinal Wiseman. This so-called 'Papal Aggression' provoked widespread indignation throughout the country and was heatedly debated in parliament from 14 to 25 March 1851, as we have seen. The revival after the famine of the Irish Orange Associations, staunchly opposed to the Pope and tenant-right as the twin evils of the day, kept 'no-Popery' controversy in the news. The recent persecution of a Genoese Protestant furnished the *Daily News* for 29 January 1853 with an opportunity to protest against Popish tyranny as if the sixteenth century had returned.[31] Meanwhile the political turmoil in the Papal states in Italy had begun to involve other European powers in the affairs of the Papacy. In 1849 Louis Napoleon brought the Pope back from exile in Gaeta and late in 1852 it was announced that the grateful pontiff was planning to crown him emperor of France, though in the event the coronation took place without the Pope.[32]

This caused profound disquiet in England. There were rumours that the new emperor might try to win popularity by avenging the national humiliation of Waterloo in an aggressive war against England. The victor of Waterloo, the Duke of Wellington, had only just passed away, in September 1852, and almost with his dying breath, it was recalled, he had recommended strengthening Britain's defences by sea and land as invasion might come at any time.[33] Before long the press had whipped up a full-scale invasion-scare. The very title of the new emperor, Napoleon III, hinted at the tradition of conquest and invasion associated with the first Napoleon. Was it significant that the French navy was expanding? Was the island race once again in danger from the fleet of her old enemy?[34] In January 1853, while Kingsley was planning *Westward Ho!*, the radical M. P. John Bright addressed a Peace Society rally in Manchester convened in an attempt to stem the tide of aggressive anti-French feeling. *The Times* trounced Bright's speech as 'imprudent, unmanly and unpatriotic'.[35] This manly and patriotic hysteria, linked with anti-Catholic feeling in that emperor and Pope were political allies, was just the stimulus Kingsley needed for his rousing patriotic tale about an earlier aggressor in alliance with an earlier Pope.

Long before Kingsley's novel was finished the French invasion-scare had been forgotten. The French aggressor of 1853 had become Britain's ally in the Crimean war by 1854. But one patriotic cause could be very much like another. Kingsley knew that his novel would 'make a book which people will read in these war-times and learn what glorious fellows their forbears were'.[36] Anti-French feeling was overlaid with anti-Russian feeling, reflected in contemporary *Punch* cartoons (illustration 3). Fighting against the Spanish Armada or against the Russians at Sebastopol could be easily assimilated to Kingsley's manly Christian rhetoric of perpetual warfare on the side of righteousness against evil. In his war-pamphlet *Brave Words for Brave Soldiers and Sailors*, published the same month as *Westward Ho!* for distribution among the troops at Sebastopol, Kingsley assured them that

he who fights for Queen and country in a just cause, is fighting not only in the Queen's army but in Christ's army . . . Believe that you are sharing in . . . the everlasting war which the Lord Jesus wages against all sin, and cruelty, and wrong . . .[37]

In *Westward Ho!* he treated the defeat of the Armada as an episode in the same ever-lasting war, a victory of the angels of light over the

"SALUTE THE ROOSHIANS? AYE, AYE, SIR."

3 Crimean manliness: cartoon by John Leech in *Punch* (1854)

fiends of darkness.[38] Kingsley and his countrymen needed to
reassure themselves that there could be such a thing as a just war
attracting divine assistance for the Crimean adventure almost
foundered through military blunders and administrative short-
comings which even Florence Nightingale could not put right. Even
at the outset many had wondered at the wisdom and justice of
fighting for Islamic Turkey against Christian Russia.[39] In February
1854 the Evangelical Lord Shaftesbury argued in the House of
Lords that the Bible was more easily available in European Turkey

than in Russia: where the Czar had actively discouraged Christian
missions and suppressed the Russian Bible Society the Turks had
been surprisingly co-operative.[40] But Tractarians and others more
sympathetic to the Russian Church than to biblicist Evangelicalism
were unimpressed. They could reasonably claim that the presence of
Christian missions in the Czar's domains, already well served by the
Russian Orthodox Church, had been an unwarrantable imperti-
nence in the first place, not unreasonably resented. Newman's
lectures on Turkish history, delivered in 1853 just before the war
broke out, painted an unflattering picture of Turkey as 'an infamous
Power, the enemy of God and man', observed that the Czars of
Russia had fortunately inhibited Turkish expansion in Europe, and
suggested that no Christian reader could possibly refuse to wish
Godspeed to 'any Christian Power, which aims at delivering the
East of Europe from the Turkish yoke'.[41] When Britain went on to
declare war on just such a Christian Power and then bungled the
whole affair Newman felt that the British people themselves were to
blame, 'the ignorant, intemperate public, who clamour for an
unwise war'. In a series of articles entitled 'Who's to Blame?'
Newman argued that the British constitution itself, admirably
liberal and permissive in peacetime, discouraged and frustrated the
strong and effective government action which was needed to win
wars: it would suit Britain much better to avoid war altogether,
particularly this one.[42] Not surprisingly Kingsley resented such
unpatriotic murmurings: one almost suspects that he supported the
war because the Puseyites and Newman, now a Roman Catholic,
were so much against it. 'I am tired of these men's falsehood', he
complained in a letter.[43] Coleridge had questioned the national
loyalties of the Catholic priesthood twenty-five years before[44] and
Newman's articles on the war seemed to confirm his misgivings,
which Kingsley shared. The well-documented treachery of English
Jesuits and other Catholics during the Elizabethan war with Spain
provided a sinister parallel which would not have been lost on the
first readers of *Westward Ho!*: at moments of national crisis one could
not trust the Catholic clergy.

The Crimean war was one of the events of 'two years ago' which
Kingsley had in mind in his next novel *Two Years Ago* published
early in 1857. The other was a further outbreak of cholera in 1853–4.
Kingsley was emotionally involved with the war and practically
involved with the cholera: there are numerous references to both in
his letters at the time. But the novel is more concerned with fighting

disease and unmanliness at home than fighting the Russians on the Black Sea. Kingsley exploits the glamour and the challenge of war as a testing-ground for manly virtue and towards the end of the book several of the principal characters actually get to the seat of war, but the novel does not follow them there. Tennyson's famous 'Charge of the Light Brigade' had bestowed on Balaclava and indeed the entire war a patina of glory which it badly needed. Kingsley's brother Henry, also a novelist, and G. A. Lawrence, often linked with Kingsley as a 'muscular Christian' writer though his books were distinctly unChristian, both took advantage of this and included their fictional heroes among the gallant six hundred of the Light Brigade.[45] Kingsley deliberately relinquished his opportunity to describe the heroism of war to make the point that a truer heroism could be found at home, a tactic often adopted by the apologists of moral manliness, discussed in an earlier chapter. His hero Tom Thurnall is an adventurous doctor, modelled on the well-travelled Dr George Kingsley, another brother.[46] Thurnall may think that his path to glory will be his posting as an undercover agent in the Crimea but he has already covered himself with glory in the less glamorous task of combatting the cholera in a west-country village. To emphasize the point Kingsley makes his Crimean adventure an absurd fiasco which so chastens the self-sufficient adventurer that he becomes a manly Christian at the last.

Kingsley's Christian manliness had changed direction since he wrote *Yeast*. His Christian socialist ardour had cooled a little, though the increased prosperity of the country had done something to alleviate the social distress which gave rise to it in the first place. The manly Christian warfare against evil continued, but the specific adversary was now preventable disease. This was a more limited area of concern than the social, political and economic organization of the nation but Carlyle had urged men to be practical and know what they could work at. Like Tom Thurnall Kingsley was a little chastened by experience and abandoned some of his wilder and more utopian projects to concentrate on sanitary reform. In the spring of 1854 he was living in Bideford, hard at work on *Westward Ho!*, when the cholera reached the district. Though he was only a visitor, without parish responsibilities in the area, he joined in the work of house-to-house visitation and did what he could to halt the disease.[47] Aberalva, scene of the cholera in *Two Years Ago*, is based partly on Bideford and partly on nearby Clovelly, Kingsley's boyhood home. But the novel ranges far beyond Aberalva: Tom

Thurnall happened to be shipwrecked there and Kingsley just
happened to be staying in Bideford but both had business elsewhere.
In February 1854 Kingsley had been in London with a deputation
which had waited on the Prime Minister, Lord Palmerston, to
discuss sanitary matters. Lives were at stake in England as well as the
Crimea but Kingsley hoped he had done some good, melodramatically observing 'Remember, it is now a question of blood-guiltiness –
that is all'.[48] In fact he had plenty of confidence in Palmerston's
practical attitude towards the cholera. The Prime Minister had
infuriated the Edinburgh Presbytery of the Church of Scotland and
the Evangelical *Record* in October 1853 by refusing their request to
proclaim a national fast-day with public prayers against the
cholera. Scientific measures to check the disease seemed to him
rather more in keeping with the spirit of practical Christianity, he
said. Kingsley was delighted by this reply and agreed whole-
heartedly.[49] In *Two Years Ago* the Aberalva dissenting congregation
are convulsed with hysteria when urged to abase themselves in the
face of the pestilence visited upon them for their sins. This needless
panic only makes them more liable to be carried off by the disease.
Both Palmerston and Kingsley subscribed to the 'sanitary idea'
propounded by Edwin Chadwick, whose labours at the Board of
Health had helped to contain the cholera epidemic of 1848–9.
Chadwick was convinced that

man could, by getting at first principles, and by arriving at causes which
affect health, mould life altogether into its natural cast, and beat what had
hitherto been accepted as fate, by getting behind fate itself.[50]

Fatalism and moral inertia were the worst enemies of all, a point
which Kingsley dramatized in the contrast between the manly and
energetic doctor Tom Thurnall and the effeminate poet Elsley
Vavasour who neglects his own health and does nothing to improve
the health of his wife and family. By 1857, when *Two Years Ago* was
published, Chadwick was a frequent visitor in Eversley Rectory,
Kingsley's collaborator in the campaign for sanitary reform and
health education.[51]

The cholera and the Crimean war by themselves could have
supplied material for more than one novel but Kingsley extends the
scope of *Two Years Ago*, and rather confuses the reader, by
incorporating an extended satire on the so-called 'spasmodic' poets
such as P. J. Bailey in his portrait of Elsley Vavasour. He also tackles
the issue of the abolition of slavery in America. There is a
preposterous sub-plot about a runaway slave turned opera-singer

and her vaguely Emersonian lover Stangrave, who hesitates to commit himself manfully to the cause of the black man.

Elsley Vavasour is the best example of an unhealthy mind in an unhealthy body in Kingsley's fiction. Like Coleridge before him, Kingsley distrusted the extravagant sentimentalism of the eighteenth century and thought it an unsound foundation for a moral and manly life. He regretted that the literary tradition of voluble emotionalism had continued with Shelley and with lesser poets under Shelley's influence.[52] P. J. Bailey, author of *Festus* (1839), Alexander Smith who published his *Life Drama* in 1853, and Sidney Dobell the poet of *Balder* (1854) devoted themselves to undisciplined exploration of the violent sensations of emotionally unstable *personae* whom it was tempting to identify with the poets themselves. Rape, suicide, madness, ecstatic delight and the ultimate despair in which men curse God provided a large part of the poetic stock-in-trade of these 'spasmodic' rhapsodists. Anticipating Kingsley, the literary journalist W. E. Aytoun had ridiculed their absurdities in his wicked parody *Firmilian: a Tragedy* (1854). The artistic and dramatic potential of the half-crazed *persona* was realized most effectively not by any of the 'spasmodic' poets but by Tennyson in *Maud*, published in 1855.[53]

Like Carlyle, who celebrated strong and inarticulate heroes, Kingsley thought it was healthier not to bring the emotional life too much into the open or to be the puppet of one's momentary sensations. Mind and body should be devoted to the bracing work of social improvement rather than poisoned by morbid introspection. Elsley Vavasour demonstrates the dangers of this: he is an excitable and hyper-sensitive poet in the 'spasmodic' tradition, with traces perhaps of the foolish Castruccio Cesarini in *Ernest Maltravers* as well. He becomes inflamed with jealousy (for no good reason), runs amok on Snowdon and eventually dies from opium.

By way of contrast Kingsley invents two healthy and kindhearted mountain-rescuers for Vavasour, Rugby-educated undergraduates who are part of a reading-party in the area. They owe a good deal to that manly Christian Tom Hughes, with whom Kingsley spent a climbing holiday in Wales. Their clean-limbed energy also reflects the vigour of the most famous reading-party in Victorian literature described by the Rugbeian A. H. Clough in *The Bothie of Tober-na-Vuolich*, a narrative poem Kingsley greatly admired.[54]

One might expect Kingsley to hold Byron at least partly

responsible for the excesses of Elsley Vavasour. After all, the
romantic despair of *Manfred* contributed to the immature melancholy of Lancelot Smith in *Yeast*. But Byron redeemed himself in
Kingsley's eyes by his sturdy manliness and his life of action as well as
sensation which came to an heroic and self-sacrificing end among
the ruffians at Missolonghi, his comrades in the struggle for Greek
independence.[55]

The abolitionist sub-plot is an attempt to liberate the notion of
righteous quest which helps to make manliness Christian manliness
from the confines of the English experience. Maurice had taught
that the battle for truth and right was universal and everlasting and
the cosmopolitan Stangrave helps to open up wider perspectives. He
is a modern knight-errant who is chivalrously protective of his lady,
Marie, but needs to find a knightly cause before he can win her.
Kenelm Digby's revival of chivalric idealism in *The Broad Stone of
Honour* (1822) had attracted the interest of Disraeli and the 'Young
England' movement and more recently of Edward Fitzgerald,
translator of Omar Kayyám and author of *Euphranor* (1851), a
Platonic dialogue about education.[56] Kingsley makes Stangrave
visit the original 'Broad Stone of Honour', the enormous fortress of
Ehrenbreitstein at Coblentz which Kingsley himself had seen on his
German holiday and noted 'for professional purposes'.[57] Honour
eventually summons Stangrave to fight against slavery. Harriet
Beecher Stowe's *Uncle Tom's Cabin* (1852), a best-seller in England
as well as America, had publicized the plight of negro slaves and
impressed Kingsley so much that he entertained the author at
Eversley Rectory when she came to England in 1856.[58] They
probably discussed the presidential elections of 1856, mentioned at
the beginning of *Two Years Ago*, in which the abolitionist candidate
John Charles Frémont was defeated. In the novel Claude Mellot
thinks this is a disaster but Stangrave merely hopes that by the next
election the abolitionist cause will be better organized. Mellot wants
all the slaves freed at once but Stangrave favours a more gradual
approach which will not drive the slave-owning southern states into
open rebellion. This rather cautious abolitionism reflects Kingsley's
ambivalence on the issue. The trouble was that he always wanted to
be both roundhead and cavalier, liberal and conservative. Like
Carlyle he was attracted by the moral fervour of Puritanism in
seventeenth-century England, and in abolitionist New England for
that matter, but he came from the landed gentry and was
sympathetic to the chivalry and the broad acres of the Old South.

He shared Mrs Stowe's passionate concern for the slaves and his hero
Tom Thurnall helps Marie to escape from slavery by way of the
'underground railway' described in *Uncle Tom's Cabin*, but he
remembered that his maternal grandfather Nathaniel Lucas had
been a judge on Barbados and a member of a long-established slave-
owning family.[59] Some years later, during the civil war which broke
out despite Stangrave's hopes that it could be avoided, Kingsley
lectured his Cambridge undergraduates on the background to the
conflict and annoyed his more radical friends such as J. M. Ludlow
and Thomas Hughes by his sympathy for the slave-owning south
and his lukewarm attitude to Abraham Lincoln.[60] He never really
liked the negro but he could think of him as a man and a brother in
the honourable tradition of William Wilberforce and he largely
avoided the racist hysteria of his former master Carlyle.

American affairs and a continuing concern with sanitary reform
provide part of the background for Kingsley's next novel *The Water-
Babies* (1863). Yankee self-righteousness and democratic bump-
tiousness were an easy target in the book and in the England of the
1860s since they could be blamed for leading the northern states into
a civil war which Kingsley and many of his countrymen thought
could have been avoided. The moralistic American Cousin
Cramchild and the abusive annual caucus of the hoodie-crows
which feature in the book reflect the contemporary undercurrent of
irritation with America in Britain.[61] Water in *The Water-Babies* is a
cleansing agent in a literal sense as well as a symbol of baptismal
renewal. The physical health obtainable through cleanliness and
adequate sanitation is a precondition of the moral and religious
purification Tom the chimney-sweep's climbing-boy has exper-
ienced by the end of the book: Tom's early dirtiness and physical
degradation had not given his soul much of a chance. But almost
every aspect of the current affairs of the 1850s and early 1860s makes
an appearance in the novel.[62] What had begun as a whimsical fairy-
story for his youngest son Grenville grew into a freewheeling
commentary on the issues of the day. The 1861 Children's
Employment Commission had agreed to include the problem of
climbing-boys in its terms of reference. After publication of its report
in 1863 the success of Kingsley's novel helped Lord Shaftesbury to
get parliamentary backing for a more effective ban on climbing-
boys in the form of the 1864 Chimney Sweepers' Regulation Act.
Jonas Hanway had first drawn attention to the problem ninety years
before and Blake had sung of child chimney-sweeps in *Songs of*

Innocence and Experience (1794), but climbing-boys were still suffocating in chimneys as late as 1875, when further parliamentary action was taken.[63] Little Grenville Kingsley (who later ran away from school)[64] would have relished his father's repeated gibes in the story against the rote-learning of useless information in the classroom, but he might not have realized that they were an enlightened and sardonic commentary on Robert Lowe's 'Revised Code' of 1862. This set up the iniquitous system of payment by results for elementary schoolteachers who were thus encouraged to cram their protégés to convince government inspectors of their efficiency. The novel also pokes fun at competitive examinations. The unending series of public and professional examinations which overshadows middle-class youth to the present day was a very recent development in 1863: the Committee on Nominating and Selecting Candidates for Junior Appointments in the Civil Service had introduced open competition by examination only in 1860. Twenty years later, in *Iolanthe*, Gilbert and Sullivan were still making fun of competitive examinations and of 'that annual blister, / Marriage to deceased wife's sister', a controversial reform in the Marriage Laws which Kingsley mocks in *The Water-Babies* though it had first been proposed as long ago as 1849.[65]

But the most significant influence on the novel was the publication of Darwin's *Origin of Species* in 1859 and the subsequent warfare or, as it has recently been argued, pseudo-warfare between science and religion,[66] in which 'Darwin's bulldog' T. H. Huxley played a major role. Kingsley was on friendly terms with Huxley at the time despite their disagreements on religious matters. Huxley's famous confrontation with Bishop Wilberforce in 1860, when he claimed he would rather be descended from an ape than a bishop who abused his intelligence, is genially represented in the novel as a civilized exchange of insults between a professor and a divine.[67] In the course of a prolonged controversy in the pages of the *Athenaeum* in 1861 Huxley had demonstrated that Sir Richard Owen, the eminent anatomist, was quite wrong when he claimed that the human brain was anatomically significantly different from that of other primates because it had a distinctive lobe or hippocampus minor, and that this helped to disprove the Darwinian theory. This becomes the absurd 'hippopotamus major' in the slapstick of *The Water-Babies*.[68] Huxley had written to Kingsley in 1860 saying he would like to believe in the immortality of the soul but he could find no empirical evidence to convince him.[69] The romantic intuitionism which

Kingsley had learnt from Coleridge allowed him to go beyond empiricism: in Coleridge's terminology Huxley was enslaved by the 'mechanico-corpuscular' philosophy stemming from Locke and Descartes. *The Water-Babies* is Kingsley's extended answer to Huxley. He pokes fun at sceptical scientists and with mock gravity raises the epistemological problem of whether one can say water-babies exist or not. The strange blend of accurate marine biology, one of Kingsley's hobbies, and surreal fantasy which makes use of observed realities but juggles them into bizarre patterns, is a conscious strategy for marrying science to mystery. It remains unclear whether Tom has died and passed into another world or whether he is still alive and caught up in some sort of dream-vision. Maurice's teaching on eternal life, to which death made no difference, lies behind this deliberate confusion. As he said in a letter to Maurice, Kingsley's whole object was

to make children & grown folks understand that there is a quite miraculous & divine element underlying all physical nature; & that nobody knows anything about anything, in the sense in wh[ich] they may *know* God in Christ, & right & wrong.[70]

Morality, religion and evolutionary science are brought together in Kingsley's idiosyncratic notion, illustrated at length in the novel, that the soul secretes or moulds the body. This too is a response to Huxley's teaching. In a series of popular scientific lectures published in the same year as the novel Huxley said that the moral and intellectual faculty in man was made possible by physiological structure and organization, though not directly ordered by them. Kingsley chose to regard this as a species of physiological determinism, though Huxley made no such claim, and insisted that it was the other way round: the soul determined the body, not the body the soul.[71] In *The Water-Babies* the Doasyoulikes who live at the foot of the Happy-go-lucky Mountains were once human beings but through sheer idleness they gradually lost the skills and capacities of men and the characteristic human physique that went with them. The survivors of the species had tree-climbing propensities and were very strong, with feet that could grip branches. In fact they were very like apes: their evolution reversed the direction of Darwinian evolution, because their subhuman moral and practical capacities gradually attracted a subhuman physiology. On a much smaller scale Tom's moral condition is reflected in the kind of body he has at any given stage in his personal evolution: when he has behaved in

an anti-social way he discovers he has grown a prickly,
unapproachable body which expresses his uncongenial soul.[72]

Kingsley's whimsical commentary on Darwinism and current
affairs in the form of a children's book makes rather disconcerting
reading today and even contemporary readers found it vaguely
unsatisfactory. The *Spectator* complained that 'his chaff is neither
subtle to men nor intelligible to children'.[73] It is the most extreme
example of Kingsley's ambitious, perhaps over-ambitious attempt
to be serious and entertaining at the same time in fiction which both
exercised private hobby-horses and made a contribution to public
discussion. A fishing holiday by Malham Tarn in the Yorkshire
Dales in 1858[74] supplied him not only with the geographical setting
of the story but with the unbuttoned and inconsequential manner of
fisherman's anecdote after dinner. At the end of the book he makes
fun of the idea that there is a moral to the tale by saying it teaches
thirty-seven or thirty-nine things, he is not quite sure which. He was
never very happy with the demands of a moral age that everything
in literature should have a moral 'wh[ich] you can pick out with a
penknife'.[75] Children's books of the pious variety, particularly
American ones such as Maria Cummins' enormously popular *The
Lamplighter; or an orphan girl's struggles and triumphs* (1854) or Susan
Warner's equally popular *Queechy* (1852), also about an orphan,
offered sentimentally improving accounts of children almost as
deprived and oppressed as Tom the climbing-boy who survived
their troubles and came at last through tears to 'holy peace'.[76] The
moral hardly needed a penknife to isolate it. *The Water-Babies* was
deliberately not that kind of book. Tom ended up as a successful
engineer, involved in vigorous work rather than 'holy peace'.
Kingsley's novel was an entertaining fantasy which had some of the
features of Heinrich Hoffman's *Struwwelpeter* (1847), a grotesque
illustrated children's book which was widely read in England as well
as in Germany. But it used the games fantasy plays with reality to
make a profoundly serious point about higher realities underpinned
by the ever-living God who judges and controls the moral and
physical world. The moral could not be extracted in reductive
fashion because the tale in some sense was the moral, an extended
parable 'wrapped up . . . in seeming Tom-fooleries'.[77] For all its
burlesque and whimsy *The Water-Babies* is a more moral and
religious book than *Hereward the Wake* (1866), Kingsley's last novel.

The legend of Hereward and the last days of Saxon England had
gripped Kingsley's imagination ever since he came across Thomas

Wright's essay on 'The Adventures of Hereward the Saxon' (1846). He had lectured on Anglo-Saxon literature and history at Queen's College in 1848.[78] But the fenland setting of the Hereward story had been familiar to him from early childhood. His father was Rector of Barnack in Lincolnshire from 1824 to 1830, until Kingsley's eleventh year, when the family moved to the west country.[79] Barnack is just to the west of the fens, midway between Bourne and Peterborough and not much more than a dozen miles from either. Kingsley's sources for his novel make Hereward the son of Leofric, Lord of Bourne, and describe his part in the sack of Peterborough in 1070.[80] Kingsley often revisited the fens in later years when he was in Cambridge to give his lectures as Professor of Modern History, a post he held from 1860 to 1869. Though he continued as Rector of Eversley during these years *Hereward*, closely based on mediaeval sources, is more the work of Kingsley the historian than Kingsley the clerical moralist and social critic. The historical Hereward whom Kingsley faithfully renders began as a juvenile delinquent, went on to join with the Danes in the pillage of one of the great minsters of England, was unfaithful to his wife and finally compromised rather shamefully with the Conqueror. In the novel this rather unattractive hero is redeemed only by his savage cunning, his prowess in combat and his long service to the lost cause of Saxon England.

Kingsley treats him fairly indulgently, with only occasional lapses into moralizing. The modish Darwinian theory of the survival of the fittest is invoked in defence of Hereward and the lawless men of his time: in such a primitive age only the savage and the strong could expect to survive at all.[81] Darwin and the historical record provided a convenient excuse for indulging in romantic primitivism: Hereward the Saxon or Anglo-Danish hero is a wild, semi-mythical figure in the same tradition as Carlyle's early Norsemen and Odin their god, but he is also like the wild man Kingsley had once been himself. A certain savagery remained. Even in the midst of his Christian socialist enthusiasms he had offended the more liberal-minded J. M. Ludlow with his unclerical, and uncritical, admiration for that cut-throat adventurer Rajah Brooke of Sarawak, to whom he later dedicated *Westward Ho!* In the year that *Hereward* was published he joined Carlyle in defence of the brutal Governor of Jamaica.[82]

Kingsley's personal hankerings after manly Saxon savagery coincided usefully with the cultural climate of the 1860s in which the

Anglo-Saxons were in high favour. Their finest hour arrived in
1867, a year after *Hereward*, when William Theed completed his
statue of Queen Victoria and her late lamented Albert in Anglo-
Saxon dress and installed it in the Royal Mausoleum at Frogmore.[83]
In the same year the historian E. A. Freeman published the first
volume of his *History of the Norman Conquest*, a magnificent elegy for
'Teutonic England' whose brightest light sank forever at the Battle
of Hastings.[84] Two years previously John Earle had published his
invaluable edition of *Two of the Anglo-Saxon Chronicles Parallel* which
included the *Peterborough Chronicle*, one of Kingsley's sources for
Hereward.

Behind the historical and antiquarian vogue of the Anglo-Saxons
lie two currents of feeling: a radical tradition of resenting the
'Norman yoke' for destroying an ideally liberal political constitution stemming from Teutonic antiquity, and a popular patriotic
tradition of enthusiasm for sturdy English resistance to the French or
rather Norman-French invader.[85] Freeman and Kingsley were in a
sense heirs to both traditions. It was unfortunate for Kingsley that
Freeman was a much more profound and pedantically accurate
historian who probably resented the enormous popularity of
Kingsley's Cambridge historical lectures. His vitriolic review of
Kingsley's *The Roman and the Teuton* (1864), a quirky and spirited
essay in the romantic Teutonism which Freeman also espoused, was
followed up by an onslaught on *Hereward* which rather unfairly
ignored the fact that the book was a novel rather than a piece of
academic history.[86] Both Kingsley and Freeman had studied
Augustin Thierry's romantic nationalist account of the Norman
Conquest, a liberal French version of the 'Norman yoke' theory
which sentimentally grieved over the suffering of the Saxons under
Norman rule and went on to link it with the miseries of other subject
peoples such as the Scots and the Irish later in British history.[87] As
John Burrow observes of Freeman, 'the Norman Conquest was his
historical consolation for not belonging to an oppressed nation.'[88]
Much the same could be said of Kingsley. He had read Bulwer
Lytton's preposterously chauvinistic novel *Harold, the last of the Saxon
Kings* as soon as it was published in 1848 and rather liked it.[89] The
irregular condition of the English church before the conquest had
prompted the Pope to support William's invasion in the hope that
this would give him the chance to impose reforms. Bulwer Lytton
seized on this to give the Saxons the status of honorary protestants
manfully indignant that the Pope has presumed to 'dispose of a free

people and an ancient kingdom'. Harold at Hastings is made to
sound like Kingsley's Amyas Leigh fighting the Spanish Armada:
'Foreign priest is a tyrant as ruthless and stern as ye shall find foreign
baron and king!'[90] Kingsley relished this religious variation on the
well-established theme of manly English *versus* tyrannical Normans
which approximated to his own favourite antithesis of sturdy
protestant manliness and encroaching priestly 'Manichaeism'. It
gave him a special interest in the libertarian rhetoric of romantic
Teutonism which had been endowed with scholarly respectability
by the assiduous researches of J. M. Kemble and of Freeman himself
into 'the immemorial rights of Teutonic freemen'.[91] Like Kingsley,
Freeman had been deeply impressed with the historical work of
Thomas Arnold who sang the praises of Arminius or Hermann for
preserving Teutonic freedoms from the Romans. He paid tribute to
Arminius as 'the first of a roll call which goes on to Hampden and to
Washington'.[92]

But Kingsley, descended from both a Royalist and a regicide,[93]
was a cavalier as well as a roundhead, imaginatively disposed to ride
with Prince Rupert as well as to defend English liberties and take
moral stands with Hampden and the Puritans. William may have
been an invader but he also introduced the continental traditions of
chivalry and romance to Saxon England and who would have had it
otherwise? The genius of Chaucer, for example, had both a Saxon
and a Norman component, Kingsley maintained.[94] He takes
account of this in the novel by exposing Hereward to continental
influences through his travels and his Flemish wife Torfrida and by
trying to teach him something of chivalry, as if to prepare him for the
Conquest. This concession weakens the strain of romantic Teutonism in the novel and by implication unflatteringly aligns Hereward
and his Saxons with the barbarians of pre-Conquest England as
Carlyle had described them, 'lumbering about in pot-bellied
equanimity'.[95] There was also a political argument in favour of the
Normans, advanced by Carlyle and, in much more sophisticated
form, by the historian William Stubbs, romantic Saxonist though he
was: it could be shown that the Conquest brought strong and stable
government.[96] Kingsley accepted Carlyle's hero-worshipping esti-
mate of William as necessary tyrant and 'master-personage'.
Perhaps Hereward, like the Cavaliers or the Jacobites of a later era,
was 'wrong but romantic'.[97]

The mixed heritage of Saxon and Norman in contemporary
England ran parallel to the mingling of highlands and lowlands,

Jacobites and Hanoverians in modern Scotland as Sir Walter Scott
had perceived it. Just as *Waverley* sympathetically describes both
sides in 1745, so *Hereward* seeks to do justice to conqueror and
conquered in 1066. Scott's novel recollects in tranquillity the
partisan emotion of sixty years before. In Kingsley's novel two of his
characters attempt a similar retrospect eighty years after the main
action: in the last chapter Hereward's daughter and her Norman
husband (prototype of the Tory squire) enjoy a peaceful old age
together and muse serenely on past antagonisms. Unfortunately
Kingsley himself was too much of a partisan to make such a
reconciliation very convincing. His novel falls rather awkwardly
between the ardours of romantic Saxonism and pride in the strength
and chivalry of Normandy even while trying to bring them together.

Kingsley retreats from the tradition of romantic Saxonism in
another way by bringing in the Danes. Hereward's status as the
champion of undying national freedoms is badly compromised
when he takes part in a Danish invasion of his own country. As long
ago as 1849 Kingsley had felt that the later Anglo-Saxons were a
rather enfeebled race who needed the masculine vigour of the
Danes.[98] This is reflected in the novel: many of the monks and priests
are degenerate Anglo-Saxons, but the fighting men tend to be
Anglo-Danish. The Danish expedition of 1070 was a matter of
historical record, and the fen country was in any case an area of
Danish settlement, part of the Danelaw. These circumstances
complicate and confuse the pattern of oppositions in the novel, not
least because Kingsley acknowledges the Viking antecedents of the
Norman conquerors. In this case his imagination needed simpler
polarities than his historical information could yield to produce a
compelling historical fiction. Most people find *Hereward* a disappointment after *Westward Ho!*

The Danes rather get in the way in the novel, but Kingsley tried to
make the best of it by half-heartedly tapping the contemporary vein
of pro-Danish sentiment. The Prince of Wales, whom he had tutored
at Cambridge, had married Princess Alexandra of Denmark in 1863
and the Kingsleys had been guests at the wedding. This Danish
marriage contributed to the outraged feeling in England on
Denmark's behalf when Prussia invaded the Danish territory of
Schleswig-Holstein in 1863–4.[99] Kingsley shared this feeling and
went out of his way in *Hereward* to trace a connection between the
family of Princess Alexandra and the family of the Anglo-Danish
Harold who fell at Hastings (ch. 18). But popular enthusiasm for the

Danish cause was much feebler than the wartime patriotism and anti-Catholic feeling which helped to make *Westward Ho!* a best-seller. In the event the British government took no action against Prussia in the Schleswig-Holstein affair and less than a year after finishing *Hereward* Kingsley himself was reconciled to Prussian policy.[100] The parallels with the contemporary scene which had contributed so much polemical energy and excitement to *Hypatia* and *Westward Ho!* were less striking in *Hereward* and did not do much to enliven the narrative. It remains a grim and brutal saga in which sturdy and aggressive manliness, however graphically described, merges all too infrequently into manly Christianity.

5

Kingsleyan manliness (II): some versions of virtue

Kingsley's Christian manliness, or 'muscular Christianity' as it was so often called, was derided from time to time by bright young journalists. One of the most distinguished offenders was Leslie Stephen, later editor of the *Dictionary of National Biography* and father of Virginia Woolf. A fanatical rowing-coach and Alpinist as well as a former clergyman, the agnostic Stephen may have felt that Kingsley was pushing him out of his playground and trying to make it a church preserve. The year before *Hereward* was published Stephen wickedly travestied Kingsley's 'muscular Christianity' as a combination of the muscularity of Bell's *Life* (a sporting journal) and the Christianity of F. D. Maurice's sermons, for which Stephen never had much respect.[1]

Both the manliness and the Christianity of the novels are broader than this implies, but Stephen's remark draws attention to the two audiences Kingsley was always trying to address, and to the problems this involved. On the one hand as a clergyman-novelist he wanted to gain the interest of the Esaus, the rough and sturdy men of the fields whose lives and enthusiasms seemed to themselves and others to lie outside the church altogether. On the other hand he wanted to convince Jacob the smooth churchman that it was because his religion was more exclusive and narrowly focused than Christianity ought to be that so many manly Esaus had so little to do with it. The first audience, like Kingsley himself, might well browse through sporting magazines, newspaper accounts of current affairs or scientific discovery or military matters, books of travel or history and the odd popular novel before riding to hounds or returning to the gold-diggings or rejoining the regiment. The second audience, also like Kingsley, read sermons and serious and improving literature, but unlike him tended to deplore both the life-style and the reading-matter of breezy sportsmen and adventurers and men of the world. Even those who moved between both worlds, Esaus on Saturdays and on holiday but Jacobs on Sundays and during the week, might resent Kingsley's serious designs upon their diversions and his attack on the inadequacy of their seriousness. In his fiction as much as in his parish Kingsley could be relentlessly interfering: the coarse squireen Trebooze in *Two Years Ago* is not allowed to enjoy his sport and his drink in peace but is pestered to join a militia regiment and be made a man of, while the austere and high-minded curate Frank Headley in the same novel is brow-beaten into fighting the cholera, falling in love and developing a burning desire to go out to the Crimea before Kingsley is finished with him. Natural prowess and passion are seen as good things when Jacob tries to ignore them, or good things which could be better used when Esau thinks that that is all there is to life. Kingsley's considerable popular success as a novelist suggests that he usually persuaded both Esau and Jacob to listen, even if Esau retaliated with gibes at 'muscular Christianity' and Jacob denounced him in the partisan religious press.

The message was the same for both. It can be briefly summarized. Physical strength, courage and health are attractive, valuable and useful in themselves and in the eyes of God. The emotional ties of family and of romantic and married love are natural and pleasing to God and should help to give a man a just sense of values and responsibilities. The natural world was created for man to admire and to understand and subdue through sustained intellectual and scientific enquiry which would also disclose the pattern of the moral universe underlying the natural world. Man, endowed with strength and natural affections and the capacity to explore and understand the natural and moral order, should put all these gifts to work in the service of his brother man and of God, as patriot or social reformer or crusading doctor. These four fundamentals of Kingsleyan Christian manliness can be attributed variously to different aspects of the secular and religious background surveyed in earlier chapters and to personal concerns highlighted by the specific circumstances which have just been discussed. They are the constants of a varied literary output and a varied life.

Physical manliness had a long tradition behind it in English life and letters, but it particularly commended itself to Kingsley the hunting parson who had been sickly as a child and whose adult life was characterized by frantic energy punctuated with attacks of nervous exhaustion and physical collapse. Carlyle's strong and silent heroes made a special appeal to a man who valued strength and energy and must often have wished for more of them. The closest he came to desperate adventure himself was when he was arrested and put in jail overnight through an absurd misunderstanding on his German holiday,[2] but his doctor brother George had been wounded in Paris in the February Revolution of 1848, and his ne'er-do-well brother Henry had sampled the rigours of the Australian outback, and a third brother, Gerald, a naval officer, had died of fever in the Torres Straits aboard HMS *Royalist*.[3] In the next generation one of his sons worked as a railroad engineer and surveyor in South America and the other tried his hand at sheep-farming in Queensland, while his niece Mary became one of the most famous African explorers of her day.[4]

Kingsley had been unusually close to his mother as a child because of his frequent illnesses,[5] he was happily married to someone who had contemplated a celibate life, and he was an affectionate father to his children, so natural affections of his own made him sympathetic to F. D. Maurice's theological adaptations of the language of family. It was appropriate that Maurice stood godfather to Kingsley's eldest son, called Maurice after him, in 1847, and the following year wrote a preface for *The Saint's Tragedy*, Kingsley's dramatic account of St Elizabeth the married saint. This had its origins in the unpublished fragment *Elizabeth of Hungary* which he began to write and illustrate as a wedding-present for his wife in 1842. *Hypatia* was dedicated to his parents with a note that 'the view of human relationships which is set forth in it' arose out of his own affectionate relationship with them.[6] *The Water-Babies*, written for his youngest child, may be arch and condescending at times, particularly to modern taste, but it catches something of the child's sense of wonder and sense of fun. Kingsley must have been an interesting father as well as a passionate husband and a dutiful son.

Kingsley's passion for nature which began with his country childhood never left him but it was disciplined by the theology he learnt from Coleridge and by the scientific method which he came to regard as educationally indispensable. The young Kingsley who savagely attacked the vague Emersonian nature-worship which almost seduced him from duty and the Anglican God gradually modulated into the middle-aged Canon of Chester whose adult-education lectures on geology and botany were as popular as the history lectures delivered from the Cambridge chair he had just relinquished. God and nature had been theorized over by Bacon and put in order for the Church of England by Bishop Butler's *Analogy of Religion, Natural and Revealed, to the Constitution and Course of Nature* more than a century before.[7] Taking a hint from the neo-Baconianism of his friend William Whewell,[8] Kingsley breezily updated Bacon and Butler in children's books on popular science and in his scientific lectures and suggested that God's world offered excitement and purpose and moral and spiritual enlightenment to the scientific inquirer as well as to the social reformer, the patriot and the strong man.

Scientists, social-reformers, patriots and strong men could be Christian as well as manly only if they acknowledged Christ as the basis of their activity as Kingsley did and directed that activity to benefit their fellow men and brothers in Christ. Coleridge and Maurice, Carlyle and Arnold had all preached the importance of action and fighting the battles of righteousness, but apart from Arnold, who carried the battle into the classroom, they were mainly paper-warriors. Kingsley's preaching was sustained by his practice. Like Arnold he was an inspiring teacher. In his countless popular lectures he tried to do something about the educational short-comings of his time as he perceived them. In his sanitary campaigns in particular he taught by example. His daughter Rose wanted to nurse the wounded in Germany during the Franco-Prussian War. She was a qualified nurse but Kingsley's letter of recommendation could add, without false modesty, that

As my daughter, I need not say that she has been brought up in a thorough understanding of practical matters relating to cleanliness, ventilation, & sanitary matters in general.[9]

Christian manliness was not just an ideal in Kingsley's fiction, it was the basis of his practical work as pastor, teacher and reformer and the essence of his life and experience.

PHYSICAL MANLINESS

The attractiveness of physical vigour leaps off the page in Kingsley. One expects it in *Yeast*, where the hero is a 'poor wild uneducated sportsman', 'full of manhood' and understandably exasperated with the sweet-natured but feminine spirituality of the Roman Catholic priest in the novel who seems to be a thumb-nail sketch of Newman:

'What a man!' said he to himself, 'or rather the wreck of what a man! Oh, for such a heart, with the thews and sinews of a truly English brain!' (ch. 14)

He prefers the physical discomforts of duck-shooting to hair-shirts (ch. 14) and side-by-side with the Cornish gamekeeper Tregarva, 'some six feet three in height, with thews and sinews in proportion' (ch. 3), he joins in the pleasure of a fist-fight with Cockney poachers (ch. 9). This is in the best traditions of the hard-riding, hard-living manliness described in Bell's *Life* or in C. J. Apperley's *Memoirs of John Mytton*, foxhunter and duck-shooter extraordinary. But it comes as a surprise that Bishop Synesius of Ptolemais is cast in the same mould in *Hypatia*. In a chapter with the splendidly anachronistic title 'Squire-Bishop' Kingsley recreates this rather misty historical figure in his own image as manic-depressive man of action, an ostrich-hunter and dashing horseman who leads his household into battle with a band of marauding Ausurians. Where Lancelot Smith's technically unregenerate manliness shames the churchmen of the book Synesius' technically regenerate manliness attracts converts. The Jewish Raphael Aben Ezra found him 'the only Christian from who he had ever heard a hearty laugh' (ch. 21). He provides a kind of touchstone for other manly Christians or manly men in the novel. The young Philammon has grown up among the monks of the Nitrian desert but that is no place for a man. Kingsley asks indignantly 'What did his glorious young humanity among the tombs?' (ch. 1) and removes him to Alexandria as quickly as possible so that he can fight and glory in his strength in a less restricted atmosphere. On the way he almost literally falls in with a boatload of Goths when his own frail craft is destroyed by a hippopotamus: the friendly barbarians who happen to be passing harpoon the hippo and pull him out of the water (ch. 3). Ostrich-hunting bishop and barbarous Goth are brothers under the skin in that both revel in sport and fighting as Philammon soon will himself. Roman accounts of the barbarians of northern Europe had stressed their enormous size and strength and their contempt for the relatively diminutive Romans, and the modern romantic Teutonists cherished the myth of the superior physical stamina of the Teutonic race.[10] Kingsley was following this tradition when he made the Amal of the Goths complain that there were few real men in Roman Alexandria and that they tended to fall down if you boxed their ears. These Gothic bullies, hearty, 'thoroughly good-natured, honest fellows', were perhaps a little inclined to robbery and murder, but Philammon soon learns to prefer their company to that of the sinister and unhealthy monks of Alexandria (ch. 3). At the end of the book the 'murder grim and great' which the Goths inflict on the besieging mob of monks is artfully juxtaposed with the far more horrible murder of the defenceless Hypatia. Kingsley even wrings a moral out of it by making the Goths the unconscious instruments of Providence avenging the blood of Hypatia (ch. 29).

This rather alarming relish for good-natured brutality comes to a climax with Hereward the Wake, another Teutonic hero whose wild career as Berserker and 'brain-hewer' is largely Kingsley's own invention though he could have found plenty of Berserker blood-lust in Bulwer Lytton's *Harold*. When Hereward piously asks for masses for the souls of all those he has slain he admits complacently that there may be some that have slipped his mind (ch. 15). Amyas Leigh is not much better in *Westward Ho!* He first comes to notice when he breaks the head of his schoolmaster Vindex Brimblecombe, an unpleasant incident modelled on the cruel trick played on the tyrannical Mr Vindex in Henry Brooke's *Fool of Quality*.[11] But where Brooke's story is used to point the sentimental moral that schoolboys must be treated kindly or they retaliate, Kingsley robustly hints that boys will be boys and one should be prepared to forgive a bit of horseplay, though of course such things should not happen.

All this celebration of physical strength, shading over into brutality, did something to justify all the allegations of merely muscular Christianity. The muscular shepherd-boy David was one of Kingsley's heroes. But David put his strength to good use by killing Goliath. Lancelot Smith did much the same in *Yeast*, wrenching off the rail of a bridge by main force, before an admiring Argemone, in an attempt to rescue Tregarva from drowning. When he took part in the fight with the poachers this was to rescue the old game-keeper Harry Verney who was sprawling on the ground with two poachers on top of him. The glorious young humanity and fighting zeal of Philammon in *Hypatia* justify their existence when he is able to use his strength to protect the negress wife of the porter. Amyas Leigh and Hereward can be bullies in a good cause when it comes to fighting for their country against Spaniards or Normans. Sir Richard Grenvile is presented as the supreme hero of physical hardihood in *Westward Ho!* Kingsley abandons the chronological sequence of his narrative to report how he 'died as he lived, without a shudder, and without a whine' and he reproduces his last words, as Froude had done, from a seventeenth-century source:

'I have ended my life as a true soldier, fighting for his country, queen, religion, and honour: my soul willingly departing from this body, leaving behind the lasting fame of having behaved as every valiant soldier is in his duty bound to do.'

Those were the last words of Richard Grenvile. The pulpits of those days had taught them to him.[12]

Kingsley's campaign against the 'Manichee' pulpits of his own day which would have totally shunned physical manliness, even in the service of the country, predictably leads him to uncritical extremes: his praise of Grenvile ignores contemporary accounts of his unpopularity and tyrannical pride.[13]

But Kingsley is not completely uncritical of healthy animalism and physical manliness. Even the excitements of an otter-hunt in *Two Years Ago* fail to redeem its brutish organizer Trebooze. Hereward the invincible loses his strength when he loses his virtue, as he realizes in his strange fight with Sir Letwold, symbolic representation of his abandoned best self in the novel though a perfectly ordinary knight in the sources.[14] In *The Water-Babies* crude physical sturdiness is the beginning rather than the end of manly character. At the beginning of the book Tom is ensnared in a web of animal imagery, enduring the miseries of his life 'like a donkey in a hailstorm', sleeping like a pig in the evening and rising like a gamecock in the morning. Life with Grimes is associated with bulldogs and brutality. But being a man is more than this. Tom's energy and hardihood are good qualities but they can be exhausted and he has to learn that 'you must expect to be beat a few times . . . let you be as strong and healthy as you may' (ch. 1, ch.2). The moral significance of the animal imagery is made explicit later in the novel when the Queen of the Fairies comments that 'He is but a savage now, and like the beasts that perish; and from the beasts that perish he must learn' (ch. 2). He embarks on the process of moral regeneration which eventually equips him with a redeemed sturdiness to sustain him in his manly expedition to the Other-end-of-Nowhere at the end of the book.

Physical manliness is not only attractive and useful in Kingsley, the basis at least for a higher manliness: it is also an index and a condition of psychological, moral and spiritual health. Kingsley's idiosyncratic variant of the old association of healthy mind and healthy body emerges at the outset of his literary career. In *The Saint's Tragedy*, his first published work, the contrast between unhealthily effeminate professional religion and robust practical manliness is deliberately contrived. The perverted monkish asceticism of Conrad of Marburg, focused not on human life and love but on visions of the saints, is roundly denounced by the loyal and plain-spoken Walter of Varila, transformed by Kingsley from a colourless man of prudence and integrity in his thirteenth-century source into a reincarnation of the blunt and faithful Kent in *King Lear*.[15] A good meal and some manly exercise would induce in Conrad a more wholesome spirituality:

> Will you be cozened, sir, by these air-blown fancies,
> This male green-sickness, by starvation bred
> And huge conceit? Cast off God's gift of manhood,
> And like the dog in the adage, drop the true bone
> With snapping at the sham one in the water?
> What were you born a man for?[16]

In the unpublished *Elizabeth of Hungary* from which *The Saint's Tragedy* evolved Kingsley wrote indignantly that this 'Manichee' ideal of holiness was no more than physical privation.[17] Christian manliness involved the sanctified fulfilment rather than the hysterical negation of one's physical nature. The intensely physical young Lancelot Smith argues along the same lines with his less vigorous cousin Luke, lured by the aura of peace of the unmanly Church of Rome. The church Lancelot does not yet belong to, unlike the Church of Rome, would have to acknowledge rather than repudiate connections between the spiritual and the physical:

> My body, and brain, and faculties, and appetites must be His will, whatever else is not . . . the spiritual cannot be intended to be perfected by ignoring or crushing the physical, unless God is a deceiver, and His universe a self-contradiction. (ch. 5)

The theology of the Incarnation which Kingsley had learnt from Coleridge and Maurice sanctified and redeemed man's physical nature since Christ Himself had assumed it. Kingsley drew the eccentric corollary that wilful injury to one's physical nature also injured the moral and spiritual capacity through which one could participate in the divine nature of Christ. Emotional instability, treachery and sadistic cruelty tend to be the characteristics of the physically unhealthy, the celibate and the ascetic in Kingsley's fiction. This is particularly noticeable in *Hereward*, where the disciplines of prayer and fasting, or at least fasting, render Edward the Confessor a priest-ridden fool, Waltheof a monkish incompetent and unreliable ally, and the monks of Ely traitors to Hereward's cause when their temporalities are threatened.

There are exceptions. The city-bred Alton Locke is hardly to blame for his unhealthiness, so after falling in love with the wrong girl and giving way momentarily to the temptations of the mob-orator he is allowed to be a manly Christian in the end. The physically unimpressive John Brimblecombe in *Westward Ho!* is allowed to be more fool than knave and redeems himself in a short bout of absurd heroics against the Spaniards.

Kingsley drew attention to this episode in an attempt to counter those tiresome allegations of merely muscular Christianity.[18] He would have been more convincing if Brimblecombe had been a more serious and important character in the novel. The physically overwhelming figure of Amyas Leigh dominates the action and terrifies not only his schoolmaster but also his less manly Catholic cousin Eustace. Sexually repressed but hopelessly in love with Rose Salterne, weak-natured, treacherous and vacillating, Eustace finally becomes a Jesuit. This ultimate capitulation to the unhealthy religion which has already ruined his character is described in terms which almost suggest castration:

Eustace is a man no longer; he is become a thing, a tool, a Jesuit . . . which, by an act of moral suicide, has lost its soul, in the hope of saving it; without a will, a conscience, a responsibility. (ch. 2)

The most startling examples of unhealthy souls in unhealthily celibate and ascetic bodies are the monks in *Hypatia*. The young Philammon, deliberately secluded from women by his monkish upbringing, reacts with prurient fascination and guilty horror to the wall-paintings of beautiful women in a ruined temple. Kingsley's source for the unwholesome sexual fantasies of the celibate in the novel seems to have been the mentally tormented life of St Antony of the Desert, recounted by Athanasius.[19] Interestingly Newman, the supreme 'Manichee' in Kingsley's demonology, had included some judicious chapters on St Antony in his book *The Church of the Fathers*. The horrible murder of Hypatia by a mob of celibate monks has the same overtones of repressed and perverted sexuality, so much so that it shocked the usually broad-minded Tennyson.[20] The fact that Kingsley could point to the historical record for many of the details of this appalling crime, which was committed in Alexandria in 415, powerfully strengthened his case against monkish religion.[21]

But Kingsley admitted that there were moral health-hazards besides the wrong sort of religion. In *Hypatia* he seems to hint that long-established homosexual practices have contributed to the physical degeneracy of the Roman citizens of Alexandria: for all their casual brutality the lustily heterosexual Goths are given a rather unconvincing moral as well as physical ascendancy over them since they are 'untainted by hereditary effeminacy' (Preface). Kingsley is never explicit about homosexuality, in common with most of his contemporaries, but he leaves it open to the reader to suspect that the 'maundering, die-away effeminacy'[22] of the 'Manichees' who repress the instinct to marry and be conventionally manly may include this element of unspoken and unspeakable sin. Unnatural vice, unnatural at least by the standards of the 1850s, would be an appropriately awful consequence of unnatural contempt for one's ordinary physical nature.

Marriage for Kingsley's manly heroes is however much more than the legitimate outlet for God-given sexual energy. It is the reward of ennobling romantic love and the most enriching of those ordinary relations of life which require a man to lose selfish concerns in care for others and to open himself to influences outside the hard shell of his own self-sufficiency.

NATURAL AFFECTIONS

Kingsley saw these ordinary relations of life as fundamental to human dignity. In the strange evolutionary dream-sequence at the end of *Alton Locke*, which was published eight years before *The Origin of Species*, Kingsley mingles the Lamarckian notions of development popularized in Robert Chambers' *Vestiges of Creation* with recent theories of primitive Aryan migration[23] to offer a poetic vision of humanity in its physical and moral aspect. A crucial stage in man's moral evolution, Kingsley suggests, is when he becomes aware of himself as part of a family, for this can lead him on to a sense of the Divine as Maurice had taught. Alton the dreamer becomes aware of

The music of loving voices, the sacred names of child and father, mother, brother, sister, first of all inspirations. – Had we not an All-Father, whose eyes looked down upon us from among those stars above; whose hand upheld the mountain roots below us? Did He not love us, too, even as we loved each other? (ch. 36)

Kingsley's prose-lyric of family love owed something to the investigation of ancient eastern civilizations with the aid of comparative philology in which his friends Baron Bunsen the scholarly Prussian ambassador and his young protégé Max Müller had played a part, reporting some of their findings to the 1847 meeting of the British Association in Oxford. Sir William Jones, whose papers read to the Asiatic Society of Calcutta at the end of the eighteenth century laid the foundations of comparative philology and comparative ethnology, had long since noted the affinity of Sanskrit with Latin and Greek and had argued for a common origin for all three languages from which the Germanic and Celtic languages, as well as the ancient language of Persia, might also be derived. Ancient Persian religion perhaps gave a hint of the value-system of this prehistoric Indo-European or Aryan civilization and Jones described this as belief in one supreme God, creator of all, source and inspiration of love, particularly the love of men for their brother-man, their parents and their God. Later scholars such as Bunsen and Jakob Grimm noticed that the affinities between the various Indo-European languages were most noticeable with family-words such as 'father', 'mother' and 'brother'. Obviously the language of family had been important even at the dawn of history.[24] Kingsley's reference to the 'All-Father', a title of the Scandinavian Odin, is designed to link the value-system of primitive Indo-European man with specifically Germanic tradition.

Even in primitive times in their remote pine-forests the Germanic peoples had reverenced their womenfolk and laid great stress on the value of the family, if Tacitus was to be believed. The Victorian romantic Teutonists, Kingsley included, deplored the implied challenge to these values represented by the gradual rise of a rule of celibacy in the Roman church, a development which disastrously separated the clergy from ordinary life and family and national responsibilities.[25] If the western church had been administered from Potsdam or Berlin rather than Rome, they seemed to imply, this would never have happened. Instead, perhaps, one might have had the spectacle any time from the fifth century onwards of some flaxen-haired Gothic priest, part-time chaplain to a warrior-band, frowning at his unruly offspring before pronouncing a blessing on a Sunday dinner of roast boar washed down with mead.

This vision of a Germanic clerisy of good family men and patriotic citizens was not entirely a Protestant fantasy. Before the Norman Conquest some of the English clergy were married, a source of scandal to the rest of the church. One of the motives behind the Pope's support of William the Conqueror was that Norman domination of England would make it easier to impose reform on the English church in this matter. When the Norman Abbot Lanfranc of Bec became Archbishop of Canterbury in 1070 this is what actually happened.[26] Kingsley makes use of this in *Hereward the Wake*: the national cause which Hereward represents receives support from English churchmen because their traditions are English rather than Roman and so, unlike the Elizabethan Jesuits in *Westward Ho!*, their first political loyalty is to England. Kingsley might have made more of this than he does: the trouble is that he is so contemptuous of any kind of churchman in the novel and so determined to celebrate the secular heroics of Hereward that this theme tends to languish.

It is much more vigorously pursued in *Hypatia*, though chiefly from a negative point of view. If the monks of Alexandria, led by the formidable Cyril, had been more like Anglican clergymen of the right stamp, married and settled in parishes and with an interest in the social and political welfare of the community and the state, they would have been much less of a political threat to the Roman authorities and Alexandria would have been a less turbulent place. As it is one has a sneaking sympathy for the ambition of Hypatia and the Roman prefect Orestes to repeat the unsuccessful experiment of Julian the Apostate and banish Christianity from the Empire altogether: there were no problems of this nature in the great days of the Empire when Jupiter rather than Jesus and His church held sway. Bishop Synesius is the only honorary Anglican in the novel, historically notorious for being married and not caring whether this cost him his chance of a bishopric. The sinister and celibate Peter the Reader sneers at the wife of Synesius on principle (ch. 7), which naturally disposes the reader in her favour. Kingsley presents Synesius as a man whose pastoral usefulness stems from a broad human sympathy deepened by the joys and sorrows of family life. This admirably Germanic virtue in a north African churchman leads to amusing anachronism: when he leads the loyal members of his household in the skirmish with the Ausurians he is not so much a Christian bishop as some Germanic hero supported by his faithful *comitatus*. The manly bishop makes a good impression on Raphael Aben Ezra, but the Jewish intellectual is finally won to Christianity when he befriends the exemplary close-knit Christian family of Majoricus and seeks to become a member of it himself by marrying the daughter Victoria.

Kingsley's stress on family relationships as the proper context of manly Christianity was pushed well beyond the conventional self-satisfaction of the middle-class Victorian paterfamilias by Maurice's theology of brotherhood and sonship in Christ and by his rampant anti-Catholicism which smoulders in his novels of contemporary life as well as in his historical romances. Lancelot Smith in *Yeast*, improved by his love for the Puseyite Argemone as she is restored to a more humane Christianity by her love for him, is ready to be a manly Christian and Christian socialist by the end of the book. But his cousin Luke has taken a different route out of spiritual perplexity and has become a Roman Catholic priest, turning his back on the customary duties of 'Parent, Englishman, Citizen' (ch. 14). If Kingsleyan parents have duties and responsibilities which knit them into the social fabric of the nation they also have rather extraordinary privileges. Both Grace Harvey in *Two Years Ago* and Alton Locke are saddled with thoroughly tiresome mothers, one a humbug and a thief and the other pious and intolerant. Instead of disowning her mother Grace loyally stays with her and keeps silence as her suspicions deepen. She suffers vicariously for her mother's crime: 'her mother's sin was to her her own sin' and her agony was like Christ's agony in Gethsemane (ch. 26). Sandy Mackaye sternly reproves Alton Locke for his disrespect to his mother (ch. 3).

Tom Thurnall's much more satisfactory parent helps to bring out the best in his wild and wandering son. For all his hard-baked self-sufficiency and godlessness Thurnall has a soft spot for his father and comes back from his wanderings to help him in his blind old age. This acknowledging of a relationship and acting upon it is the beginning of a higher life and Kingsley manipulates the plot to sustain the moral momentum. Thurnall's feeling for his father brings him back to England and places him within reach of the benign Christian influence of Frank Headley and of Grace Harvey, with whom he falls in love. Needless to say his vigorous manliness and his practical effectiveness as a humanitarian doctor help to enrich the Christianity of his friend and his beloved alike.

Kingsley's fictional parents presumably merit love and respect from their children as a return for their early care and protection which may well continue into later life. The love of parents for their children is a slightly risky literary topic, fraught with the dangers of sentimentality, and Kingsley's touch is a little uncertain in this respect. When Miriam the hideous old Jewess in *Hypatia* turns out in the end to be the doting mother of Raphael Aben Ezra, scheming to promote his well-being though he is unaware of her existence, this does less honour to family relationships than Kingsley may have intended. When Hypatia refers in a lecture to Hector's touching farewell to his son Astyanax and his wife Andromache in the *Iliad* there is a kind of inverted sentimentality about the way in which she dismisses the emotional poignancy of the story as 'earthly commonplaces' and brutally allegorizes it as a parable of the elect soul and its spiritual father (ch.8). There is a kind of parallel in *The Saint's Tragedy*: the preposterously nasty and perverted Conrad, spiritual adviser to the saintly Elizabeth and probably half in love with her in the best tradition of Protestant *canards* against Catholic confessors, deliberately outrages the sentiment of motherhood on which Kingsley is trading heavily by suggesting Elizabeth cannot be a saint and a mother, 'hate the flesh and love its fruit'.[27] At his best

Kingsley can present motherhood with tenderness and dignity. In the midst of all the blatant heroics and catchpenny patriotism and prejudice of *Westward Ho!* the mother of Frank and Amyas Leigh stands as a centre of stillness and peace in a violent world. Her uncanny intuition that Amyas is returning for the third time but without his brother who has been murdered by the Inquisition raises her motherly affection to an almost mystical plane. The novel is brought to an elegiac close when the careful love of a mother is mingled with joy at new beginnings. Mrs Leigh blesses the union of Ayacanora and a humbled, blinded Amyas: ' "Fear not to take her to your heart again; for it is your mother who has laid her there" ' (ch. 33).

Rather surprisingly, while there are plenty of parents and of course actual or aspiring husbands and wives in Kingsley's fiction there are not many brothers and sisters to reinforce the sentiment of family. Kingsley had no sisters and does not seem to have been on particularly easy terms with either his dissolute and spendthrift brother Henry or his godless doctor-brother George who was hardly ever in England anyway, which may help to explain it. The only important brother–sister relationship is between Pelagia and Philammon in *Hypatia*, and this is clumsily handled. Nor are there many young children. Most of his manly heroes will have children in due course but the main interest of the novels is in getting them suitably married first: their subsequent career as parents, Englishmen and citizens is usually taken for granted rather than described. Elsley Vavasour has children and neglects them, but he had never much hope of being a manly Christian in the first place. Even in Kingsley's children's book *The Water-Babies* the child-hero is not part of a loving family but an orphan, which is of course how he falls into the clutches of the brutal Grimes. He eventually acquires a kind of extended family as he comes across other water-babies and marine creatures, and by the end of the book he meets a mythic mother-figure, but this is more an allegory of the family solidarity of Maurice's Kingdom of Christ than an imaginatively displaced human family. Tom's ultimate destiny is to be another manly Christian hero. Kingsley playfully and tiresomely neither affirms nor denies the fairy-tale ending that would make Tom marry Ellie, the beautiful little girl he found when he came down the wrong chimney. But it is clear that the cleansed and purified Tom, perhaps washed clean of sexual defilement if one attends closely to the protean water-symbolism of the novel, will need a good wife to keep him that way when he embarks on his great career as a successful engineer.

Kingsley lays so much stress on the ennobling power of sexual love and marriage that he runs into difficulties in his presentation of the beautiful and voluptuous Pelagia in *Hypatia*. On the one hand he associates her with the hearty and wholesome Goths: it is better for her to be the concubine of the Amal of the Goths than to repress her sexuality altogether like Hypatia. The rivalry between Pelagia and Hypatia for the attention of the youth of Alexandria is described in the chapter entitled 'Venus and Pallas' which assimilates them to the mythic roles of Pallas Athena and Venus/Aphrodite, the sterile, virginal, intellectual principle and the triumphantly nubile. Pelagia's mythic dignity is emphasized when she dances the role of Venus rising from the waves, anticipating the famous painting by Botticelli *The Birth of Venus*. The very name 'Pelagia' could be a Greek form of 'Marina' which is an epithet of Venus arisen from the sea in Horace.[28] On the other hand Kingsley does not quite approve of concubinage. The obvious solution would have been to marry her to the Amal whom she loves dearly. But perhaps that would have been one concession too many to Gothic paganism which already outshone the Alexandrian Christianity of the novel in a rather embarrassing fashion. Kingsley tries to make an honest woman of her in a different way by making her the long-lost sister of the virtuous and manly Philammon. When the relationship is revealed Philammon is rather improbably delighted to have discovered in the person of a freebooter's mistress the 'deep, everlasting, divine reality of kindred' (ch. 16). Though the Amal had appeared in a reasonably sympathetic, even heroic light earlier in the novel he now represents a stumbling-block to Pelagia's return to the Christian fold and Philammon has to fight him to the death with questionably Christian gusto to get him out of the way so brother and sister can end their days together as saints of the desert.

This rather disappointing conclusion to the novel, perhaps suggested by the legend of St Pelagia of Antioch who had been a pantomime-dancer and luxurious wanton until her conversion,[29] is Kingsley's way of suggesting that the Christianity of the fifth century was not generous and liberal enough to offer a satisfactory role for a fair penitent which did not involve the extremes of self-renunciation and sainthood. But it does violence to Kingsley's own narrative instincts to join heroic brawn with tender beauty. This is the customary pattern in his novels: the manly hero is redeemed and enlisted as a soldier of Christ by his love for a good woman, and the woman usually benefits as well. Paradoxically Pelagia is not good enough, or at least not Christian enough at the right time, for this to work with the Amal, so she becomes a saint instead.

Though the muscular Philammon is a Christian and the beautiful Hypatia is a pagan the formula of mutually enriching love works in the usual way with them. Each comes to a more Kingsleyan tolerance and understanding of human nature through love for the other. Monks and philosophers alike are represented as shut off from the liberal humanitarian spirit of true Christianity in the novel. Kingsley carefully selects out of his historical sources a narrative thread which allows him to stress this point. He rejects the tradition embodied in the *Suda*, a Byzantine encyclopaedia, that Hypatia was married so that she can pride herself on an austerely sexless and passionless philosophy and so that Philammon can legitimately fall in love with her. On the other hand he takes up a hint in the *Suda* that one of Hypatia's lecture-audience declared passionate love to her and was austerely rebuffed and makes Philammon the man in question.[30] Ascetic Christianity and ascetic paganism confront each other in some embarrassment, awakened by sexual excitement but unable to cope with it properly. The witch-like Miriam contrives to expose Hypatia's repressed sexual feelings in a scene which is both preposterous and imaginatively vivid and compelling, like so much of Kingsley. She arranges for Hypatia's prophetic trance of devotion to Phoebus Apollo, which is manifestly sublimated sexual ecstasy, to coincide with Philammon's half-concealed presence in the room so that when she kneels abjectly before him as to the apparition of a god she expresses devotion to a man (ch. 26).

The Goths had had other plans for Hypatia. They had hoped that she would have married the Amal and become his 'Alruna' or wise woman, a companion who could counsel and sustain his doughty heroism. Hereward's wife Torfrida is represented as another 'Alruna', a woman of uncanny powers who helps her husband to win battles. When he abandons her for another his failure and defeat are assured. Though Kingsley follows his sources quite closely in *Hereward* Torfrida as Alruna is largely his own invention. All through Kingsley's fiction the good women who help their lovers or husbands or, occasionally, their sons to be Christian as well as manly converge upon the stereotype of the Alruna. This is a Germanic myth-figure more or less invented by Jakob Grimm, one of the famous story-telling brothers, on the basis of stray fragments of northern tradition and legend.[31] The special moral function of the Alruna seems to be original to Kingsley. Lancelot Smith sees in his beloved Argemone an Alruna of the nineteenth century, one who can 'look at the heart and have mercy' as in older days she might have 'charmed our old fighting, hunting forefather into purity and sweet obedience among their Saxon forests' (ch.3). In *Alton Locke* the Alruna-figure is the good and wise Eleanor, a far more appropriate inspiration to Christian socialism than the beautiful nonentity Lillian with whom the hero first falls in love. Eleanor acquires full mythic status when she appears as the veiled prophetess-figure in Alton Locke's dream towards the end of the book.

Kingsley was a firm believer in the benign influence of a man's 'mother, his sister, the maid whom he may love'.[32] But the Alruna is not just a fancy-dress version of the conventional Victorian 'angel-in-the-house', the man-civilizing paragon of Ruskin's moral and aesthetic imagination.[33] J. M. Ludlow noted shrewdly that 'the good part' of Eleanor in *Alton Locke* was drawn from Kingsley's wife and implied that her severity and aloofness could be attributed to the same source.[34] Fanny Grenfell as she then was could take the credit for saving the soul of the young Charles Kingsley in his undergraduate days. In later years her husband often asked her to give advice to young men such as his pupil John Martineau because he felt that, like the Alrunas of his fiction, she had a special intuitive understanding of their problems which no man could emulate.[35] The Alruna has a special place in Kingsley's imagination as the mythic embodiment of all that is needed to complement the wild and vigorous Kingsleyan *alter egos* who dominate his fiction and to complete them in authentic Christian manliness.

GOD, NATURE AND MORALITY

But what is the wisdom the Alruna intuitively possesses which she can impart to her manly consort? It seems to vary from novel to novel, depending on the state of enlightenment of either party, but the aim is always that both should end up with a proper moral and spiritual understanding of the world God created. There are two dangers to be avoided: the over-religious 'Manichee' attitude which shuns the world in an ultimately self-centred cult of personal holiness and the over-worldly attitude of complacent materialism, pragmatism or nature-worship which perilously ignores the dread imperatives of the moral law and, curiously enough, rushes into the same moral *cul-de-sac* of absorption in self to the neglect of suitably Christian-manly altruism and activity. *The Saint's Tragedy* and *Hypatia* contain Kingsley's most sustained exploration of the first hazard, while the novels of contemporary life, including *The Water-Babies*, consider the second. There are important shifts of emphasis, because Kingsley begins by thinking about the natural world chiefly as a poet and ends by thinking about it chiefly as a scientist, but there is an underlying consistency in that Kingsley keeps faith with the God of nature who had been disclosed to him by Coleridge and Carlyle.

The unmanly approach to nature is magnificently represented by the unspeakable Conrad of Marburg in *The Saint's Tragedy*:

> Nature's corrupt throughout –
> A gaudy snake, which must be crushed, not tamed,
> A cage of unclean birds, deceitful ever;[36]

This attitude had encouraged the young Elizabeth to distrust the beauty and majesty of the earth as it pressed upon her senses and to repudiate such seductions by an act of will as she struggled to attain to the vision of God. But despite Conrad's endeavours to make a saint of her Elizabeth's proto-Protestant common sense comes to the rescue in the form of Luther's (and St Paul's) conviction that faith and not works, divine grace rather than individual effort is the means of access to glory. She brings herself up short with the question

> And who am I, that my own will's intent
> Should put me face to face with the living God?

The Lutheran Prince Albert was most impressed by Kingsley's St Elizabeth.[37] Before long Elizabeth has come to reject the 'vain conceits / Of self-contained sainthood' in favour of a more outward-going practical Christianity based on the principle of self-sacrifice as Maurice had commended it:

> Nought lives for self – All, all – from crown to footstool – [. . .]
> The oak, ennobled by the shipwright's axe –
> The soil, which yields its marrow to the flower –
> The flower, which feeds a thousand velvet worms,
> Born only to be prey for every bird –
> All spend themselves for others.

Nature properly understood in this way, with the help of some poetic licence, is not foul and corrupt but radiant with divine meaning, pattern of the moral and spiritual life inaugurated by Christ Himself, 'The Lamb, before the world's foundations slain'.[38]

This perception was not widespread in Hypatia's Alexandria. With the exception of Synesius, philosophers and religious alike were engaged in the futile attempt to escape from the natural world and to 'scale the heavens' by a conscious effort of the ego. Kingsley's Hypatia had devoted herself to a Universal Soul identifiable with the idea of the One in Plotinus, father of the neo-Platonist school to which the historical Hypatia is known to have belonged. The One is constantly 'warring with the brute forces of gross matter': man's physical body and the natural world of matter apprehended through the senses obstruct access to it, which leads Hypatia to ascetic repudiation of 'this prison-house of our degradation'. Her ambition is to attain mystical union with the One by 'one continuous effort of her practised will', in a self-induced hypnotic trance. Plotinus' treatise 'On Beauty' seems to have provided Kingsley with an appropriate pattern for Hypatia's planned ascent to the source of original good and beauty beyond the intelligible and sensuous world. But such high aspirations, which Hypatia is uncomfortably aware are very like the ascetic quest for the beatific vision of Christian monks and nuns, can easily be brought down to earth. In the middle of her trance Hypatia is interrupted by a vision of her enemy Pelagia, as voluptuous and worldly as Hypatia is cold and aloof and a far more generous and likeable human being.[39]

Pelagia and Raphael Aben Ezra are the two pivotal figures of the novel, the outsiders, whore and Jew, whom true Christianity eventually includes in its embrace. False Christianity, which abhors the worldly Pelagia, and the false philosophy which Raphael pursues for so long are remarkably similar: Philammon thinks he is drawn to Hypatia because she speaks of 'the unseen world, of the hope of immortality, of the conquest of the spirit over the flesh, just as a Christian might have done' (ch. 8). But he is unphilosophically in love with her and more firmly linked to the flesh and the world than he imagined. He is Pelagia's brother after all, though he does not yet know it. The newly Christianized Raphael, who has passed beyond Hypatia's otherworldly neo-Platonism to a Platonized Christianity which accepts the world and sees Christ as the archetype of man, promises to tell her about the man Jesus 'At the ninth hour'. Raphael's unintended suggestion of the crucifixion, which took place in darkness between the sixth and the ninth hour, prepares the reader for Hypatia's hideous death in front of a crucifix to which she appeals in her last moments, 'appealing – and who dare say, in vain? – from man to God' (ch. 29). God who was made man in Christ and lived and suffered in the world was more generous than the philosophers and the monks who scorned the world.

At the end of the novel Raphael goes off to Berenice 'to labour and to succour', a 'much loved and much-loving man' embarked on manly Christian work in the world like that other vigorous and unselfish Christian Synesius (ch. 30). F. D. Maurice had explained the vigour and manliness of the Elizabethan achievement as the result of accepting the living presence of Christ in the world as Synesius and Raphael had done. *Westward Ho!* dramatizes this insight and simplifies the work of Christian manliness into selfless dedication to the cause of Protestant England. Eustace Leigh's self-conscious and self-centred attempts to be virtuous are as inappropriate as Will Cary's selfish pursuit of his own quarrel. Frank Leigh describes Cary's private preoccupations as a waste of *thumos*, the dynamic of manliness, 'that divine wrath which, as Plato says, is the very root of all virtues' (ch. 5). Selfishness, private greed and private quarrels were part of the Elizabethan experience. The expedition of John Oxenham, an historical figure, foundered through greed for gold. Sir Thomas Stukely, another historical figure who becomes Amyas Leigh's uncle in the novel, embarked on a vainglorious and self-centred career which ended in despicable treachery.[40] Amyas himself, constantly distracted from his highest responsibilities as a patriot by his selfish quarrel with the Spanish Don Guzman, needs to be kept up to the mark by the historical example of the heroic Sir Richard Grenvile. Even at the climax of the battle with the Armada he turns aside determined only on personal vengeance. But the natural world which Amyas can usually master as mariner and adventurer in good causes snatches vengeance from his grasp when the Don's ship founders off Lundy. Nature inflicts the punishment of the God of nature for deserting God's cause when Amyas is melodramatically blinded by lightning.

Westward Ho! despite its absurdities demonstrates both Kingsley's poetic and imaginative responsiveness to the natural world, particularly in the exotic South American scenes, and his moralist's view of nature as both instrument of the moral law and potential seduction from which one must establish moral independence. In the manner of Tennyson's and Homer's lotos-eaters two of Amyas' mariners desert their epic quest for self-indulgent sloth in a natural paradise and urge Amyas to do the same, fortunately to no avail (ch. 24). For all his furious energy Kingsley was lured by lotos-eating too: he whimsically described his favourite occupation as doing nothing and his favourite amusement as sleeping.[41] In his early poetry he registers the influence upon him of mountains, winds and waves, as he rested on Nature's bosom 'where my young spirit dreamt its years away'.[42] The Coleridgean image of the Aeolian harp on which the winds of nature play the tune springs to mind, and Kingsley actually gives a literal Aeolian harp to the morally passive Argemone in *Yeast*. Emerson and other seemingly pantheist authors such as Fichte and Schiller, 'Anythingarians' in Kingsley's unflattering vocabulary, encouraged the nature-worshipping Lancelot Smith to abandon himself to mere contemplation. Kingsley complains of writers who 'talk as if Christians were cabbages' with Emerson very much in mind: one cannot be a manly Christian if one is a moral vegetable, and Emerson had enthused about man's unity with nature which implied 'an occult relation between man and the vegetable'.[43]

Alton Locke was impressed by the Anythingarian address of Professor Windrush with its Emersonian doctrine of 'Self-Reliance' which assimilated man into a harmonious system of nature requiring him only to do 'what is after my constitution'.[44] But he found it no help in moral extremity, when he was driven to contemplate suicide. Nor was it any help to the American Stangrave in *Two Years Ago* when he had to face up to the moral challenge of the Abolitionist issue. The scientist, on the other hand, devoted himself to understanding rather than being ruled by nature, manfully acting on Bacon's principle of conquering nature by obeying her, and the vigorous hero of *Two Years Ago* is a man of science.[45]

Tom Thurnall's status in *Two Years Ago* is curiously ambivalent: he is both scientific hero and over-worldly adventurer, unselfish doctor and self-centred materialist. This reflects Kingsley's ambivalence about scientific achievements. He was interested in the natural sciences as a proficient amateur geologist and naturalist, and he was interested in the applied sciences as a sanitary reformer on scientific principles and as a man of his time impressed by Britain's technological and industrial triumphs and the wonders of the Great Exhibition.[46] On the other hand as clergyman and moralist he was opposed to self-satisfied materialism, as an heir to the teaching of Coleridge and Carlyle he was unhappy about the dehumanizing consequences of the industrial revolution, and as an historian he was usually unwilling to patronize the pre-industrial past to sing the praises of the present. His comparison of the puny British squadron which defeated the Armada with the larger but less glorious Crimean expeditionary fleet is a deliberate taunt to Macaulay and the brash apologists of the progress of science and intellect (ch. 30). The scientific response to the natural world, like the poet's, could be justified only if it could be moralized and spiritualized.

Kingsley contrived this justification by trading on the ambiguity of the term 'law' which can imply both solemn edict to be flouted at one's peril and scientific rationale of the behaviour of natural phenomena. The God of righteousness and justice who was also the creator of the natural world could be regarded as the originator and administrator of both kinds of law. Tom Thurnall needs to make the connection between objective scientific laws which he recognizes and understands and moral and spiritual laws, equally objective and absolute in Kingsley's view, which he rather tends to ignore. As it happens, most of his sins are discreetly but disappointingly confined to foreign parts where the novel does not follow him.

Scientific and moral laws are firmly allied in *Alton Locke* and *The Water-Babies*. An unmoralized and unspiritual science was perverse and wrong, and this was painfully apparent among the devotees of the 'dismal science' of political economy denounced by Carlyle and by Alton Locke. Kingsley was intelligent enough to realize that political economy had its part to play in the development of the nation, but not when it purported to subject mankind to the mindless tyranny of economic laws without applying these laws to the benefit of humanity. It was man's moral duty to conquer his economic problems through attentive obedience to the laws of economic behaviour in the Baconian tradition instead of giving up in despair. The moralizing of Darwinian science in *The Water-Babies* has already been discussed. The morally inexorable Mrs Bedonebyasyoudid represents the capacity of Nature and Nature's God to reward and punish in terms of the natural world, a role which Kingsley later assigned to Madam How, the general course of scientific law in nature, in his book of popular science *Madam How and Lady Why* (1870).

The shifting physical forms and environments which Mrs Bedonebyasyoudid bestows upon Tom at different stages of his moral evolution are parallel to the adventures of the soul of Alton Locke in his strangely significant dream. Alton's infatuation with the empty beauty of Lillian and his lapse into the selfish and irresponsible passion of the demagogue (Kingsley's moralizing addition to the true story of Thomas Cooper) have temporarily robbed him of the moral dignity of the manly Christian. In his dream he is punished for this self-centred neglect of the noble cause of Christian socialism by being stripped of his discredited human identity and allowed to fall down the Lamarckian evolutionary scale until he becomes a mere madrepore, a perforate coral. Slowly he works his way back up again, a consciousness without a moral will. He becomes a prehistoric mylodon, as much a slave to the crude sense of power as he was as a demagogue, and this causes him to rampage around and uproot trees in wanton destruction only to suffer for it when they crash down on him and fracture his skull. This extremely rough justice extends to George Locke and Jemmy Downes elsewhere in the novel. George's economic behaviour is governed by purely economic considerations, though one might have expected some morality from a clergyman. The coat he buys so cheaply has been made at the cost of misery and disease on the part of the half-starved tailor, and the coat carries infection to George and kills him. Jemmy Downes dies horribly in the inhuman squalor into which he had been prepared to deliver his workmates by sabotaging their protest against the change to the appalling outworker system of sweated labour. In all three cases nature exacts a terrible penalty for moral failure which offends against the God of nature and of justice: God and nature ensure that the punishment fits the crime. In effect Kingsley's novel individualizes Carlyle's dire rhetoric of social and political sin and inevitable retribution, most effectively articulated in *Past and Present* and *The French Revolution*. Kingsley's God is shown to execute justice by means of the inexorable laws of nature.

THE CHRISTIAN MANLY QUEST

Alton Locke's dream soon passes beyond the passions of the mylodon. The process of rehumanization is complete with the acknowledgement of the All-Father, the Mauricean God from whom stem all human relationships. Alton's new sense of himself as a son of God and therefore a brother to all humanity prepares him for the final stage of the dream-sequence which explores the nature of human society and the opportunities for manly Christian work within it and for it. This offers a more fully Christian vision of the possibilities of Christian socialism than Alton Locke the literary Chartist has yet perceived. Unfortunately it comes too late. Alton

Locke is sent off to the New World and to new beginnings at the end of the novel but he dies before he gets there. Lancelot Smith's work as a manly Christian is kept for the future: he is made to confront '"Jesus Christ – THE MAN"' and half-unconsciously follows his master Barnakill through a cathedral door to find his own place in a kind of Mauricean eternity labouring to build up the kingdom of Christ (ch. 17). Tom Thurnall is finally reclaimed for Christianity very hurriedly in the last few pages of *Two Years Ago*, which leaves the author no space to describe his life and work in his fully regenerate state. Only little Tom in *The Water-Babies* is given any opportunity to do anything much after he has evolved from a selfish and malicious creature into a socially-responsible water-baby. His final expedition to the Other-end-of-Nowhere gives the dignity of romantic quest to the unselfish work in the world which is required of manly Christians. But of course this is all nonsense 'even if it is true', fantasy rather than realistic narrative.

There is a similar pattern of disappointment or at least of unrealized possibility in Kingsley's historical novels. *Hypatia*, for example, ends sombrely: Hypatia herself was murdered and Pelagia and Philammon went 'to the only place where such in such days could find rest; to the desert and the hermit's cell' (ch. 30). Philammon's longing for the busy world beyond the Laura or monastic community where he has grown up causes him to ' "pant for the battle" ', and near the beginning of the novel the friendly Goth Wulf lays claim to him as a sort of heroic protégé, but this never really comes to anything (ch. 1). His attempts to engage manfully in the battle for truth and right are embarrassing and incompetent: he fails to champion Christianity effectively against Hypatia's philosophy; his dash into the arena of the theatre to rescue Pelagia from 'this infernal place: this world of devils!' almost gets him trodden on by an elephant, and though he does all he can to save Hypatia from the monks it is to no avail (ch. 22). Raphael Aben Ezra, a much more interesting character, shows signs of doing rather better by the end of the book as a practical Christian, helped by his wealth, but this is not described in detail. Only Synesius, curiously peripheral to the main action of the book, is allowed to appear as a fully-functional manly Christian.

Some of this sense of disappointment can be attributed to Kingsley's own temperament, at once sanguine and liable to profound melancholy like his manic-depressive Bishop Synesius. The moral and practical difficulties which beset the Christian manly

quest and hinder Kingsley's dramatic and imaginative realization
of it in his novels owe something to his intermittent sense of his own
incapacity as he plodded along trying to make ends meet instead of
plunging heart and soul into the battles of righteousness. Sometimes
he felt he was no longer a

> Joyous knight-errant of God, thirsting for labour and strife;
> No more on magical steed borne free through the regions of ether,
> But, like the hack which I ride, selling my sinew for gold.
> Fruit-bearing autumn is gone; let the sad quiet winter hang o'er me –
> What were the spring to a soul laden with sorrow and shame?[47]

Some of the difficulty could be described as relatively short-term,
the realistic perception of the liberal optimist that things will
improve but 'no, not yet' and 'no, not there' as E. M. Forster was to
put it.[48] In time Christianity largely purged itself of the
'Manichaeism' of the fifth century which darkens the pages of
Hypatia. Hereward's doomed battles are overlaid by the myth of
imperishable freedom to which he has subscribed and the grimness
and defeat of his last days merge into the glories of a new and greater
England two generations later. The misery and social unrest of the
1840s which seemed to defy immediate practical solution and drove
Kingsley to fantasy and mystery at the end of *Yeast* and *Alton Locke*
gradually passed away in the more stable and affluent 1850s, as
Kingsley noted in his preface to the fourth edition of *Yeast* in 1859.
Three years earlier he had revisited some of the scenes of *Yeast* in the
opening pages of *Two Years Ago* to draw attention to the increased
prosperity of country areas.

But this is not the whole story. Kingsley's acute perception of how
the world progresses puts him into the position of having to assert,
half-embarrassed, half-defiant, that such good work as is done in it is
not the perquisite of manly Christians alone. Tom Thurnall the
selfless doctor and sanitary reformer and Alton Locke the Chartist
fight manfully against evil and wrong, fully aware in the Carlylean
phrase of Sandy Mackaye that ' "All around ye . . . are God and
Satan at death grips" ' (ch. 8), even though they are not yet fully
regenerate Christian heroes. God is with Hereward and Amyas
Leigh in many of their more righteous adventures even though His
presence is not much acknowledged. Kingsley was trapped rather
awkwardly by his conflicting responsibilities as secular novelist and
as Christian moralist. He tried to extricate himself by alternating
between the roles of the biographer who follows the fortunes of an
individual and the social observer or historian whose interest is in

larger patterns. The excitement and interest of Kingsley's novels cannot always wait for the church to catch up with them and Kingsley did not see why they should: the vigorous activities of Esau did not need Jacob's blessing. Kingsley the social commentator or historian could take a comfortably broad view of Esau's doings since he could see the overall good that always resulted. God could usually be relied upon to do the same. Carlyle's praise of massive unconscious virtue, inarticulate and unselfconscious compliance with some intuitively apprehended divine imperative, gave Kingsley a convenient if heretical justification for the unregenerate doing good in his novels. Tom Thurnall shocks Frank Headley by describing the unselfish kindness of a murderer (ch. 10). But this seemed to make conversion to Christianity unimportant and incidental, a purely private matter. Kingsley tried to redress the balance by switching from historical or epic to biographical narrative, insisting from time to time that Amyas Leigh and Hereward and Tom Thurnall confront the moral inadequacy and godlessness of their lives. He wanted to argue that only Christianity could guarantee that the hero would act rightly and in the right spirit. But self-denying right action, whether consciously Christian or not, could always gain his approval. Not surprisingly, the religious press was offended.[49]

Like Thomas Arnold's pre-Christian Greeks and Romans, who were dignified as instruments of Divine Providence irrespective of their wishes or intentions in the matter, Kingsley's heroes could be worldly adventurers or classical mythological figures without Christian credentials. Provided they did right and helped others God would help them and would reward their altruistic virtue, their generosity, magnanimity and chivalry, by conferring a kind of quasi-divinity upon them.[50] The Greeks had made their heroes the kinsmen of the gods and Kingsley was pagan enough to do the same,[51] falling back almost as an afterthought on Maurice's theology of men as brothers of Christ and sons of God. Unlike Carlyle, unlike the Greeks, Kingsley democratically took the Mauricean line that all men had this divine heroic potential. The moral of his children's book *The Heroes* is that there is a golden fleece for everyone to seek, a blow to strike for humanity before the end.[52]

This simple ethic, deliberately blurring the frontier between secular and sacred, was not always sufficiently emphasized in specifically religious accounts of man's earthly pilgrimage, Kingsley felt. He was never entirely happy with Bunyan's *Pilgrim's Progress*

4   Manly quest in *The Water-Babies*: 'Tom's journey', by Linley Sambourne (1890 edition)

because of its inward-looking, single-minded concentration on the world to come rather than the contemporary world with its problems and opportunities for Christian service.[53] The vision of Bunyan's Beulah or happy land is not repudiated at the end of *Yeast* but the route to it is altered to pass through the social distress of the 'hungry forties'. Kingsley always preferred an adventurous openness to the things of the present world, combining the courage of the pilgrim or questing knight with the intelligent alertness of the Baconian scientist. Spenser's *The Faerie Queene*, full of knights and moral and physical adventures, was a much better manual of manliness.[54] Tom's pilgrimage to the Other-end-of-Nowhere in *The Water-Babies* (illustration 4) is knightly quest, moral ordeal, voyage of exploration and scientific expedition all in one. Mother Cary tells Tom he must always look at her, and insofar as she stands for God the benign and all-powerful architect of everything this represents the religious imperative of the Christian manly quest. But Tom cannot see her all the time, so he is given her dog to look at instead, a whimsical counterpart to the Christ who was God in human and visible form. According to Coleridge Christ was the embodiment of the Divine *Logos* which underpinned all scientific law. Since Bacon had taught that human achievement, the conquest of nature, came through obedience to this law, Tom is sent forth looking backwards at the dog, the Christ-figure which inspires him and encourages him to consider the patterns of past experience as he looks back and use them as his guide to future achievement.

The Baconian conquest of nature and Maurice's easily secularized ideal of brotherly co-operation which was realized in the Christian socialist co-operative associations are brought together in the parable of social evolution in the later stages of Alton Locke's dream. Here the manly quest is identified with the great westward migrations of the adventurous Indo-European peoples. A mountain barrier blocks their progress but they form a social contract, agreeing to work together to tunnel through the mountain and conquer the natural obstacle and to till the ground in equal shares to feed themselves. The sense of brotherhood in a common task sustains and regulates their labours for a time but their king loses his authority, the stronger labourers gradually become an aristocracy of wealth who neglect and oppress their weaker brothers, and finally the downtrodden rise in revolt and slay the aristocrats. They prepare for a life of idleness until reminded of their responsibility to work together as 'brothers of the Son of God' and to resume digging through the mountain.

This is a co-operative version of Carlyle's injunction to find one's duty in the work lying nearest to hand. But collective enterprise, however manly and unselfish, can make for dull reading. Individual achievement, especially of an unusual or distinguished kind, is always more interesting, especially in novels. Kingsley was well aware of this. He embellished his version of the Christian manly quest, more often individual than co-operative, with the Platonic doctrine of *thumos*, or righteous indignation, with the glitter of chivalry and with the rhetoric of cosmic battle for righteousness assimilated from Maurice, Carlyle and Arnold. But as we have seen, the quest is more important than the person who undertakes it. As Tom Thurnall remarks of the (not very significant) social criticism and righteous indignation of Elsley Vavasour,

'he began by trying to set the world right, when he hadn't yet set himself right; but wasn't it some credit to see that the world was wrong?' (ch. 25)

Tom Thurnall's heroic fight against the evils of disease and apathy in sanitary matters, Stangrave's chivalric quest on behalf of negro slaves and his beloved Marie, Frank Headley's self-sacrificing exercise of his priestly vocation 'as chivalrous as a knight-errant of old' are different versions of the manly quest and manly achieve-ment. This convergence on the theme of Christian manliness in action gives *Two Years Ago* the only real unity it possesses.

Westward Ho! is Kingsley's best and most unified as well as his most exciting novel because he simplifies the national and religious circumstances within which Christian manliness operates. Alexandrian Christianity is no help to anyone in *Hypatia*. The monkish religion of the eleventh century is not much better in *Hereward*. Kingsley labours the point by departing from his sources to blame Hereward's over-religious mother rather than his father for making Hereward an outlaw and so inaugurating his manly career without benefit of clergy.[55] Apart from the Goths, who carry their national traditions around with them, there is very little sense of nationality and patriotism in *Hypatia*. Danes, Saxons and Normans muddle the issue of English patriotism to a hopeless extent in *Hereward*. Neither novel has a sufficiently noble cause or noble woman to sustain either chivalry or righteous manliness for very long. But the national Protestant crusade against Catholic Spain in *Westward Ho!* kindles the *thumos* or righteous indignation of every true Englishman and imparts its own virtue to all who take part in it. The chivalrous defence of the honour and virginity of Queen

Elizabeth forms a part of this national battle for righteousness against Spain, the Pope, the Inquisition and the Devil. Kingsley simplifies things even more by displacing some of this chivalric feeling, caught from Froude's defence of Elizabeth, into the absurd but noble quest of the Brotherhood of the Rose. The dangers Rose Salterne encounters in the clutches of the Spaniard Don Guzman and his Catholic countrymen do duty for the dangers from which Rose's band of lovers and all the other brave sailors of the time are seeking to protect Queen Elizabeth, England and protestantism. This was the epoch, the nation and the religion which produced Kingsley's favourite poet Spenser: in *Westward Ho!* Kingsley successfully and vividly dramatized the manliness he perceived in Spenser's *The Faerie Queene* where he believed that 'man is considered as striving to do noble work in this world'.[56]

The work Charles Kingsley did in this world has been variously assessed. In politics he managed to offend liberals and conservatives, in church matters he wilfully antagonized Evangelicals and Tractarians alike, as an historian he exasperated Freeman, as a thinker he exasperated Leslie Stephen. But he was listened to as a teacher and loved as a parson. His chaotic energies, his infectious enthusiasms and his plain-spoken truculence would have given him a reputation for aggressively manly Christianity if he had never written a single novel. By dramatizing his concerns and convictions and enlivening them with a luridly vivid imagination Kingsley did as much as anyone of his generation to articulate the triumphs and tensions of church and world for a popular audience. There was no-one quite like him, except, perhaps, the author of *Tom Brown's Schooldays*.

6

Tom Brown's manliness

Like his friend Charles Kingsley, Thomas Hughes was a vigorous sportsman, a pupil of Carlyle and Maurice, a pioneer Christian socialist and an energetic and combative campaigner for social reform. With the publication of *Tom Brown's Schooldays* in 1857 he became a popular novelist as well. Like Kingsley, he wanted to preach through the medium of fiction. Not surprisingly, his gospel was rapidly assimilated to the 'muscular Christianity' of Charles Kingsley, the established novelist and preacher, by *The Times* and the *Edinburgh Review* among others.[1]

The similarities between Kingsley and Hughes as men and novelists are obvious but should not be exaggerated. Kingsley wrote as he lived, with fierce, spasmodic vehemence, in the intervals of ill-health and depression. Hughes, no less energetic and with almost as wide a range of enthusiasms, was both healthier and happier, buoyant and cheerful by temperament, less brilliantly imaginative but more fluent and business-like in his writing. Where Kingsley stuttered nervously and excitedly except in the pulpit Hughes had the brisk and well-articulated delivery of the professional advocate. This helped him not only in the courts, where he became a Queen's Counsel and eventually a County Court Judge, but also in parliament where he was a Liberal member for nine years, from 1865 to 1874.

His greatest talent at the bar was not as an advocate, however, but as an equity draftsman, preparing long, detailed statements of fact for legal deeds such as those appointing new trustees.[2] By its very nature such an occupation encouraged orderly exposition and discouraged the wilder flights of fancy. Though he strenuously denied that Tom Brown was a self-portrait[3] he invented very little of his hero except his vacillating moral character and his moral and political adventures. The deliberately humdrum name 'Tom Brown' implies someone as ordinary as Tom Hughes thought he was himself. The background and education of Tom Hughes and Tom Brown are much the same: sons of Berkshire squires educated at private school, Arnold's Rugby and the unreformed Oxford of the 1840s before contracting early marriages and embarking on socially responsible work in the world. The most vivid and exciting parts of *Tom Brown's Schooldays* and the sequel *Tom Brown at Oxford* (1861) are the accounts of football and cricket and fighting and the more informal aspects of life at school and college and in rural Berkshire which draw most directly on Hughes' personal experience. These are the bait to win the reader's interest. The moral struggles which Hughes invents for his otherwise interesting manly hero have the effect of concentrating much of the seriousness of the Tom Brown stories on questions of personal conduct in the first instance rather than broader social and national questions which loom so large in the much more ambitious novels of Charles Kingsley. In *Tom Brown at Oxford* the 'condition of England' question becomes the 'Harry Winburn problem' in which Tom's interest is largely personal. Social and national concerns are very much present in the background, often indicated by direct incidental reference: they represent the final testing-ground for emerging manly character, but questions of character come first. This self-imposed restriction to the life and times of Tom Brown, a not particularly heroic middle-class everyman, delivered Hughes from some of the embarrassments of Kingsley, obliged to be both social commentator and moralist, epic historian and individual biographer, but it caused other problems. Both Tom Brown stories are trapped into structural anachronism, illustrating the author's response to the contemporary situation of the 1850s but based on the experiences of the younger Tom Hughes in the 1830s and early 1840s. The relations between Tom Brown and his surprisingly little-known author must be inspected a little more closely.

TOM BROWN'S AUTHOR

Hughes was born in 1822 at Uffington in the Berkshire Vale of the White Horse. The famous White Horse incised in the chalk-down just above the village in some prehistoric ritual may already have been ancient when the Romans came and venerable indeed when Alfred fought the Danes less than a mile away. The rich deposit of history and tradition in that particular corner of Berkshire left traces in the Tom Brown stories and was brought to life in Tom Hughes' tale *The Scouring of the White Horse*, 1859, a lightly fictionalized account of the celebrations associated with a recent refurbishing of the familiar landmark. The Hughes family had been associated with the area for generations, but its most notable member was Tom's grandmother Mary Ann Hughes.[4] This rather formidable lady, friend of Sir Walter Scott and of that lesser historical novelist Harrison Ainsworth, imparted to her son John Hughes and her grandson Tom a taste for literature and history as well as country pursuits. In the intervals of cricket and rowing and occasional academic work at Oxford Tom Hughes found himself reading Scott to a broken-down jockey to keep him out of the public house.[5] Scott confirmed in Hughes a taste inherited from his father for the chivalric idealism of the middle ages: this gave glamour and dignity to the moralized manliness of his writings. He loved to allude to the old Spanish legend of Durandarte at Roncesvalles which represented for him 'the beau ideal of knighthood summed up in a few words':

> Kind in manners, fair in favour,
> Mild in temper, fierce in fight, –
> Warrior purer, gentler, braver,
> Never shall behold the light.[6]

Scott also indicated ways of keeping faith with the past even when that past involved conflicting traditions. The clash of Cavalier and Roundhead, romantic traditionalism and a politics of moral indignation, was an energizing tension in Hughes as well as in Kingsley. His father was a staunch Tory landowner who devoted his literary leisure to editing the Boscobel Tracts which detailed the escape of Charles II after the Battle of Worcester.[7] But John Hughes was also a staunch moralist who respected the moral character of his Oxford friend Thomas Arnold. He swallowed his indignation at Arnold's Whiggish politics and sent Tom to Rugby in 1834 together with his eldest son George. This seems to have had little political effect on George, who turned out a benevolent Tory paternalist like his father.[8] But in Tom it sowed the seeds of a principled radicalism on social and political questions. Undergraduate Oxford, still dominated by a Church of England largely unmoved by Arnold's appeals for reform, was as Royalist and as conservative as John Hughes. In 1842, Hughes' second year at Oxford, the Oxford Union defeated a motion supporting Hampden's stand against ship-money and the tyranny of Charles I and in his final year the Union voted in favour of retaining the Corn Laws, just a year before they were finally repealed.[9] By that time Hughes had learnt to think differently after his travels in the north of England where anti-Corn-Law feeling was strongest.[10] He could now quote Byron's sneer to his Oxford companions and to his father:

> For what were all these country patriots born?
> To hunt, and vote, and raise the price of corn?[11]

It is unlikly that he was so tactless. He was still a country patriot himself, up to a point. He never lost his enthusiasm for the customs and traditions of his own locality in Berkshire. But his early life in the country was no idyll. Agricultural distress had led to the Captain Swing riots in his childhood; the New Poor Law of 1834, the year he went to Rugby, had seemed to make things worse rather than better, and rural poverty still continued in the 'hungry forties' when he was at Oriel. All this could now be understood rather differently. Carlyle as well as Arnold and the opponents of the Corn Laws convinced him that social distress was not a divine visitation but a moral challenge, the result not of irresistible forces but of the failure of men and governments to take action. Tom Brown's politics moved rather more violently in the same direction in his Oxford career: he derided the conservative heritage Tom Hughes had moved away from by displaying a copy of the death-warrant of Charles I in his rooms. When Squire Brown came to visit he manfully refused to take it down but tried desperately to keep it out of his father's field of vision (ch. 42). Tom Hughes seems to have avoided the family feud that Tom Brown was almost comically afraid of: in 1853 Squire Hughes gave a generous subscription to the cause of co-operative labour associations to which his now Christian socialist son was devoting a great deal of his time and money.[12]

The theme of co-operation, reinforced by Maurice's theology of universal brotherhood in Christ, is important in the Tom Brown novels even though Hughes developed his interest in co-operative associations when school and college experiences were behind him. He remained a Rugby schoolboy all his life: later experience complemented and enlarged rather than effaced earlier interests and enthusiasms. This may be why *Tom Brown's Schooldays*, moralizing and all, has lasted so well as a boy's book while its graver rivals such as F. W. Farrar's *Eric or Little by Little* (1858) now seem unreadable and absurd. Tom Hughes, like Tom Brown, had been an enthusiastic cricketer at Rugby and had played in an exciting match against a visiting MCC side in his last year at school. Sixteen years later in *Tom Brown's Schooldays* this is replayed over by over, almost ball by ball, as Tom Brown's last match.[13] Hughes had been able to keep his eye in in the interval by playing for Oxford and later organizing a cricket club at the Working Men's College. The plucky fist-fighting in *Tom Brown's Schooldays* and the rowing in *Tom Brown at Oxford* also reflect enthusiasms which had never died and which Hughes had put to good use. Hughes had probably studied boxing more seriously than anything else at Oxford, taking lessons with 'the Flying Tailor', a retired prize-fighter. He had rowed in the Oriel boat though he never quite attained the distinction of his brother George who stroked the heroic Oxford crew which won the 1834 boat-race against all odds and a man short. Hughes kept himself fit and enlivened the Working Men's College through the 1850s by teaching boxing there: he also founded the WMC rowing-club.[14] In 1860 his decidedly useful pair of hands was at the disposal of the London dockland church of St George-in-the-East where an extreme ritualist rector had caused so much disquiet that hooligans had disrupted services and damaged church furnishings. Hughes led a police force of volunteers which soon restored order.[15]

Co-operation rather than sport prompted Tom Hughes' earliest literary work. He took a very active part in the setting up of co-operative workshops, the main practical result of the Christian socialist movement of 1848. His legal background and his professional work in London made him a more useful man for this type of work than Kingsley, who was enthusiastic but never had any head for business and had parish responsibilities in Hampshire. Soon Hughes became editor of the co-operative *Journal of Association*. In 1850 he wrote a Christian socialist tract outlining the history of the Working Tailors' Association which had been set up to bring relief to the distressed Alton Lockes of the city, and he appeared as an expert witness before a House of Commons Committee to give evidence about the savings of the working classes and to promote the cause of co-operation in high places.[16] None of the co-operative associations survived for long in the form the Christian socialists had intended, but Hughes kept faith with the co-operative movement, as he kept faith with his Tory father's legacy of strict integrity and humanitarianism and Arnold's training in principled liberalism, to the end of his life. In 1869 he was chairman of the first Co-operative Congress and in 1881 he was co-author of *A Manual for Co-operators* prepared at the request of the 1879 Co-operative Congress. He actually wrote *Tom Brown's Schooldays* in a house in Wimbledon built by the North London Working Builders' Association, the most long-lived and successful of the Christian socialist co-operatives. It would be an exaggeration to call the house a 'commune' but it was shared between the Hughes family and the family of his fellow-Christian socialist J. M. Ludlow.[17]

The sense of co-operative purpose as a basis for life and society inspired Hughes in his parliamentary career from 1865 to 1874. He was a man of principle rather than party and had no special skills or finesse as a politician, but his early experience of working men's associations led to sympathy with the cause of labour and the struggling Trade Union movement. He published an account of a prolonged lock-out of engineers in 1860 and in 1869 tried hard but unsuccessfully to promote a Trade Union Bill in the House of Commons.[18] He remained closer to the spirit of Maurice's doctrine of universal brotherhood than Kingsley: the institution of slavery appalled him and during the American Civil War he fought vigorously to publicize the northern cause in England on moral and humanitarian grounds where Kingsley was noticeably unenthusiastic. The American abolitionist poet James Russell Lowell was both his friend and his guide to American politics before and after the Civil War. In Lowell's sometimes eloquent, sometimes embarrassingly bad verse, especially in the *Biglow Papers*, Hughes found a parallel to the combative rhetoric of the just cause which Arnold and Carlyle had developed and applied to English social problems. Lowell's *Vision of Sir Launfal* contrived to mingle the trappings of mediaeval chivalry and romance which Hughes had loved as a child with a democratic morality of respect for all men which he had learnt as a co-operator and Christian socialist. Lowell supplies several of the epigraphs in the Tom Brown novels.[19]

But Hughes was no internationalist: he was interested in America, and in India and the colonies, mainly from the point of view of a right-thinking patriotic Englishman. In this he remained true to the tradition of Coleridge, Arnold and Maurice for whom the Church usually meant the Church of England and the State usually meant Britain south of the Tweed. Arnold had written a Prize essay on colonization in 1818. One of his sons, William Delafield, a friend of Hughes with whom he occasionally corresponded, became director of education in the Punjab; another, Thomas the younger, settled for a time in Tasmania.[20] But the title of the elder Arnold's essay, significantly, was *The effects of distant colonization on the parent state*. Hughes thought more about the surplus of middle-class youths in the parent state than about the specific nature of the territories to which they could be exported.[21] His utopian scheme in 1879 for a co-operative colony of public-school men at Rugby, Tennessee, perhaps the last experiment in the tradition of Coleridge and Southey's Susquehanna project, was an embarrassing failure which almost ruined Hughes financially. Not for the first time he put too much trust in his fellow men and allowed his optimism and his enthusiasm to distract his attention from practical difficulties. Agriculture would have to be the basis of the new colony but none of the colonists knew enough about farming and many of them were well-bred idlers lacking Hughes' energy and determination, more interested in tennis than Tennessee. Encouraged by Tom Brown's author, they liked to think of themselves as Tom Browns abroad, but the more practical Davy Crockett would have been a far better model.[22] Hughes had a similarly insular view of India. Kipling had not yet invented the white man's burden, and though William Delafield Arnold had made heavy weather of India as a location for Arnoldian moral ordeal in his novel *Oakfield* (1853) Hughes was content to make it the subaltern Harry East's adventure-playground in *Tom Brown at Oxford* before finally transporting him to New Zealand.

Hughes' interest in foreign affairs seems to have been almost confined to wars and rumours of wars. Like his school friend and contemporary A. H. Clough, whose narrative poem *Amours de Voyage* is set amidst the political disturbance of Italy in 1848, the year of revolutions in Europe made a profound impression upon him. Christian socialism which began in that year was intended to be a bloodless revolution in the social outreach of the Church. His fellow Christian socialist J. M. Ludlow had actually been in Paris in 1848 to see revolution at first hand. Like many Englishmen from Palmerston downwards Hughes admired Kossuth the leader of the Hungarian rebellion of 1848 and Mazzini the hero of Italian liberation.[23] The War of Independence fought by Tom and East against the tyranny of the Fifth in *Tom Brown's Schooldays* is described very much in terms of these popular revolutions (I, ch. 8). But fighting the Fifth, or Flashman, or tyrants in France or Italy or Hungary, can all be assimilated to the eternal battle for truth and right which is central to the ideal of Christian manliness.

It was all too easy to sanctify chauvinistic sabre-rattling by invoking this infinitely adaptable rhetoric of the just war, and the Tom Brown novels, like Kingsley's *Westward Ho!*, reflected the popular patriotism first revived by Francophobia and the Crimean War. In *Tom Brown's Schooldays* Old Brooke is described as an

autocrat kinder and wiser than the Czar (I, ch. 5). Evil has to be
fought and vanquished in the individual and the school, in Arthur's
father's slum-parish and among the Queen's enemies, particularly
Russians and border-villains (II, ch. 5). This anti-Russian animus
probably relates not merely to the Crimean expedition against
Russia but to the even more recent Persian expedition against Herat
in Afghanistan, close to the Persian border, which had secret
Russian backing and alarmed the British in India. The Victorian
dread of Russia was only incidentally associated with the Crimea:
the dominant fear was that the Russians would gain an ascendancy
in Constantinople, in Persia and in Afghanistan and so have a clear
passage from their own territories into British India.[24] In 1856 two
divisions were despatched from India to save Herat from the
Persians and the Russians, and British gunboats appeared in the
Persian gulf. After months of sporadic and inconclusive fighting and
some much more effective diplomacy the issue was resolved and the
Persians withdrew in April 1857, just as *Tom Brown's Schooldays* was
published.[25]

This rather obscure campaign was almost immediately forgotten
when the Indian Mutiny broke out a month later, though some
observers felt afterwards that the mutiny could have been contained
more quickly if the Persian expeditionary force had not still been out
of the country. The horrors and heroism of the siege of Lucknow
displaced the siege of Sebastopol in the public imagination so that
India rather than the Crimea was the natural setting for Harry
East's military adventures in *Tom Brown at Oxford*. One of the heroes
of the mutiny was Hughes' schoolfriend William Hodson, 'Hodson
of Hodson's Horse', killed at Lucknow. Neither Hodson nor Harry
East had been very distinguished at Rugby but Hughes felt he could
now celebrate them both as models of the 'glorious Christian soldier
and Englishman', able to 'take his place, and do his work in his
world battle'.[26]

By 1860 military manliness was on review in Hyde Park as well as
Hyderabad. The fear of French invasion and Napoleon III which
Kingsley hoped to exploit in the early 1850s revived again after the
Crimean War. The first Napoleon had been banished to St Helena
before Hughes was born but he knew all about him. He had talked to
veterans of the Peninsular War as a child and his father had grown
up a staunch patriot in an England at war with the French on land
and sea.[27] There was a rich heritage of patriotic sea-songs from this
era and on social occasions Tom Hughes could always be prevailed

upon to sing Prince Hoare's 'The Arethusa'. The 'saucy Arethusa'
had fearlessly engaged a much larger French vessel in the Channel

> Though the Frenchman laughed and thought it stuff,
> But they knew not the handful of men, how tough,
> On board of the Arethusa.[28]

Tom Hughes' lifelong interest in the navy[29] and in the armies which
defeated Napoleon I was prompted by the reminiscences of his
elders, and so perhaps was his enthusiastic service with the
Volunteers, set up in 1859 to drive the third Napoleon from British
soil in the event of a French invasion. For Hughes this provided an
opportunity to combine his co-operative and aggressively patriotic
instincts: he felt that in volunteering all classes of Englishmen could
find 'a bond which may in the end bind the nation together again'.[30]
He commanded two companies of Volunteers associated with the
Working Men's College and gladly accepted a commission to revise
the Military Regulations for Volunteers. He also played a very
active part in the 1860 Volunteer review in the presence of Queen
Victoria in Hyde park.[31] This was one of the high points of Victorian
military manliness. The Volunteer review attracted enormous
publicity, even in *Punch*. The cheerfully unmilitary Mr Punch was
there in person, manfully supporting the armed might of Her
Majesty, whose rifle was shown resting on his head (illustration 5).

For Hughes as for Kingsley soldiering, or at least part-time
soldiering, was a noble and natural occupation for a gentleman of
manly sporting instincts. All that cricket and rowing and boxing
kept Hughes fit for the physical ardours of volunteering. He found it
natural, even necessary, to link Harry East's athletic prowess at
Rugby with his success as a soldier. For Harry at least war in India
has little to do with the Great Game of international politics: it is a
physically exhilarating game or sport in its own right. He describes
artillery going into action:

Nothing stops those fellows. Places you would crane at out hunting they go
right over, guns, carriages, men, and all, leaving any cavalry we've got out
here well behind. (ch. 44)

As a clergyman Kingsley could have only indirect contact with
military manliness, celebrating Saxon and Elizabethan soldiers,
sending his patriotic pamphlet *Brave Words for Brave Men* to the
troops before Sebastopol and enjoying the company of officers from
nearby Aldershot at home in Eversley. As a Volunteer Officer Major
Hughes of the 19th Middlesex could write about fighting manfully

BEST REST FOR THE QUEEN'S RIFLE.

5   Mr Punch and the Volunteers: cartoon in *Punch*, 1860

in good causes with the authority of some technical information, though Napoleon III never risked an engagement with the Working Men's College Volunteers.

TOM BROWN'S SCHOOLDAYS

Morality, sport, social concern, co-operation and aggressive patriotism are the major ingredients of the Tom Brown novels. Hughes' skill as an equity draftsman ensures, in *Tom Brown's Schooldays* at least, that these elements are cunningly arranged to lead the reader by pleasant paths to a hard centre of sub-Arnoldian moral seriousness which seeks to teach a young person his duty to himself and to his society. The result is impressive, if not completely convincing. Hughes began to think about *Tom Brown's Schooldays* when he was facing Squire Brown's dilemma of what to tell his son before sending him off to school. The death of his daughter Evie in 1856 halted work on the novel for a time and may have been partly responsible for the more sombre vision of darkness and death and eternal manliness in the later chapters, but Hughes' early letters to his publisher indicate that he had always intended to work up to moral manliness by way of sturdy manliness.[32] The age-structure of school life helped him, though the social structure of school life made things harder.

Hughes knew that there was an enormous gulf fixed between junior and senior boys at school: even the boys of the Fifth were puny creatures beside the majesty of the Sixth. This meant that school life was dominated by a hierarchy of respect for seniority which Arnold had tried to exploit in his system of praepostors and which Hughes exploited in the person of Old Brooke, a sporting hero used to mediate the reforms of the Doctor to the younger boys who hang on his every word. Until Tom Brown is in the sixth form himself, aware of the impending challenge of the world beyond the school and capable of quasi-adult conversation with a young master, his moral and intellectual consciousness is distinctly rudimentary. As with most boys, for a long time his values are hero-worship, directed at the Doctor and at sportsmen like Brooke, and an ethic of pluck and physical hardihood.

Hughes' earlier chapters operate very much in these boyish terms. The simple paternalistic goodness of Squire Brown and his wife is accepted as a moral base-line at the start of the novel. It is linked with a retrospect of the traditional usefulness and courage of the Brown dynasty, the upper-middle-class backbone of Britain. Heroism and pluck are represented as the heritage of Britain and the Browns for the thousand years that separate Alfred's onslaught on the Danes and the storming of the heights at the Alma in the Crimean war. A single sentence encompasses both events and links Berkshire with the Black Sea as arenas of English manliness: 'And up the heights came the Saxons, as they did at the Alma' (1, ch. 1). Old Benjy initiates the young Tom Brown into the sturdy outdoor life of the country which is the foundation of glories such as these. He aids and abets his fishing and riding and introduces him to the hearty traditional games and 'veasts' of the area, a meeting-place for different classes which Tom Hughes particularly valued as Christian socialist and co-operator as well as Berkshire patriot. He developed this theme at much greater length in *The Scouring of the White Horse*. Wrestling and back-swording are at least as rough as the football and fighting Tom is to encounter at school but they can be just as healthy and wholesome. Back-swording, if played with proper coolness and self-control, is 'by no means a punishing pastime'. Joe Willis rather loses his cool in his bout with the unknown old man, plays wildly and loses the match. The older man has acquired moral maturity as well as physical skills, part of the lesson Squire Brown will send Tom to Arnold's Rugby to learn. He keeps his temper, takes no arrogant delight in his victory, and generously waives his right to the prize (1, ch. 2).

Hughes draws the same simple moral from Tom Brown's first football match at Rugby. Young Brooke is cool, careful and deadly accurate, fully in command of himself in the scrum where the more hasty boys push too hard and miss the ball completely. He would make a brave and resourceful army officer and Hughes works in passing references to the Old Guard at Waterloo and the light and heavy brigades whose Crimean exploits had been glorified by the poet laureate as an implicit patriotic sanction for the sturdy manliness the game brings forth (1, ch. 5). Tom Brown makes a good start at Rugby by risking life and limb to cover the ball with his body and earning the commendation of 'plucky youngster' (1, ch. 4). His long journey to Rugby through the night on the outside of the coach must have been quite a physical ordeal for a small boy but he survives it with the stout-hearted resilience which sustains him later on when Flashman roasts him by the fire and he refuses to give in (1, ch. 8).

This rather primitive first stage of manliness is contrasted with feeble womanliness: young Tom very soon outwits Charity Lamb, his incompetent nurse, and causes consternation in a girls' school in the village by riding his pony round the table where the cowering schoolmistress and her pupils are seated (1, ch. 3). But Hughes acknowledges that women represent more than apron-strings and hysterics: a later stage of manliness is reached when Tom befriends Arthur, who is associated with the gentleness and goodness rather than the weakness of women. Arthur is first mentioned by the little matron, is invited to tea with Tom by Mrs Arnold, and is responsible for bringing his gracious mother to the school and into the novel. Victorian religious painters such as Holman Hunt and apologists of Christian manliness such as S. S. Pugh stressed both the masculine strength and the womanly tenderness of the Christ.[33] The Christian manliness Tom Brown develops needs the corrective of the best kind of womanliness associated with Arthur, as well as the challenge of chivalrous protection of the weak, though the well-aimed boot which ensures Arthur has peace to say his prayers is a very down-to-earth substitute for the lance of Sir Galahad. Arthur, for his part, needs the invigoration of the healthy outdoor life at Rugby and Tom obligingly introduces him to tree-climbing and cricket, even including him in the Eleven, against his better judgement, for his last match.

As Tom gradually rises through the school it becomes clear that sporting manliness and the ethic of pluck and hardihood can be extended into a more adult and a more specifically Christian ethic. As Hughes argued later on in his book *The Manliness of Christ*, Jesus demonstrated his manhood in His self-sacrifice and moral courage. Sturdy manliness leads on to and in a sense becomes a metaphor for unflinching moral resolution. Tom Brown comes to admire Shadrach, Meshach and Abednego: like himself they had undergone an ordeal by fire; unlike him they had bravely witnessed to the God of Israel in the burning fiery furnace. In the school context moral courage involved 'facing the music' like the boys on the Rugby coach whose pea-shooters pepper an irate yeoman: they offer to go before the magistrate to answer for it. Moral courage also enabled boys to stand against the stream of public opinion in school as Arnold's sermons had urged: Arthur's kneeling to say his prayers in the cheerfully godless dormitory is a brave act, and so, much later on, is Tom Brown's determination to give up using cribs in preparing his classical work. Tom Brown's private school, unlike Tom Hughes', is not a happy place because there is no encouragement to be brave and manly and own up of your own accord: instead there is an insidious system of tale-bearing and espionage which upholds the oppressive discipline of the place. This helps to define by negation the specific characteristics of Rugby where Arnold fostered self-respect by trusting the boys and it became the custom never to lie to the Doctor or shirk the blame for one's own misdeeds. Hughes probably borrowed this tactic of tendentiously comparing public and private schools from the autobiographical *School Experiences of a*

Fag at a Private and a Public School (1854) by his fellow-Rugbeian George Melly.[34]

Public-school sturdiness and self-reliant manliness come into their own in the fight chapter and in Tom and East's 'war of independence' against the unwarrantable tyranny of the Fifth form. But it is here that the nature of schoolboy society begins to present Hughes the moralist with problems. He approves of fighting in good causes, supported by Maurice's rhetoric of truth and right ranged in apocalyptic battle against evil. Russians and Border-Ruffians and the struggle for a free Hungary or Italy offer justification for fighting in the contemporary world, as we have seen, and Hughes was no more impressed than Kingsley with the activities of the Peace Party and its leaders Cobden and Bright. On the other hand fights rather disrupt the good order one might wish to see in school life. Hughes wishes to lead Tom Brown by stages from sturdy manliness to Arnoldian manliness, but this involves making a kind of quantum leap from the closed system of schoolboy life with its uninhibited freedoms and amoral traditions to the reformist values of the Doctor who was aware that the 'spirit of combination in evil' among boys represented his biggest challenge as a Christian headmaster. The age-old division between boys and masters, 'us' and 'them', was particularly apparent in unreformed Rugby, and in his praise of fighting Hughes sided very definitely with 'us'. The terse dialogue of the fight chapter, the breathless excitement conveyed in the present tense of the description, express Hughes' boyish exuberance and enthusiasm for a good clean scrap. Slogger Williams is bigger and stronger than either Tom or Arthur, so Tom deserves full marks for courage and chivalry in taking him on to stop him bullying Arthur. His simple and manly ambition to leave behind him 'the name of a fellow who never bullied a little boy, or turned his back on a big one' is almost achieved in this single heroic encounter. But Arthur and the Doctor are left outside the ring of cheering spectators. Arthur is genuinely distressed at the fight, and Hughes draws back a little from his own enthusiasm by importing adult morality in the shape of the under-porter, unheroically equipped with brush and dustpan, who tries to intervene and warns that the Doctor knows of the fight and is on his way. Young Brooke, who has made no attempt to stop the fight despite being one of the Doctor's praepostors, and the other onlookers including Tom Hughes himself are uneasy and embarrassed until the Doctor goes away again (II, ch. 5).

The Doctor had intended that praepostors and senior boys would bridge the gap between the lawless rough-and-tumble of school life and the ideal of Christian gentlemanliness which he hoped to inculcate. But even good praepostors like young Brooke can find themselves unwilling and unable to take decisive action against the tendency of boys to be boys. The hierarchy of seniority upheld by the boys themselves is liable to abuse if seniors exert power without assuming responsibility, yet the Rugby principle of self-reliance precludes complaint to a sixth-former let alone a master. After the heroic Old Brooke departs the School-house gradually loses the sense of fellowship and common purpose which he had fostered and which had contributed so much to the prowess of the house in games. Instead of leaders the house is left with bullies. Hughes the co-operator and friend of labour and champion of liberal causes seeks to relocate the lost sense of common purpose in the house in the strike against tyranny and unlawful fagging initiated by Tom and East.

'Down with the tyrants!' cried East; 'I'm all for law and order, and hurrah for a revolution'. (1, ch. 8)

The possibility of just law and order in schoolboy society, which depends on the neglected principle of older boys accepting responsibilities towards younger boys as well as exercising power over them, is reasserted when the revolution and the strike succeed. But this triumph of a righteous cause still occasions some disquiet because it upsets the hierarchy of the school and defies the dignity of the Fifth.

This indicates that schoolboy custom and schoolboy sturdiness are not quite enough to guarantee the righteousness which is the objective of Hughes and of the Doctor. After victory in the 'War of Independence' Tom and East drift along thoughtlessly and lawlessly enough and the Doctor fears he may have to expel them '"if I don't see them gaining character and manliness"' (1, ch. 9). Exactly halfway through the book Hughes has to go beyond the framework of robust autonomous boy-society, with some regret, and introduce Arthur and Rugby Chapel to perfect Tom and East in Christian manliness. He makes Arthur the son of a dedicated Christian socialist parson, perhaps loosely based on Charles Kingsley. Mr Arthur's death just before Arthur comes to Rugby is an occasion for introducing a higher seriousness for which the circumscribed world of school is at best a preparation. Like Kingsley and Maurice, like Ludlow and Hughes himself, the elder Arthur, set down 'in that smoky hole Turley, a very nest of Chartism and Atheism', had striven in the midst of grim economic conditions to remove class-hatred and restore men to a sense of their brotherhood in Christ.

He had battled like a man, and gotten a man's reward. No silver teapots or salvers . . . but a manly respect, wrung from the unwilling souls of men who fancied his order their natural enemies; the fear and hatred of everyone who was false or unjust in the district, were he master or man; and the blessed sight of women and children daily becoming more human and more homely, a comfort to themselves and to their husbands and fathers.

His funeral, at which six labouring men and two members of the local Freethinking Club bore him to his grave, afforded a glimpse of co-operative Christian manliness and 'of what this old world would be, if people would live for God and each other, instead of themselves' (II, ch. 2).

By insisting that 'the spirit of his father was in him' Hughes contrives to make young Arthur an ambassador of adult manliness of this quality within the school. For all his apparent weakness he has inherited a moral and spiritual strength which is the counterpart and necessary complement to Tom Brown's physical strength. Wholesome friendship like that between Tom and Arthur, carefully distinguished from the homosexual patronage of the 'small-friend system' as it is delicately phrased (II, ch. 2), can be a source of moral benefit within the school but Hughes goes beyond the school and beyond ordinary temporal reality altogether to round off his message. Arthur's illness, his journey through the valley of the shadow to the boundaries of another world, draws particular attention to the religious faith he has inherited from his father. Arthur did not die because God had work for him to do. His dream hints at the nature of the work God intends for him and for Tom and for every manly Christian. Pluck and hardihood and the spirit of fellowship and co-operation in the school-house and in team games are caught up into a vision of dauntless and everlasting service of the Lord on either side of the river of death. Arthur's father who has gone before is a model worker in this co-operative Mauricean eternity, but Tom and Arthur and the Doctor are involved in the work as well and so are 'many a hard, stern man, who never came to church, and whom they called atheist and infidel' (II, ch. 6). This recalls the freethinkers of Turley who grieved at the death of Mr Arthur. Macmillan, Hughes' publisher, was nervous about this passage, afraid of offending religious orthodoxy, but Hughes insisted that it should go in. Like his master Maurice, like Kingsley singing the praises of Goths and Esau-figures, Hughes felt he had no right to usurp God's prerogative and exclude anyone from doing God's work in the world, or to doubt that the Father would finally reconcile all His children to Himself. For many years he worked side by side with freethinkers such as John Stuart Mill and the veteran secularist G. J. Holyoake in the service of co-operation and Trade Unions and never doubted that they were all of them doing the work of the Lord.[35]

Arthur's dream provides a wider setting for the final reconciliation of Tom, and later East also, to the moral seriousness of the Doctor. But this needs to be accommodated to the relatively trivial concerns of school life, which imposes a certain strain on the remaining three chapters of the novel. Mrs Arthur's present of a fishing-rod and a Bible symbolizes the new alliance of manliness and adult Christianity in Tom Brown, but he is still only a boy. Christian socialism will have to wait for a year or two (until the later chapters of *Tom Brown at Oxford,* in fact): in the meantime it seems Tom can only forswear the use of cribs, rather priggishly as East observes, and try to 'persuade himself that he should like all his best friends to die offhand'. Hughes sensibly tries to get round this restriction not by making Tom a precociously pious adolescent like some Rugby boys of his time but by stressing the extent to which school society is a microcosm of human society in the world at large. The dishonest impulse to rely on cribs, and the evil instincts which make Flashman and Slogger Williams bully younger boys, can be attributed to the same secret reservoir of human iniquity as the injustices of economic recession and class-warfare and the villainies of 'Russians and Border-Ruffians'. Tom comes to realize the existence of what some have called the Devil, 'some great, dark, strong power which is crushing you, and everybody else'. If moral evil in the individual, the school and the world outside has a single source there is also a single antidote in the redeeming and uniting love of God conveyed through the Eucharist. This is a solemn act of sharing which is celebrated in Rugby Chapel and throughout the world as an expression of human interrelatedness and mutual dependence within the family of God. Tom finally persuades East to go and see the Doctor about taking the Sacrament when he describes how he took the bread and wine from the Doctor and found himself praying for Flashman '"as if it had been you or Arthur"' (II, ch. 7). The epigraph from Lowell's *Vision of Sir Launfal* which heads the whole chapter demonstrates a point of intersection of Tom Brown at the altar-rail, co-operative Christian socialism and Maurice's vision of church and world as Christ's family of love:

> The Holy Supper is kept indeed,
> In whatso we share with another's need – . . .

Who bestows himself with his alms feeds three,
Himself, his hungering neighbour, and Me.

Tom Brown's last match, and his final act of hero-worship before
the Doctor's tomb, underline the same lesson. The magnificent co-
operative efforts of the Rugby Eleven demonstrate how cricket is not
just a game but an institution, as noble a heritage as *habeas corpus* and
trial by jury, as Arthur boyishly puts it. Chapel and cricket-pitch
can convey the same moral, the importance of unselfishly submit-
ting one's individuality to the service of a common cause. Hughes
knows from all that has happened since his own last match at Rugby
how life dismantles the comradeship of cricket and school enthusiasms and how death in the Crimea and in India can make that sense
of separation seem irrevocable. He quotes the wistful but manly
musings of his Rugby contemporary A. H. Clough.[36] But this
suddenly distant prospect of schooldays and school friends gone for
ever is rescued from sadness by a further reference to Maurice's God
of infinite and all-embracing love who will bring all men home again
at last, however wayward, however distant from each other. The
Rugby experience, with its fighting, its intense excitements and
common loyalties given religious meaning by devotion to Arnold
and (possibly) to the God of righteousness mediated by him, can be
seen as both a preparation for and a metaphor of the outside world of
struggle and dedication to noble causes. Tom Brown, aroused from
selfish sorrow, realizes that he shares his hero-worship and his grief
at Arnold's death with many others who have lost a friend in him:
this offers a hint to the adult Christian who must express his love of
Christ by sharing it with all men, who are his brothers in Christ. As
the young master says, Rugby is a model of how the country and the
world should be governed, 'the only corner of the British Empire
which is thoroughly, wisely, and strongly ruled just now' (II, ch. 8).
Arnold could have wished for no better epitaph.

TOM BROWN AT OXFORD

Tom Brown at Oxford is a more adult book, as one might expect. It
is longer and more diffuse than its predecessor and has never been as
popular. It is tempting to dismiss it as an unsuccessful attempt to
cash in on the success of *Tom Brown's Schooldays*. But Hughes'
correspondence with his publishers reveals that he had always
intended to go on to Tom Brown's experiences at college and after.[37]
The result is an interesting and unjustly neglected novel. There are

some lively vignettes of Oxford, Berkshire and London, and invaluable glimpses of the world of the 1840s as it had struck a representative middle-class observer who was devout but unclerical, thoughtful without being an intellectual, and socially and politically alert without being unduly partisan or extreme. But the sparkle and the concentrated energy of *Tom Brown's Schooldays* are missing. The writing dragged on for nearly four years, interrupted by other work and by the writing of *The Scouring of the White Horse*. Hughes had begun to feel old: the death in 1859 of his son Maurice, for whom *Tom Brown's Schooldays* was written, was a severe blow, following hard on the death of his daughter Evie in 1856.[38] For Hughes as for later public-school men such as Cyril Connolly[39] Oxford was not such a vital and exciting experience as school and it was less vividly recalled. Undergraduates spent less than half the year in residence so that home life in Berkshire, quietly abandoned after a few chapters in *Tom Brown's Schooldays* to allow Tom to concentrate on being a fulltime schoolboy, comes to play an important part in the later novel. Harry Winburn, a childhood friend of Tom Brown but forgotten even before the end of his schooldays, is resurrected as the central figure of the Berkshire scenes and the 'condition of England' theme associated with them. Hughes offers a simple parallelism between Harry Winburn in trouble and Tom Brown in trouble but Oxford and Berkshire are kept together in the same novel only by an audibly creaking plot which eventually identifies Tom Brown's Oxford sweetheart Patty, barmaid of the *Choughs*, with the beloved of Harry Winburn in Berkshire. Where Tom Brown and Tom Hughes spent some eight years at Rugby, growing from small boy to whiskered sixth former, the undergraduate career lasted only half as long and did not involve the same complex hierarchies of seniority within a closed society which helped to structure *Tom Brown's Schooldays*. In any case, as the *Saturday Review* pointed out, Tom Brown may have been a typical schoolboy but he was hardly a typical undergraduate since he was neither an earnest bookman nor an extravagant idler.[40] Harry East, an equally typical schoolboy, did not go to Oxford at all. Rugby boys in Arnold's time were entrusted with considerable responsibilities by the time they reached the Sixth but undergraduate life was less demanding and more individualistic, as Tom Brown ruefully observes: '"here one has only just to take care of oneself, and keep out of scrapes; and that's what I never could do."' (ch. 5)

Tom Brown's higher education in manliness necessarily involves

6 Tom's visit to Dr Arnold's tomb: Arthur Hughes' illustration for *Tom Brown's Schooldays* (1869 edition)

new departures. On the face of it the almost-adult Tom Brown,
brought into a right relation with his maker and his fellow man as he
stands before Arnold's tomb, has already learnt the Arnoldian
lessons of moral maturity (illustration 6). Hughes has to make him
regress a little between school and college to get his new novel
started. Cricket and field sports, manliness without very much
Christianity, fill Tom's life in the interval and give Hughes his
excuse to claim that 'the whole man had not grown'.[41] Unfortunately there is no continuing Arnoldian régime of phased moral
growth, no carefully delimited arena of ethical perseverance and
responsibility, to help Tom in the final stages of the maturing
process. This makes it harder for him, and presents Hughes with the
artistic problem of divising an alternative context for personal
development. To begin with he tries to adapt the paradigm of school
experience to the college situation. The iniquitous 'fast set', feckless
and extravagant, abandoned to self-indulgence and an unregenerate enthusiasm for the less disciplined sports, stand at one pole of a
simple moral analysis of college life, corresponding roughly to the
lawless world of school custom at Rugby. The difference is that there
is no compulsion upon Tom to become a member of this set and he
never really does. At the other pole stands the crusading righteous
man in some sense outside the system, represented by the servitor
Hardy who corresponds roughly to the virtuous Arthur and like him
needs to be brought into the system a little to benefit from it and help
redeem it. Hardy is elected to a fellowship and sets about reforming
the college, but he does not stay long in Oxford to consolidate this
achievement. There is also, at the outset of the novel, a rather pallid
reflection of the perpetual warfare of boys and masters at school in
the situation of the dons hopelessly at odds with the sporting
undergraduates they had originally welcomed for financial reasons.
Arnold eventually makes Rugby a more harmonious place. But
Hughes finds it more difficult to resolve a college into a sort of
Christian socialist co-operative association. He suggests that by
temperament and inclination the tutors are often impossibly remote
from the majority of the undergraduates. This is certainly Tom's
experience at a breakfast party with his own tutor: nervousness
masquerading as a cold formality inhibits the man from giving an
adequate answer to a query about private reading (ch. 5). A system
of praepostor-substitutes to mediate the donnish values of academic
seriousness, industry and moral integrity to undergraduates might
have helped to bridge the gap. But the most likely candidates for this
role, the dedicated reading men, have little life beyond their books

and so have no social contact with, let alone influence upon, their more irresponsible contemporaries.

Hughes soon realizes not only that the school paradigm is inappropriate to college life but that Oxford itself is insufficient as a training in manliness. Tom Brown gets by as well as he can. Collegiate manliness is fostered by the ardours and disciplines of rowing and by personal contact with thoroughly good men such as the magnificent all-rounder Hardy, a 'servitor' who earns his higher education by acting as a college servant. Hardy was probably modelled on Hughes' tutor at Oriel, James Fraser, later Bishop of Manchester and known as 'Tom Brown in lawn sleeves'. Like Hardy, Fraser had been very poor as an undergraduate: his mother was a widow in straitened circumstances. He became a Fellow of Oriel in 1840, just before Hughes went up to the same college, and proceeded to a country living in Hughes' beloved Berkshire before becoming a highly successful Bishop of Manchester noted for his constructive intervention in labour disputes. As a young don he indulged an appetite for manly sports, particularly hunting, which he had been unable to afford as an undergraduate. Hughes wrote his biography in 1887.[42] The name 'Hardy' which Hughes gives to this sturdy servitor recalls the traditions of loyalty and service associated with Nelson's Navy and particularly with Sir Thomas Hardy, Nelson's flag-captain at Trafalgar. To stress the point Hughes makes Hardy's admirable father a retired naval officer related to Sir Thomas Hardy. The naive idealizing of Oxford by the elder Hardy, whose comically exaggerated naval idiom is manifestly borrowed from Smollett's Commodore Trunnion in *Peregrine Pickle*, is used to draw ironic attention to the moral short-comings of Oxford life in practice (ch. 19, ch. 22). Since the principal sport in the novel is rowing it is appropriate enough that Hughes should give naval names to Hardy the servitor and to Blake and Jervis, the undergraduates who recall admirals of the Cromwellian and Napoleonic wars respectively, but this is also a device to test Oxford manhood by the highest standards of patriotic English manliness. For all his brilliance the self-centred Blake fails to make the grade. Jervis, the captain of boats, is almost a great man but lacks moral energy, too optimistic and too easily contented with things as they are. Only Hardy passes the test, though much poorer than any of his contemporaries. He illustrates that in the closed society of college life, vitiated by snobbery and ill-spent wealth, it is still possible for a man to be a man 'for a' that', regardless of wealth and social position.

This democratic manliness helps to teach Tom Brown lessons in

wholesome and robust physical sturdiness, in responsible attitudes
to collegiate extravagance, and in a vigorously moral and practical
Christianity. He first encounters Hardy on the river. The pattern of
their friendship is established at the outset in that Tom has got
himself into difficulties and Hardy is able to rescue him with the
benefit of greater wisdom and experience. As a freshman Tom
Brown has plenty of pluck and determination but not much skill as
an oarsman or knowledge of the river. Hardy tries to warn him of the
perils of the lasher near Sandford but Tom cannot hear him
properly and the next thing he knows is that his old tub has been
swept over the rapids to capsize in the tumbling waters of the lasher
below. Hardy shoots the rapids in his skiff with great coolness and
skill and rescues Tom and his boat. Instead of humiliating Tom
further by reflecting on his incompetence he coaches him in sculling
on the way back and greatly improves both his technique and his
self-confidence, which is more than can be said for most of the more
formal teaching which the university has to offer (ch. 2). But Tom is
no scholar, so it is not surprising that rowing does more for his
character than reading, and that he enjoys it more.

In *Tom Brown's Schooldays* and *The Scouring of the White Horse*,
written in the intervals of work on *Tom Brown at Oxford*, the sturdy
traditions of physical manliness had been praised for their own sake
and as socially beneficial opportunities for individuals and social
classes to come together in a common enthusiasm. Pierce Egan had
made similar claims in the 1820s.[43] But he had also indulgently
described the dissipations too often associated with the sporting life.
One of the leading characters of Egan's *Life in London* (1822) was Bob
Logic the Oxonian, who patronized the ring and the cockpit in
London as well as hunting enthusiastically at Oxford. So far one
might have expected Hughes to approve, suggesting only that Bob
should try the gloves himself as well as watching others in the ring.
But Bob and his friends are reckless and ruinously extravagant and
seem to have no interest in sharing their enthusiasms with others
outside their particular 'set' or engaging in any kind of group-
activity requiring discipline or sustained effort. Nearly forty years
later they are pilloried as the 'fast set' in *Tom Brown at Oxford*,
representatives of the wrong sort of physical manliness.

The chronological gap is not as great as it might appear. The
novel is set in the early 1840s, Hughes' own Oxford years, when
Egan was still lecturing and writing about 'The Art of Self-Defence',
elderly but impenitent in the midst of Victorian respectability and

nostalgic for the glories of Gentleman Jackson and Lifeguardsman Shaw.[44] The most extreme example of Egan's old-fashioned sporting manliness gone to seed is not actually any of Tom Brown's 'fast' contemporaries but the coarsely sensual Wurley whose mind cannot rise above the unregenerate manliness of sporting periodicals and whose drunken physical degeneracy is in stark contrast to Tom Brown's athletic and clean-limbed virility (ch. 33). Wurley stands as a dreadful warning to Tom Brown and the fast set. Discipline, competitive effort and team-work, all demanded by serious rowing, can do something to rescue the undergraduate sportsman from eventually becoming like Wurley. The boating set, to which Tom belongs, had links with the fast set but represented a reaction against their physical lassitude, preferring oars and blisters to billiard cues (ch. 1).

Hughes is as enthusiastic about rowing as he was about cricket and football in *Tom Brown's Schooldays*. 'Two bishops at least does our brotherhood boast', he claims (ch. 13). The bishops in question were probably Bishop Patteson of Melanesia and Bishop Selwyn of New Zealand, the manly dedicatee of *Westward Ho!* Rowing might actually be a suitable enough preparation for the enormous physical strain of administering a far-flung colonial diocese, but there is also a hint that rowing, like cricket, is an institution for fostering moral virtue even to the level of the episcopal bench. Hardy, modelled on the future Bishop Fraser, helps to make the point. Drysdale, a member of the fast set but with 'good manly stuff in him', has tried to redeem himself by taking up rowing but loses his place in the boat by being out of training, flabby from luxurious living so that he fails to pull his weight at a critical stage of the bumping races. Hardy takes his place. His proud self-respect, even in the despised role of servitor, and the necessary frugality and self-discipline of his life, have kept him in superb physical condition so that his earning a place in the boat can be represented as a moral achievement (ch. 14).

Hughes rather overdoes the morality of rowing by linking it with Tom's potentially immoral association with Patty the pretty barmaid of the *Choughs*. As moral recklessness darkens his soul his rowing goes to pieces too – not perhaps an inevitable consequence. Matters come to a head when Tom undertakes to accompany Patty to Abingdon Fair with Drysdale and a lady who turns out to be his mistress. This final, iniquitous association with one of the fast set who had failed in stamina and discipline at his oar would have set the seal on Tom's moral corruption but the timely advice of Hardy,

Tom's moral as well as physical rescuer, finally saves the day. Drysdale himself is actually rather relieved when Tom refuses to follow him on his road to the bad (ch. 16).

Physical manliness has a social as well as an individual dimension. The rigours of rowing help to keep Tom from worse things and offer a useful discipline but this 'muscular Christianity' is not ultimately of much value unless it serves society as a whole. Hughes devotes a whole chapter to discussing 'muscular Christianity'. Glancing over his shoulder at the womanizing bullies of G. A. Lawrence's 'muscular' novels, discussed in the opening chapter, Hughes insists that the manly hero must use his strength for nobler purposes than 'belabouring men and captivating women for his benefit or pleasure'. Like Kingsley he maintains that chivalry and service are required of the strong man, 'the protection of the weak, the advancement of all righteous causes, and the subduing of the earth which God has given to the children of men' (ch. 11). Again, like Kingsley, Hughes runs into difficulties when he tries to be too specific about 'righteous causes', and for Tom Brown at least these tend to be represented as future possibilities rather than actualities. Later in the book Tom Brown's confused and intemperate radicalism stimulated by agrarian troubles and the plight of Harry Winburn seems to be a kind of failed Christian socialism with not quite enough Christianity and nothing of the sometimes frustrating, sometimes salutary moderation of F. D. Maurice. But in the confines of college and on the streets of Oxford there seems to be little scope for even failed Christian socialism. Tom Brown uses his fists in a town-and-gown fracas and uses main force to expel a trouble-maker from Grey's night-school for the poor in the town but neither of these actions is represented as particularly satisfactory or Christian. Nor is the cause specially righteous.

This is particularly so in the town-and-gown affray. Hughes had been well taught by Arnold. He knew that popular disturbances could be viewed in an historical perspective as recurring manifestations of eternal problems compounded of impatience and injustice. Hughes had also sympathized more fundamentally and had been far more involved at a practical level with the popular disquiets of his own day, in 1848 and after, than Arnold had ever been. From the time of the march of the Roman plebs upon Mons Sacer (a favourite example of popular protest used several times in the novel) up to the Chartist Demonstration of 1848 Hughes acknowledges that the ruling classes were usually to blame. This is manifestly the case in

Oxford when a drunken Irish undergraduate, one Donovan, causes a disturbance at Wombwell's travelling menagerie which gradually involves other privileged undergraduates in irresponsible hooliganism. This in its turn provokes the town mob and when Donovan breaks loose from his friends and attacks the townsmen the gownsmen feel they must try to rescue him from himself, irrespective of the very doubtful justice of his cause. A general mêlée ensues and Tom Brown gets caught up in it. Hughes tries to disapprove, mocking Tom's vision of himself as the manly hero of the hour, but as in the 'Fight' chapter of *Tom Brown's Schooldays* the excitement of a good scrap is too much for him. He is more amused than shocked by the warlike posturing of the drunken Donovan. Tom and Drysdale ignore a Proctorial warning to return to their colleges but Hughes is not much disposed to blame them. When renewed fighting breaks out he indulgently allows them to join in after making it clear that gown is heavily outnumbered by town so that that is the chivalrous thing to do (ch. 11).

There is no chivalry involved in the incident at Grey's night-school. Tom Brown's temper, dangerously ill-controlled at moments in the town and gown affair, is too near the surface. Grey is a pious and physically insignificant reading man, not immediately congenial to Tom Brown or the breezy Tom Hughes because of his total lack of interest in sport. Besides, he was probably a Tractarian. The Tractarian ideal of university life, summed up in works such as Revd T. Whytehead's *College Life* (1845), recommended to Hughes as background reading by his publisher, was austere and devout, a bookish knightly vigil undertaken as a preparation for girding on the sword of the spirit and taking Holy Orders.[45] Sport formed no part of the programme: its strenuousness was exclusively spiritual, mental and moral. Grey's college life is of this kind, but his moral force turns out to be much more effective than Tom's physical force in keeping order (ch. 19).

Grey helps to demonstrate Hardy's assessment of Tractarianism: 'there are some very fine fellows among them' (ch. 9). Hughes, speaking through Hardy, is much more fair-minded than Kingsley. His own Oxford career at Oriel, of which Newman was a Fellow, coincided with the publication of Newman's notorious Tract Ninety and the acrimonious controversy it provoked but this seems to have had surprisingly little effect on him. He remained the tolerant middle-of-the-road Anglican he had always been. While Kingsley was vehemently denouncing Puseyism and all its works in *Yeast*,

published in book-form in 1851, Hughes could write in the same
year of his plans for commissioning a 'Puseyite parson friend' to
spread the Christian socialist gospel in Plymouth.[46] The atmosphere
of ecclesiastical in-fighting in the Oxford of the 1840s is not ignored
in *Tom Brown at Oxford* but the issues are deliberately obscured. A
university sermon attacking the recent publications of eminent
Oxford figures is described as a noble attack on Popery and
Pantheism. One might suspect Tractarians of favouring the former
and attacking the latter, and anti-Tractarian liberals of possibly
doing the reverse, so the interests of the rival church-parties tend to
cancel out. Grey offers Tom an introduction to the dedicated life to
which his physical energies must ultimately be consecrated if he is to
qualify as a manly Christian. One of the critical moments in the
novel comes when Tom is helping Grey with his rather exhausting
children's excursion. Grey's dedication makes him no respecter of
persons: he is actually rather unfair to Tom's comfortably situated
fiancée Mary when he has tea with her in Belgravia. Tom needs
something of this uncompromising dedication. He achieves it, after
a struggle, when he is asked to carry a tired and grubby child
through a fashionable park (ch. 25). True chivalry should be
democratic, and he reasons that had the child been a heroine of
chivalry, a Lady Mary or a Lady Blanche, he would have complied
happily enough. As he carries the child he is seen by his own
temporarily estranged Mary, who is reminded of a time when he
chivalrously carried her, and this helps to effect a reconciliation and
the happy marriage which inaugurates Tom's career as a matured
manly Christian at the end of the novel.

But Grey's dedicated life is too otherworldly to offer any
satisfactory response to the 'condition of England' crisis. Manichee-
like he takes the view that the world is given over to the devil
anyway. He has faith that the Church will save England from the
fate of Tyre and Sidon, but no practical interest in ways and means
(ch. 48, ch. 49). Hardy and Tom are much more disturbed by the
plight of their society, even in the seclusion of the college. The
extravagance of the fast set, originally welcomed by the college
authorities because they could be made to pay double fees, draws
attention to the disastrous inadequacy of the 'cash nexus' as Carlyle
had called it as a basis for society both in the college and in the world
outside, and Hardy's reformist zeal relates both to microcosm and
macrocosm. Literary treatments of college life such as the early
chapters of Thackeray's *Pendennis* and J. G. Lockhart's *Reginald*

Dalton as well as the Oxford pamphlets of the day draw attention to the financial problems for undergraduates and their families and for tradesmen created by the tradition of reckless spending and unpaid bills.[47] Tom Hughes had a special horror of this because his father, an obvious model for the severe Squire Brown, had sternly instilled into him habits of financial responsibility of a high order.[48]

In Oxford and in Berkshire Hughes contrasts the 'mammonism' of economic individualism and cynical money-worship with Maurician ideals of co-operation. Hardy works hard as a reforming don to bring dons and undergraduates closer together, even persuading the president of the college to turn out and watch the St Ambrose boat. More stringent academic standards reduce the numbers of wealthy gentleman-commoners in college and help shift the basis of college life from cash to a common interest in learning. He suggests that the enormous bills for wines and extravagant dinners which undergraduates run up with Oxford tradesmen can be kept in bounds through the co-operation of the college authorities in supplying wines and dinners themselves and charging for them on a termly basis (ch. 45). The involvement of all classes of society in Harry Winburn's wedding festivities at the end of the book participates in the same co-operative ideal (ch. 47).

Hardy's indignation against the evils of collegiate mammonism derives from his experiences as a servitor: his contemporaries rather presumed upon the power of wealth and the poverty of servitors. He was furious when Chanter tried to bribe the junior servitor to sign his name for him in chapel (ch. 7) and was equally indignant on his own behalf when an invitation to a sparring session in Christ Church turned out to be a proposal to box for cash with a money-bet staked on the outcome (ch. 8). In his own college worldly adventurers such as St Cloud and Blake are lavish with money which is not their own. Tom Brown reaps the benefits of bad company when he suddenly finds himself liable for Blake's debts, having rashly stood security for him with a money-lender (ch. 10).

Blake's collapse in the Examination Schools, significantly on an elementary matter of religious knowledge, helps to show the shortcomings of the worldly hero. It is a setback to his selfish ambitions and a demonstration that his amoral cleverness has limitations. He does not impress his examiners when he tells them that he would have known the answer as a child, implying that such knowledge is of no value to an adult (ch. 24). With Hardy's help he succeeds the second time and then adjourns to London where he proceeds to wear himself out in the struggle for position and power, 'fretting his soul out that he isn't prime minister, or something of the kind' (ch. 49).

Blake's ambitions in the outside world and his ruthlessly intelligent self-interest in pursuing them focus attention on the Benthamite doctrines of the political economists denounced by Carlyle which seemed to subject everything to the iron laws of economics and to assume self-interest as the basis of economic behaviour. The story of Blake's examination débâcle is in fact based on the experience of Nassau Senior, one of the architects of the dreaded New Poor Law of 1834 and a leading political economist who happened to be the father of Hughes' brother-in-law.[49] Hughes' own dissatisfaction with mammonism and the political economists had probably been renewed by the intemperate denunciations of Ruskin's *Unto this Last*, which appeared in the *Cornhill* in the autumn of 1860 as the middle chapters of *Tom Brown at Oxford* were appearing serially in *Macmillan's Magazine*.[50] Ruskin had taught drawing at the Working Men's College, and Hughes thought that the Christian socialist ideals of its founders had rubbed off on him at last. He greeted *Unto this Last* with mingled irritation and gratification as a 'profession of Christian Socialism (though a poor enough and priggish enough profession)'.[51] This helps to account for the tone of slightly detached but not unsympathetic irony with which Hughes treats Tom Brown's intemperate attacks on mammonism and the *status quo* in the *Wessex Freeman*. Tom's prospective father-in-law insists that he should write no more and he meekly desists, confessing his opinions are in a state of flux in any case (ch. 44).

Tom might be intellectually rather confused but there is no doubt that his heart is in the right place. He shares Hardy's utopian vision of a righteous and Christianized commerce, the gospel taken into the Stock Exchange, and both men read a Carlylean message of the dangers of mammonism into ancient history, following the Arnoldian method of seeing classical and contemporary concerns as a moral continuum. Carthage is summarily dismissed by Hardy as

'a dirty, bargain-driving, buy-cheap-and-sell-dear aristocracy – of whom the world was well rid . . . Selling any amount of Brummagem wares never did nation or man much good, and never will' (ch. 10).

The root of the 'Harry Winburn problem' is the senseless acquisitiveness and tyranny of local landowners. They already have more land than they can manage but they still prevent Harry Winburn and other agricultural labourers from having allotments which could give them the economic independence and self-respect they had enjoyed in the days before wage-slavery and the cash-nexus took over (ch. 18, ch. 23). Tom's personal involvement in Harry's problems, ineffective though it is, helps to bring ancient history into focus. Whatever conservative Oxford might have thought Arnold at least would have been pleased that his pupil could now see topical significance in 'The politics of Athens, the struggle between the Roman plebs and patricians, Mons Sacer and the Agrarian Laws' (ch. 35).

Unfortunately Tom's passion for liberty outruns his prudence and his common sense. Hughes involves him in the violence and incendiarism of physical-force Chartism and the 'Swing' riots of the 1820s and 1830s, two separate expressions of popular disquiet which he combines for the purposes of the novel. This conveniently permits the author to establish a continuity between the benevolent Toryism of his country upbringing and the moderate radicalism of his Christian socialism. One can probably assume that the dashing fundamentally sensible Harry East is speaking for old Squire Hughes as well as Tom Hughes when he asks '"Who's the tyrant, I should like to know, the farmer or the mob that destroys his property? I don't call Swing's mob the weak and the poor!"' (ch. 41). Hughes had actually enrolled as a special constable to combat the possibility of violence if physical-force Chartism took over in the Chartist demonstration of 1848,[52] and the Christian socialists were anxious to find effective but peaceful ways of relieving the distress and allaying the anger and sense of outrage which lay behind Chartism. In the end Harry Winburn is united with his beloved Patty and sets off for the colonies with East, looking forward to manly opportunities and the challenges of the pioneer life denied to him at home. This was one of the solutions recommended by Carlyle and Hughes' own disastrous experiment at Rugby, Tennessee, shows that it is one he took seriously himself, but it leaves the 'condition of England' question without direct answers.

In a sense the biographical form of the novel makes this inevitable. Hughes was probably sensible to limit the scope of his novel in this way: whatever the general problems of society, a man can only do the work that lies to hand, and that is what Carlyle would have had him do. Tom Brown marries and stays at home, vaguely pledged to work for a better world as best he can. Harry East is a gallant soldier, like Hodson of Hodson's Horse, and that represents a satisfactory and sufficient service within his particular calling. The reader has little doubt that he will be equally proficient and manly in his new role as a colonist, active in 'the subduing of the earth which God has given to the children of men', as Hughes put it early in the novel (ch. 11). Even as a servitor Hardy is a good influence on those close to him like Tom Brown. He takes his degree and soon becomes an effective reforming tutor. His frustration at his inability to take the college any further in the direction of the Kingdom of Christ is conveniently relieved by the fresh opportunities offered by marriage to Katie and the parish ministry. This might seem to be another evasion of the issue but in the 1840s it represented a familiar pattern: young dons who wished to marry could only hold their fellowships as long as they remained single. They tended to stay in Oxford only until a college living became available which enabled them to marry. Hardy's Christian manliness as servitor, as tutor and as clergyman operates in terms of the channels open to him.

Hardy and East are effective manly Christians with a contribution to make to their society because they are thoroughly sound fellows. As Hughes put it in his hymn 'O God of Truth' which he wrote while working on the novel,

> . . . who can fight for truth and God
>   Enthralled by lies and sin?
> He who would wage such war on earth
>   Must first be true within.[53]

This is the final lesson Tom Brown needs to learn. His first attempt to fight for truth is a fiasco: his reckless involvement in the 'Harry Winburn problem' is really a diversion from the moral tangle of his relationship with Patty of the *Choughs*, the violence of physical-force Chartism an extension of his own ill-regulated passions which first surface in the town-and-gown riot.

Hughes makes unnecessarily heavy weather of the Patty affair. Tom's flirtation may have been ill-intentioned but thanks to the intervention of Hardy it stopped short of actual seduction. Nevertheless it continues to make life difficult for him. It gives rise to slanderous rumours which reach his beloved Mary, and Tom makes matters worse for himself by suspiciously refusing to explain to Mary his connection with Dick the ostler who knew him at the *Choughs* (ch. 26). Not only does he imperil his own happiness: he almost wrecks the life of Harry Winburn who is driven to recklessness and despair when Patty loses interest in him for a time in favour of a mysterious lover who turns out to be Tom Brown.

This melodramatic plotting is perhaps attributable to the excesses of Arnold's moral severity and pulpit rhetoric: sin and even the thought of sin lead to extravagantly appalling consequences. Harry Winburn's moral descent leads him into poaching and by a stroke of irony Tom catches him in the act. He is thoughtful enough and democratic enough gradually to appreciate the moral confusions of the situation. Is poaching to earn a living in time of difficulty more culpable than the selfish game-preserving which creates the conditions for poaching, or the gentlemanly poaching for sport of which Tom has been guilty himself? In any case what right has he to assume moral superiority over Harry, particularly when Harry's plight emerges as (indirectly) Tom's fault? The fact that Tom is acting as volunteer game-keeper for the lewd and loutish Wurley makes matters even worse (ch. 37). On another occasion Wurley insinuates that Tom intends to marry off Patty to Harry Winburn as a convenient way of disposing of a discarded mistress. This is undeserved, but only just (ch. 33).

The moral and religious darkness of Tom Brown is attributable to the same cause as the social ills Hardy and he perceive: in both cases the authority of the living God is flouted and denied. The rediscovery of God as the moral regulator of society remains as a vision of the future at the end of the novel, but Hardy is able to lighten Tom's personal darkness. Oxford liberal theology, represented by an actual sermon by A. P. Stanley, Arnold's biographer, assists in the process.[54] Hughes may also have taken a hint from that other great liberal figure Benjamin Jowett, translator of Plato and alarmingly Platonizing Biblical commentator.[55] Tom rediscovers the indwelling spirit of God by way of the notion of the 'daemon' or inner spirit in Plato's *Apologia*, one of Tom Hughes' favourite classical texts.[56] This has the effect of bringing Tom back into the family of God. The family life which the future seems to hold for him in the last pages of the book promises to be rich and fulfilling, the apotheosis of Christian manliness, because it will be sustained by the Maurician vision of the Kingdom of Christ and the Church as a family. Instead of a world given over to mammonism and darkness Tom Brown and Tom Hughes can contemplate

a world clear and bright, and ever becoming clearer and brighter to the humble, and true, and pure of heart, to every man and woman who will live in it as the children of the Maker and Lord of it, their Father (ch. 50).

7

The unmanning of manliness

The Christian manliness of Thomas Hughes and Charles Kingsley was a personal achievement, the mark of a useful and vigorous Christian life. It was also an inspiring if slightly vague literary ideal, a vision of individual and social regeneration through strenuousness and service which stemmed directly from the backgrounds and personalities of the writers. This made it highly idiosyncratic despite its close engagement with the issues of the day. Arguably Hughes and Kingsley are more interesting as men than anything they ever wrote. Certainly their strongly individual responses to the contemporary situation were more important to them than literary considerations such as the demands of the popular fiction market. Their enormous popular success[1] was in a sense a highly gratifying accident, a fortuitous coincidence of vivid and colourful personalities and attitudes and the interests of the reading public. It was suggested at the beginning of this study that Hughes and Kingsley developed their democratic notions of Christian manliness in an era of emerging individual possibility conveniently marked off by the two great Reform Bills of 1832 and 1867. The excitements of Christian manly heroism as they described them helped to bring romance to everyone, for all were the children of God, and the moral and religious emphasis of their work ensured that no-one need feel guilty about it. This was just what the expanding reading public needed as it freed itself of the old Evangelical suspicion of fiction and the secular imagination.

The idiosyncrasy of Kingsley and Hughes and the special circumstances of their own time have not seriously impaired their popularity in the twentieth century. *Westward Ho!* and *The Water-Babies* and *Tom Brown's Schooldays* have remained popular favourites, at least among children. But Christian manliness itself has not worn so well. Idiosyncrasy and Father Time have been too much for it, by and large. In various forms Christianity and manliness are with us still, in society and in literature and in the popular cult of sport, virility and masculine adventure. But they

have gone their separate ways. Aggressively Protestant Christian
socialism, topical in the 1850s, seemed quaintly conservative in the
1890s and increasingly incomprehensible in the new century. The
sporting manliness of Tom Brown ceased to be culturally respectable, if it ever was, when E. M. Forster lampooned gamesplaying
public-school men as victims of 'well-developed bodies . . . and
undeveloped hearts' in his essay 'Notes on the English Character'
(1920).[2]

Yet Christian manliness did not perish utterly. Kingsley's more or
less Christian heroes and the playing-fields of Rugby have lingered
in the national memory, hinting at enduring qualities and attitudes.
In subsequent literature and in life these qualities have tended to
recur, piecemeal and in different guises. They can be glimpsed in
later developments in British religion, culture and society even
though the Victorian synthesis of Christianity and manliness has
largely disintegrated.

RELIGION AND SOCIETY

The Church Militant may have to march unflinching through the
flames of controversy, but part of its triumph is to leave dead issues in
ashes behind it. Mid-Victorian Christian manliness was in part a
controversial reaction against religious positions which had been
abandoned or greatly modified half a century later. Evangelical and
Tractarian 'Manichees', antitypes of Kingsley's manly Christians,
had learned some of the lessons of manliness themselves by the 1920s
and the lines of battle were no longer clearly drawn. The middle
ground between Evangelical and Tractarian (later identifiable as
'Anglo-Catholic') became in a sense common ground so that the
stance of Kingsley and Hughes and F. D. Maurice lost its
distinctiveness. Their liberal religious impulse was not lost but it was
widely diffused and assimilated into other things. While full social
justice is still to be achieved the Church of England now publicly
approves of it and a Labour Party officially dedicated to it has come
into existence. As respect for theology declines it has become less
necessary to argue for the theological respectability of ordinary
human passions and enthusiasms. Secular common sense has long
been a sufficient seal of approval and the world rather than the
church increasingly provides the theological agenda.

But how did the Manichees become manly? Evangelical clergy,
less unworldly and exclusive because less self-consciously priestly

than the early Tractarians, were the first to change. They soon realized that the Evangelical outreach required significant interaction with the best aspects of the lives and enthusiasms of the unregenerate, particularly in the mushrooming cities where the old patterns of parochial organization had proved woefully inadequate. The history of the YMCA illustrates the transition from a 'Manichee' Evangelical piety set against the world and the mammon of unrighteousness to a more flexible outlook incorporating legitimate secular interests such as sporting manliness.

Founded in London in 1848 by a group of nonconformists and conservative Evangelicals, the Young Men's Christian Association emphasized Bible-study, prayer and education from the outset. But it was difficult to keep the interest of the members and to maintain the austerely spiritual standards of the founders undiluted in the face of increasing competition from secular attractions. By the end of the century, despite considerable resistance from the 'Manichee' diehards, secular society and physical fitness had invaded the YMCA in the cities and the gymnasium was indispensable in each local centre. This liberalizing tendency was supported from the beginning by enlightened Evangelicals such as the Revd Thomas Binney whose 1853 YMCA lecture about things secular and sacred, *Is it possible to make the best of both worlds?*, demanded the answer 'yes'.[3] But for a long time the answer from YMCA headquarters would have been a dour 'no'. An official letter pompously ruled that

the provision of physical recreation or other lawful amusements . . . should not be looked for in connection with the arrangements for the Young Men's Christian Association.[4]

But recreation triumphed in the end. Kingsley and Hughes had few direct literary descendants in their preaching of Christian manliness in fiction, but part of their message successfully infiltrated the ranks of the Evangelicals. Late-Victorian religious writing for young men assumed a breezy, even worldly tone noticeably lacking in earlier apologetic. Many religious liberals such as Thomas Arnold and Charles Kingsley, once much abused by the Evangelical press, were read and quoted by the new generation of Evangelicals. Frederick Atkins, long associated with the YMCA, self-consciously assumed a corner of Kingsley's mantle without ceasing to be an Evangelical in works such as *Moral Muscle and how to use it. A brotherly chat with young men* (1890).

Evangelical publicists generally began to exploit the attractiveness of outstanding physical prowess, whether in organized games or in independent adventure. As Patrick Scott has shown, cricket, the calm, disciplined gentleman's game celebrated as a great British institution in *Tom Brown's Schooldays*, was easily projected as the Christian gentleman's game. Revd Henry Venn, the early Evangelical who turned in his bat before he was ordained so it could never be said of him 'Well struck, parson!', would not have approved, but that was all in the past.[5] On the mission-field in particular cricket could be an enjoyable supplement to formal instruction in Christian conduct. It could be an advertisement as well as a qualification for the mission-field. The legend of 'muscular Christianity' took a new turn with the famous 'Cambridge Seven'. These magnificent cricketers, all converted about the time of D. L. Moody's 1884 Cambridge mission, went off amidst a blaze of publicity to work with the China Inland Mission.[6]

The Religious Tract Society, which had been the arsenal of the old Evangelical assault on the world, the flesh and the devil, found it expedient to concentrate on manly exploit and adventure and play down explicitly religious moralizing in its publications for boys such as the *Boys' Own Paper* (founded 1879). The *BOP* published a number of lively gamesplaying school stories vaguely modelled on *Tom Brown's Schooldays* though without its overtones of aggressive patriotism and co-operative Christian socialism. The best of these was Talbot Baines Reed's *The Fifth Form at St Dominic's* (1887), a well-written yarn mercifully free of the feverish moral earnestness of earlier tales such as Farrar's *Eric, or Little by Little*. Reed relied on the manly sporting enthusiasm of the average schoolboy and proposed a breezy practical morality without oppressively religious connotations. This formula endured remarkably well. As late as the 1920s the *Boys' Own Paper* office was still publishing wholesome adventure-stories such as Oswald Kendall's 'Tracy's "Reputation"'. This describes how a clean-limbed Englishman, a greenhorn as a cowboy but a good boxer, successfully disarms a wild west desperado and then insists that he should stand trial when everyone else wants to shoot him out of hand (illustration 7).[7]

Physical manliness was still serving Christianity well as an Evangelical instrument at this time, at least in Scotland. Eric Liddell, subject of the popular film *Chariots of Fire*, was the devout son of a Scottish missionary. But it was not until he was already a celebrated Rugby international and hero of the 1922 Scottish Athletics Championships that D. P. Thomson persuaded him to

7   English manliness out west: illustration for Oswald Kendall's 'Tracy's "Reputation"', in *Twenty-Six Stories of the Backwoods* [?1927], published by the Religious Tract
Society, *Boys' Own Paper* Office

address an Evangelical rally at Armadale, in Lothian, in April 1923. It was a shrewd move, for as Thomson noted years afterwards every newspaper in Scotland reported it the following day.[8] From this point until his departure for missionary work in China two years later Liddell led a hectic life as an Edinburgh University undergraduate, a record-breaking athlete and a well-publicised and popular speaker at evangelistic meetings organized by the Glasgow Students Evangelistic Union.

Like one of Kingsley's heroes, Liddell proved to be capable of moral as well as physical manliness. His controversial refusal to run on a Sunday at the 1924 Paris Olympics created a major stir at the time. The film suggests a last-minute dilemma, but in fact the crisis came months earlier, as soon as the time-table of heats was announced. Despite a barrage of hostile criticism Liddell stuck by his decision not to run in the 100 metres heats on a Sunday. Reluctantly the British Olympic officials permitted him to change his event from the 100 to the 400 metres and so keep his place in the team. Despite the change Liddell broke the world record and won a gold medal for the 400 metres in July 1924, winning undying fame as a hero of the faith and of the track. More than twenty years later he was celebrated as 'probably the most illustrious type of muscular Christianity ever known'.[9] At the time the popular press of Scotland, England and France went wild with enthusiasm. *The Times*, sober as always, pronounced his victory 'probably the most dramatic race ever seen on a running track'.[10]

It was also widely reported that Liddell improved his most shining hour by modestly withdrawing to prepare his sermon for the Scots Presbyterian Church in Paris the following Sunday. The nonconformist *British Weekly* reported both the victory and the sermon, which was a

simple manly appeal . . . characterized by the same qualities which gave him his great victory for the British flag – quiet, steady, earnest concentration on the one thing to be achieved, and the will to cast aside all weights which hindered the one purpose.[11]

There were countless tributes from churchmen to his greatest triumph, the upholding of the Christian Sabbath.[12] In religiously conservative Scotland and Ulster his fame was undiminished at the time of his death in a Japanese internment camp in 1945. But the obituaries in the English press barely mentioned his refusal to run on a Sunday. Even the *British Weekly*, a religious paper, was a little

condescending, embarrassed in its liberal way by a set of religious
principles which now seemed 'something of a throw-back to
Calvinist times'.[13] Perhaps the most perceptive tribute came not
from Christian sources but from a Jew, from Harold Abrahams, the
other hero of *Chariots of Fire* and a fellow-athlete in the 1924
Olympics. Abrahams recognized that Liddell's 'intense spiritual
convictions contributed largely to his athletic triumphs . . . but for
his profound intensity of spirit, he surely could not have achieved so
much.'[14]

Even in 1924 Eric Liddell's manly Christianity was something of
an anachronism. Secularism had already bitten deep into society.
The fickle popular press and the forces of the Establishment,
including the Duke of Sutherland and Lord Birkenhead of the
British Olympic Committee, had been unsympathetic to Liddell's
Sabbatarian sturdiness. Eighty years before, when Kingsley and
Hughes were young men, all the pressure would have been the other
way and there would have been a powerful lobby *against* Sunday
running. In 1844 Queen Victoria herself was severely criticized for
presuming to travel by train on a Sunday.[15] Conservative Scotland,
by creating and preserving the legend of Eric Liddell, carried the
neo-Evangelical version of what was essentially Victorian Christian
manliness into the middle of the twentieth century. Two other Scots,
Sir William Smith and John Buchan, did a lot to bring Christian
manliness down to our own day in modified form. Like Liddell they
grew up in the shadow of conservative religious traditions and
enriched them with a Kingsleyan vision of moral and physical
manliness, hearty, even aggressive, but without the cutting edge of
Kingsley's Christian socialist enthusiasm and zeal for sanitary
reform.

William Alexander Smith founded the Boys' Brigade in Glasgow
in 1883. Awakened to the spiritual needs of the city by Evangelical
influences, he had been associated with the work of the YMCA in
Glasgow and taught in Sunday school. But like Thomas Hughes he
was also attracted by the manly possibilities of the Volunteer
Movement and served as an officer with the Lanark Volunteers.
Military discipline, perhaps more attractive to boys then than now,
seemed to offer a better method of interesting and instructing the
youth of the city than the unrelieved standard fare of the Sunday
schools. He founded his organization on the twin pillars of weekly
drill parades and Bible-classes. The early officers of the BB, as it
came to be known, were often associated with the Volunteers. But

drill parades were supplemented by healthy sports and other activities: like Kingsley and Hughes in an earlier generation, like Eric Liddell and his publicists later on, Smith wanted to show that Christianity was not, or need not be, an unmanly, effeminate religion. The object of the BB from the outset encompassed 'all that tends towards a true Christian manliness'.[16]

There is at least one Boys' Brigade novel, published by the increasingly liberal-minded Religious Tract Society in 1907 under the title *Comrades under Canvas*. The author, F. P. Gibbon, was a frequent writer on military subjects, continuing the Victorian tradition of exploiting military manliness for religious ends in other books such as *The Disputed V.C. A Tale of the Indian Mutiny* (1904). He was also active in the Edwardian Boys' Club movement.[17] *Comrades under Canvas* tells the story of a Boys' Brigade camp in north Wales. Hero-worship, militarism and patriotism abound. The principal hero is General Whitworth, decorated for his famous exploit at the Chirga Pass and the youngest major-general in the British army. He takes some of the boys from the camp on a climbing expedition which leads them through the landscape of Elsley Vavasour's mountain ramblings in Kingsley's *Two Years Ago*. It turns out that both the general and two of the boys with him have read and enjoyed the novel and that leads into a general literary discussion in which *Tom Brown's Schooldays* and *Westward Ho!* emerge as popular favourites. For all Gibbon's religious moralizing his novel is genuinely entertaining in the manly tradition of Kingsley and Hughes which he self-consciously invokes. There are deeds of physical prowess and exciting adventures involving dreadful villains. The boys at camp come from a range of different social backgrounds but Gibbon is as responsive to the democracy of the gospels as Thomas Hughes and Tim Brady, a poor lad of the streets, wins the respect of all for his 'native wit, shrewdness, and sense of justice'.[18] Gibbon's own interests and enthusiasms made him sympathetic both to the Victorian Christian manliness of Kingsley and Hughes and to the work of the rapidly expanding Boys' Brigade in the twentieth century. He became a highly successful editor of the *Boys' Brigade Gazette* and published the first biography of Sir William Smith, the founder, in 1934.

Smith had realized that the manly excitement of organized outdoor adventure was a particularly useful point of access to the Christian manliness he hoped to instil. He was interested in the unorthodox scouting methods which had been tried in the Boer War and asked the hero of Mafeking, Baden-Powell, to rewrite his *Aids to Scouting* specifically for boys so that the Boys' Brigade could benefit from it. The new volume, *Scouting for Boys* (1907), was very popular not only with the BB and the YMCA for whom it was primarily intended but also with boys and men throughout the country. This interest could not be contained within the structure and aims of the Boys' Brigade so the Boy Scouts came into being as an independent organization.[19]

This departure illustrates the fragility of the synthesis of Christianity and manliness as Kingsley and Hughes originally developed it, for unlike the BB scouting evolved into a largely secular organization. Baden-Powell had been born into mid-Victorian religious liberalism, a son of the Baden-Powell who contributed to the controversial *Essays and Reviews* of 1860. The older Baden-Powell was a clergyman-scientist like Kingsley, like him a disciple of Coleridge who found no difficulty in coming to terms with Darwin.[20] But the Chief Scout, only three when his father died, moved right away from self-conscious theology into a bluff and hearty theism almost indistinguishable from secular morality. He imposed this general-purpose wholesomeness upon scouting and thought of his father not as a religious thinker but as an honorary boy scout 'manly, and very honest in his convictions . . . always cheery, eager to help, to raise the tone, moral and material, of the Nation'.[21] The Boys' Brigade has always kept much closer to the churches.

Both organizations have survived and flourished down to the present day. The Boys' Brigade has recently celebrated its centenary. It has substantially retained the Victorian ideology of Christian manliness which played a part in its foundation. It is particularly strong in Scotland and Ulster, where the legend of Eric Liddell had survived even before the film rediscovered it. In England, however, it has yielded a little to the more secular manliness of scouting.

John Buchan was neither a BB officer nor a scoutmaster. But like Sir William Smith he grew up with the Calvinist religion of urban Scotland; like Baden-Powell he was imaginatively fascinated by the possibilities of manly adventure in South Africa even before he went there on Milner's staff. Many of his popular novels are fantasies of Christian manly adventure almost in the Victorian mould. In *Huntingtower*, for instance, he tells the story of the Gorbals Diehards, tough, resourceful little ragamuffins who engage in far-fetched cloak-and-dagger escapades under the benignly Christian patronage of Dickson McCunn, retired grocer. These rascals represent an alternative Boys' Brigade, recruited from one of the depressed areas where Smith's organization was seeking to make headway.

Buchan has been called 'the last of the Victorians', 'as remote as can be from the modern intellectual in his tastes and judgements'.[22] He would not have minded. His old-fashioned qualities recalled Tom Brown or Amyas Leigh. They included a sense of the value of physical hardihood, an uncomplicated patriotism, a firm moral sense, and a simple unobtrusive piety, all of which fed into his wartime thrillers such as *The Thirty Nine Steps* (1915). *Mr Standfast* (1919) used Bunyan's *Pilgrim's Progress* as a key to a secret correspondence and as a linguistic resource. The passing of Peter Pienaar, the heroic South African airman, brings with it religious assurance. Richard Hannay reads from Bunyan by the graveside, seeing Peter no longer as Mr Standfast but as Mr Valiant-for-Truth, who fought God's battles and then passed over to his Father's house.[23] Buchan no less than Kingsley seems to have believed that God's battles were easily identified with the British cause in wartime. Like Kingsley he modified the tradition of Christian militarism by simplifying the time-honoured notion of the solider of Christ into the myth of the moral worth of the British soldier.

Buchan's manliness could be light-hearted, however – even whimsical. One of his short stories concerns a Free Kirk Elder, Peter Thomson, who is a sea-captain shipwrecked five days out from Singapore and in grave peril, as he thinks, from unfriendly natives. He recalls his 'sainted Covenanting fathers' and 'resolved before I died to make a declaration of my religious principles and to loosen some of the heathens' teeth with my fists'.[24] A more muscular Christianity would be hard to find!

Buchan indulged in the fantasy that simple manliness like this could preserve for righteousness a world-order threatened by ever-present anarchy and recessive primitivism. But where for Kingsley this would have been a programme for Buchan it was only a dream. Ambitious, restless, successful, dogged by ill health, Buchan would have liked to lead a more adventurous life, to have achieved even greater successes. A notable walker and climber in youth, he had planned an Everest expedition with a friend who perished at Passchendaele.[25] Despite important intelligence work for the Foreign Office and the General Staff, Colonel Buchan ruefully described his war-service as 'undistinguished' since he was almost continuously unwell the whole time.[26] His novels outline excitements and exploits denied their author. One of his most interesting fictional *alter egos* is Edward Leithen, a highly successful lawyer and politician somehow unfulfilled in his success and easily lured into sporting and other adventures. Buchan, himself a former lawyer and MP, concluded his career as Governor-General of Canada, and it was in Canada that he wrote his last Leithen story, *Sick Heart River* (1941). Leithen is dying and senses a spiritual void within him for all his worldly success. He comes to terms with himself and his Creator in one last heroic adventure as he strives to save a stricken Indian tribe in the Canadian wilds. Buchan himself did not live to see the book published.

Buchan's manliness derived ultimately from Calvinist and Evangelical sources mediated through his clergyman father.[27] But the Anglo-Catholic tradition had contrived a parallel rapprochement with quasi-Kingsleyan ideas by the First World War. The Revd Gilbert Studdert-Kennedy, better known as 'Woodbine Willie', was able to associate the manliness of moral and military conflict as Kingsley and Hughes had done:

> There's the 'ell of a scrap in the 'eart of a man
> And that scrap's never done:
> The Good and the Bad's at war, ye see,
> Same as us boys and the Boche.[28]

The secret of Woodbine Willie's success as Padre and priest was his sympathetic identification with the lives and conditions of soldiers and working men. Like Kingsley and Hughes, he saw life in terms of manly conflict both in the individual and in an unjust society. The quest for social righteousness was as much a theological imperative for him as it had been for them.

But Woodbine Willie's democratic manliness did not come directly from F. D. Maurice and the Christian socialists of the 1850s. It derived from the teaching and example of Anglo-Catholics such as Charles Gore and Henry Scott Holland and the new social awareness within the Church of England which they helped to create in the 1880s and 1890s.[29] Gore and Scott Holland knew Maurice's work[30] but this was not their only inspiration. They inherited the tradition of Newman and Pusey, and at Balliol they had encountered T. H. Green's neo-Hegelian idealist philosophy and listened to his attacks on clerical indifference to suffering and injustice.[31] Gore in particular was sympathetic to the growing Trade Union movement. Both men were eager to redress the inequalities of a society which had apparently been abandoned to the allegedly iron laws of economics.[32]

Scott Holland and Gore were contributors to *Lux Mundi* (1889), a collection of Anglo-Catholic essays which alarmed the older generation of Puseyites by taking full account of the European biblical researches and contemporary intellectual and scientific developments which had previously interested only dangerous religious liberals.[33] Like Kingsley and Maurice the *Lux Mundi* group laid great stress on the Johannine doctrine of the Incarnation and its release of redemptive possibilities for the whole of society. Gore's own essay, on 'The Holy Spirit and Inspiration', developed the theme of the social dimension of the Gospel. Man was a social being who could not realize himself in isolation, so 'the true, the redeemed humanity, is presented to us as a society'.[34] Practical expression was given to this social theology with the founding of the Christian Social Union in the same year. If the grace of God was working towards a corporate redeemed humanity, social injustice and personal failure to challenge it represented the sin which resisted the grace of God. As Scott Holland wrote to a friend, at long last 'the poor old Church is trying to show the personal sin of corporate and social sinning'.[35]

There were ageing survivors from the days of Mauricean Christian socialism to welcome this new development and trace its continuity of purpose with the earlier movement. Thomas Hughes wrote to J. M. Ludlow that the CSU was 'our old Christian socialism decently tricked' and Ludlow wrote several articles for the *Economic Review*, the CSU organ, to demonstrate some of the connections.[36] But where Hughes and Ludlow had been able to establish important links with working people through the Co-operative movement and their connections with Trade Unions the CSU proved to be more a clerical than a working-class enterprise. It performed the useful function of transforming attitudes to the 'social question' on the part of the bishops and many of the clergy, but it lost a valuable opportunity by refusing to ally with either the Fabians or the Independent Labour Party.[37] It was as if the High Churchmen had stolen Tom Brown's clothes and then found they lacked the courage to walk away in them.

In other respects the Anglo-Catholic party within the Church of England partly incorporated, partly disregarded the manly Christian impulse of Kingsley and Hughes. Though early Tractarians had rather disapproved of games, at least for clergymen, as an unseemly spiritual distraction, common sense and pragmatism soon returned. Nathaniel Woodard had founded Lancing College on largely Tractarian principles but his school did not acquire the status of a proper public school until he appointed an enthusiastic gamesplaying master, W. S. Raymond, who imbued the place with the spirit of Tom Brown's Rugby and inaugurated organized games. In 1859 Woodard appointed a new Head who was actually rather unsympathetic to Tractarianism because he realized that he badly needed a headmaster of 'demonstrably rugged Christianity' to ensure the popularity of the school.[38] On the other hand, the increasingly Catholic tone of the Church of England, the enduring legacy of Tractarianism, helped to countenance Anglican religious orders such as Charles Gore's Community of the Resurrection. These institutionalized the practices of celibacy and asceticism against which Kingsley had blustered and protested so vehemently.

The earnest Anglo-Catholic heroes of Compton Mackenzie's novels reflect this development. In *The Altar Steps* (1922) Mackenzie pokes fun at Kingsleyan muscular Christianity as the perquisite of those who take their religion as a cold bath. His hero Mark Lidderdale does not: in the sequel, *Parson's Progress* (1923), he has to choose between marriage and priestly celibacy, the path of Kingsley or the path of Newman. After a struggle he opts for celibacy.[39]

For doughty Protestants clerical celibacy might once have suggested a culpable remoteness from the everyday concerns of English life, but celibate priests such as Father Wilfred Knox of the Oratory of the Good Shepherd and the flamboyant Father Arthur Stanton were often among the most active in the manly work of combating social injustice and the horrors of the East End slums.[40] Mrs Humphry Ward fictionalized the type in her picture of Reginald Newcome, the fanatical and dedicated slum-priest in her novel *Robert Elsmere* (1888).[41] If Kingsley had lived (he died in 1875) he would have responded with very mixed feelings to this strange confusion of Manichee and manly Christian.

Evangelicals and Anglo-Catholics alike gradually incorporated elements of Kingsleyan Christian manliness. But Kingsley and Hughes and F. D. Maurice had conscientiously attempted to avoid what seemed to them the extremes of both the Evangelical and the Catholic parties within the Church of England. Did those of central churchmanship, their liberal and 'Broad Church' successors, preserve the manly Christian gospel entire? Not altogether. In a sense the alliance between Christianity and manliness was too temperamental, tactical and temporary. But it did not disintegrate immediately. Kingsley's personal example as energetic pastor, his social concern, his intellectual alertness, his sense of the modern world's

challenge to the church are all reflected in the career of Mrs Ward's
Robert Elsmere. It seems likely, in fact, that Fanny Kingsley's
biography of her husband, first published in 1877, supplied many of
the details of Elsmere's parish ministry at Murewell. Elsmere tries to
improve housing conditions and encourages interest in natural
history, and in winter he 'causticked all the diphtherick throats in
the place with [his] own hand'. Robert Elsmere is committed like
Kingsley to the integrity of body and soul, to the need for physical as
much as for spiritual health. His study contains the equipment of a
Tom Thurnall and a Tom Brown as well as a clergyman:

Books, natural history specimens, a half-written sermon, fishing-rods,
cricket bats, a huge medicine cupboard – all the main elements of Elsmere's
new existence were represented there.[42]

But Robert Elsmere cannot stay with Kingsley and Kingsley's
theological rationale for this manly activity. Doing good in the
world is a duty and a responsibility ultimately independent of the
orthodox doctrines of the Church of England which Elsmere finds
increasingly problematic. He encounters the social challenge of the
East End as a religious duty only after cutting his links with
Christian orthodoxy and leaving the church. A Broad Church
clergyman in the Midlands protests that he should have stayed and
worked to liberalize the church from within, but Elsmere, broken in
health from his labours, finds energy to reprove him, rather harshly,
for intellectual muddle and insincerity.[43]

The difficulty was that Kingsley and Hughes could insist that the
church should engage with the world, but the best causes and
noblest aspects of the world had no necessary connection with the
church. *Robert Elsmere* illustrated how the religiously motivated
ethical impulse could easily part company altogether from conventional religion. Two years later, in *The Broad Church, or What Is
Coming*, the Revd H. R. Haweis attempted a reply to *Robert Elsmere*.
Like Elsmere, Haweis was an ethical theist. Like Kingsley he was a
popular preacher and a vigorous enthusiast for good causes,
interested in the problems of working men and the Volunteer
Movement, well-known as a writer about music and about
Shakespeare.[44] But he felt awkward within the existing framework
of orthodox doctrine in the church and sought to reshape it to the
contours of the modern world in which he was so much at home.
Instead of leaving the church, like Elsmere, he proposed a 'frank and
radical formulation of doctrine' while insisting on his abiding

loyalty to 'the essential Truths underlying the Dogmas of the Church'.[45] This left the way open to a comfortable and uplifting vagueness. In practice Haweis' Christianity was no more, or less, than all that was self-evidently true and good and intellectually cogent. It was therefore ultimately indistinguishable from the wisdom of the market-place and had no particular need of the church at all. On the subject of saints, for instance, a sectarian rallying-cry in the past, Haweis could afford to be blandly ecumenical. St Simeon Stylites, John Wesley, Newman, Kingsley and F. D. Maurice all satisfy his generously imprecise criteria of embodying universal moral and spiritual passions.[46] On these grounds saints need not be Christians at all. The notorious secularist G. J. Holyoake would probably have qualified: he greatly respected Kingsley and Maurice and worked amicably with Thomas Hughes because he could meet with all of them on the common ground of concern for the secular well-being of working men.[47]

The ethical and social content of the gospel of Christian manliness could and did survive outside the church and the doctrinal reformulations designed in part to encompass it ran the risk of reducing the Gospel of Christ to meaninglessness. The controversial 'New Theology' of the Revd R. J. Campbell, an enormously popular Congregationalist preacher who filled the pulpit of the City Temple in London, is a case in point. This was an Edwardian attempt to reconcile modern thought and a burning social conscience with a simplified and easily secularizable version of Christian doctrine. An Ulster Presbyterian childhood and a respect for Charles Kingsley had imparted an irreducible Protestantism to Campbell's outlook, though he had come under the influence of Charles Gore and the Christian Social Union at Oxford. An Anglo-Catholic theologian of dogmatic severity for all his liberal leanings, Gore disliked Campbell's *The New Theology* (1907), which was partly a Protestant popularization of French Catholic Modernism, and attacked it in *New Theology and the Old Religion* in the same year. In fact Campbell soon disliked the book himself, admitting it had been hastily written, and gradually moved away from some of its teaching. By a strange irony he was eventually received into the Anglican priesthood in 1916 by none other than Charles Gore, then Bishop of Birmingham.[48] Rose Macaulay's novel *Told by an Idiot* (1923) glances sceptically at Campbell and implies that his essentially Kingsleyan 'gospel of the humanity of God and of the divinity of man' was neither very new nor very helpful, not likely to provide lasting support to doubtful minds in a difficult age.[49] Perhaps he got on too well with the freethinking George Bernard Shaw, whom he once invited to speak on social questions from the pulpit of the City Temple. Shaw's whimsical verdict on advanced Congregationalism such as Campbell's as 'sound Voltaireanism' is not altogether undeserved.[50]

It was difficult to sustain a liberal theology of the manliness of Christianity into the twentieth century without sacrificing some of the liberalism to dogma or losing most of the manliness to secularism. Cyril Norwood, president of the self-consciously liberal Modern Churchmen's Union and headmaster of Harrow, tried to cling on to Christianity and manliness in their Victorian synthesis in his book *The English Tradition of Education* (1929), but with mixed success. Essentially a romantic conservative nostalgic for the vanished or vanishing days of godliness and good learning flourishing side by side, Norwood praises games and athletics for their moral value in building up team spirit. In adult life, he claims, this manifests itself as an ethic of service. He finds a good example of this ethic in practice in the work of the Working Men's College which stemmed from the enthusiasm of Thomas Hughes. Behind Hughes lay the teaching and example of that great public-school headmaster Arnold of Rugby.[51] While Norwood presents this doctrine of service as a religious imperative, and for Arnold and Hughes, Kingsley and Maurice, it clearly was just that, its later manifestations in Oxford House, Toynbee Hall and the East End Settlement movement with which the self-consciously post-Christian author of *Robert Elsmere* was closely identified show that it did not have to be.[52] Neither public-school games nor the social service they might lead to had any necessary or lasting connection with Christianity.

MANLINESS AND SECULAR CULTURE

But even if Christianity disappeared from the picture the physical and ethical dimensions of 'muscular Christianity' could persist in other forms, stripped of the reassurance, and perhaps of the self-righteousness, of religious belief. One did not need to be a pagan to be uneasy about the wholesome but ultimately over-simplistic vehemence of the Kingsleyan gospel. The fastidious winced at its brashness and uncomplicated optimism from the start. Gerard Manley Hopkins unkindly characterized the Kingsleyan manner as a way of talking . . . with the air and spirit of a man bouncing up from table with his mouth full of bread and cheese and saying that he meant to stand no blasted nonsense.[53]

Secular critics could be even more devastating. One of the most persistent of them was Leslie Stephen, a failed muscular Christian himself as we have seen. Stephen was both an agnostic and an intellectual snob. He liked Thomas Hughes, and he could see that there was a lot of good in Kingsley and F. D. Maurice, but intellectually speaking he had no time for any of them. To the philosophic mind, and particularly to his iconoclastic and rational-ist intelligence, the simplicities and potential incoherences of Christian manliness were frankly inadmissible.[54] Stephen's *Science of Ethics* (1882) made passing reference to the Platonic doctrine of *thumos* or physically-derived spiritual energy with which Kingsley associated his ideal of manliness.[55] But for Stephen conduct was a science, not an energy of the spirit. His whole outlook was based on utilitarian and rationalist considerations where Kingsley's derived from the opposite school of thought, the romantic intuitionism of Coleridge and Carlyle compounded with his own idiosyncracies. Even allowing for this it has to be conceded that Stephen was as muscular as Kingsley and a good deal more clear-headed. But the shade of Kingsley can take comfort from the fact that far more readers enjoyed *Westward Ho!* than ever heard of *The Science of Ethics*.

Stephen's temperamental scepticism, like his enthusiasm for enormous Sunday walks, was shared by his neighbour George Meredith. Like Stephen, unlike Kingsley and Hughes, Meredith had cut himself free of conventional religious attitudes. He rather admired Kingsley, briefly sketching him as the good Parson Brawnley in *The Ordeal of Richard Feverel*, but as the name implies he did not take him very seriously. His explorations of the problems of conduct and education, sustained through a long literary career, reflect Victorian concerns with self-development, physical health and the health of the psyche, as a recent study has shown.[56] But religion, healthy or otherwise, hardly enters the picture. Meredith's manliness is neither as Christian nor as straightforward as Kingsley's. Complex ironies link his personal preoccupations with physical wellbeing and self-development to the iniquitous educa-tional 'system' of Sir Austin Feverel. Instead of emerging as a romantic hero successfully challenging the tyranny of the system and achieving the perfection of some ideological alternative (like Kingsley's spiritually emancipated Christian socialist Alton Locke)

Richard Feverel veers off into marital infidelity, quixotic duelling and a perfunctory Byronic ardour for remote and irrelevant national causes. In *The Egoist* the physically superb Sir Willoughby Patterne, a manly and accomplished cavalier, may be the butt of the novel's humour but he is also a parody of aspects of Meredith's own thinking and personality.

In a late novel, *Lord Ormont and his Aminta*, the once hero-worshipped soldier Lord Ormont seems in his decline to represent a complete inversion of mid-Victorian notions of chivalric or gentle-manly manliness grafted onto conveniently available Christian soldiers like Captain Hedley Vicars or General Havelock, or fictional heroes like Harry East and Amyas Leigh. He brutally neglects his wife and seems to have no principles to speak of. Not surprisingly his private secretary Matthew Weyburn elopes with Lady Ormont, the Aminta of the title. When Ormont forgivingly places a great-nephew at the school Weyburn has founded Meredith's tongue is firmly in his cheek when he describes Ormont as 'one of the true noble men'. The founding of Weyburn's experimental school in Switzerland seems to be a deliberate challenge to English public schools and Tom Brown's manliness since Weyburn is not a Christian gentleman but an open adulterer. Yet Meredith goes out of his way to make Weyburn a great cricketer and enthusiast in 'all things manly', like Meredith himself. He invests him with a sentimental rhetoric worthy of the original Tom Brown: the aim of the school is to

teach Old England to the Continent – the Continent to Old England: our healthy games, our scorn of the lie, manliness; their intellectual valour, diligence, considerate manners.[57]

These ambivalent, self-mocking ironies, uneasily poised between old-fashioned sterling Englishness and cosmopolitan perspectives, exploiting the idiom of heroism and manliness even while surveying it through the quizzing-glass of satire, register the disintegration of mid-Victorian self-confidence, the optimistic sense of human possibility embodied in Kingsleyan Christian manliness. Doubt insidiously supplanted faith and bluff assurance began to yield to sceptical perplexity. In *Tom Brown at Oxford* Hardy is at hand to assist in Tom Brown's deliverance from darkness but in late Victorian England deliverance became more difficult: perhaps a measure of darkness and uncertainty was man's natural heritage? It was a sign of the times that the author of *A Defence of Philosophic Doubt*

(1879), A. J. Balfour, became Prime Minister early in the new century.

Balfour's poor eyesight and physical delicacy had kept him from the traditional manly sports of Eton. Though he developed enthusiasms for the newly popular pastimes of golf and lawn-tennis in later life he always seemed a curiously lethargic figure deficient in the vigour and manly energy expected of the resolute national heroes admired by Kingsley and Carlyle. Perhaps it was no longer worth the effort? Like Joseph Conrad, Balfour was imaginatively haunted by the prospect of a cooling sun and a dying universe implied in the second law of thermodynamics. He could envisage a time when

the earth, tideless and inert, will no longer tolerate the race which has for a moment disturbed its solitude. Man will go down into the pit, and all his thoughts will perish . . .[58]

In politics this elegantly dismal vision sometimes encouraged him in an apparently fatal passivity and intellectual indolence which infuriated Lord Curzon, his successor as Foreign Secretary, and at one critical stage of the Versailles peace negotiations seemed to the young Harold Nicolson an appalling abdication of moral responsibility.[59]

Balfour's rather intermittent energies and intellectual equivocations can be partly offset by his political successes, particularly his cool and adroit management of party. Whatever Kingsley himself might have thought it would obviously be absurd to judge him as unsound in politics and morals because he was not altogether sound in wind and limb. In some ways Balfour's intellectual subtlety and absence of dogmatism, his feline shrewdness and pragmatism, make him a sympathetic and essentially modern figure. But these very qualities also make him a kind of antitype of Kingsleyan Christian manliness and illustrate how far we seem to have travelled from the simple heroics of Amyas Leigh and the terrifyingly unsubtle attitudes of Hereward the Wake to questions of national importance. Balfour and his younger contemporary Baden-Powell, only a generation removed from Kingsley and Hughes, demonstrate in different and perhaps extreme ways how short-lived devout and energetic Christian manliness had turned out to be as an ideal of conduct and a national specific. For Baden-Powell manliness had passed over into perpetual boyishness and Christianity had almost disappeared into wholesomeness. For Balfour Christianity had become more a problem than a solution and manliness had been relinquished for a masterly philosophic calm reposing on the further shores of action.

At Cambridge Balfour had seemed to be effete and a little precious, inclined to rest too long abed and noted chiefly for his fine collection of blue china.[60] The religion of aestheticism, altogether less strenuous than Christian manliness, swept into England between the yellow covers of French novels in the later nineteenth century. In place of the burning eye of the manly hero or the tranquil glow of the altar candle came the hard gem-like flame of the individual sensibility savouring the passing moment and its sensations. Walter Pater, Fellow of Brasenose, was the presiding genius of the movement. His fastidious Epicureanism and moral inertia irritated the wife of his colleague Humphry Ward. The tragically ineffectual Langham in *Robert Elsmere*, so different from Elsmere the Kingsleyan activist, is partly modelled on Pater. The philosophical and sentimental reveries of Pater's novel *Marius the Epicurean* (1885) die away on the ritualistic periphery of the Christianity of the early church, in stark contrast to the violent action and thoroughgoing Christianity of Kingsley's *Hypatia*.

But between Pater and Kingsley, between hedonistic aestheticism and manly or muscular Christianity, there was a possible meeting-point in the moralized Hellenism outlined by the Revd E. C. Lefroy. The nature of the Hellenism he tried to moralize and its connections with the religion of aestheticism call for some explanation. Rugby school had taught Thomas Hughes as well as Matthew Arnold that 'conduct is three-fourths of life'[61] but for some of the Greeks and some late Victorians the greatest thing in life was beauty.[62] The muscular development and the sheer physical grace of the male form had been nobly rendered by Greek sculptors such as Praxiteles and celebrated in Pindar's odes to athletic heroes. Plato's *Symposium* seemed to lend philosophical dignity to intense male friendship inspired by such beauty. J. A. Symonds and other classically-educated aesthetes found in the Greek cult of male beauty an attractively wistful hedonism which spoke to their religious agnosticism and perhaps to their latent (or overt) homosexuality. For them as for Pater the shadow of death, the sense of a brief day of sun and frost, gave a poignant intensity to the perceived beauties of form and feature.[63] Symonds described the elegies of Mimnermus of Colophon as 'true to one type of the Greek character' in their fascination with 'the flower of my equals in age gladsome and beautiful' and their horror of disfiguring old age. Pindar's odes particularly appealed to Symonds because they celebrated the manliness or spirit (*arete* again) of the strong victor of the games but placed it in the context of a short and inscrutable mortal life:

we are not all unlike the immortals either in our mighty soul or strength of limb, though we know not to what goal or night or day fate hath written down for us to run.

With sure knowledge only of the present world Greek art and literature sought only to 'assist the freedom of the spirit and to confirm the energies of men by bringing what is glad and beautiful into prominence', Symonds concluded, and paid tribute to this 'tranquil and manly spirit'.[64]

The Revd E. C. Lefroy read Symonds' work with interest, and Symonds later returned the compliment.[65] Lefroy was a Grecian in spirit, but how could this Greek worship of beauty be reconciled with the formularies of the Church of England? He tried to convince himself that Greeks and Christians alike aspired to perfection of life, and that some muscular Christians like Charles Kingsley met Symonds and the Hellenizing aesthetes half way by celebrating the physical perfection and the energy of the human body. Superficially at least 'manliness' could be regarded as common ground. But there was a world of difference between manliness as spectacle and manliness as practical ethic. Where Kingsley could derive his ethics from revealed religion the agnostic Symonds and the Hellenizing aesthetes had to fall back on the promptings of nature, or so Lefroy maintained. Even so, he insisted that the Greeks 'knew as well as the great Apostle of the Gentiles, that unrestrained indulgence in fleshly appetites must end in degradation and death'. In an article entitled 'Muscular Christianity' in the *Oxford and Cambridge Undergraduates' Journal* Lefroy set to work to bring the cultivated hedonism of Symonds and Pater, Matthew Arnold's vision of Hellenism as sweetness and light, and Kingsley's robustly manly Christianity into an improbable harmony, a balance of the perfections of body, soul and intellect. This emerges not as a life-long *modus vivendi* but as a religion of youth, crystallized into St Paul's imperative 'Quit you like men, be strong.' Lefroy goes on to beat Kingsley and Hughes at their own game by drawing the rather illogical inference that 'The Christian who can "stroke" an "eight" is more valuable than his brother who leads the prayer-meeting.'[66]

With Lefroy as with Kingsley personal enthusiasm is rather recklessly identified with religious principle. But if the robust religion is superficially very similar the personal enthusiasm is not. While Kingsley remained aggressively heterosexual Lefroy was more deeply affected by the homosexual atmosphere of Symonds' aestheticism than he would have cared to admit. Devout and optimistic despite the ill health which restricted him to a career of teaching private pupils, Lefroy lived vicariously in the beauty, strength and activity of youth: 'My poetic soul gets an infusion of red blood whenever I am brought into contact with vigorous, energising humanity', he wrote after watching a rugby match. This sick man's celebration of health found expression in graceful sonnets describing 'A football player' or cricketers or oarsmen, or the 'shapes more sinuous than a sculptor's thought' of a straining wrestler's limbs, or a golden lad who was 'Nature's and Fortune's gilded darling'.[67] Lefroy seems to have recognized the suppressed homosexuality of his excited reveries on the touchline. One young footballer, smiling like the Hermes of Praxiteles, made him think 'If Olympus were extinguished tomorrow, I should still have a God.' Then he remembered he was a clergyman and dismissed his fantasy as 'a passing idiocy'.[68]

This 'passing idiocy' was an occupational hazard for unmarried Victorian schoolmasters. Careers as well as morals could be destroyed by it. Lefroy's biographer W. A. Gill tries hard to impose some kind of personal and intellectual coherence on Lefroy's short life, insisting that the Greek cult of physical beauty formed 'the natural foundation of a genuine morality and a healthy religion',[69] but Lefroy's own sense of moral revulsion suggests that the alliance between Hellenism and manly Christianity was uneasy at best. Perhaps the Greek ideal could be over-idealized? The Eton master and poet W. J. Cory, one of A. J. Balfour's teachers, illustrates the problem. Like Symonds, he was emotionally involved with the wistful hedonism of the Greek poets. His verse-translation of the famous elegy for Heraclitus laments the passing of a beloved friend:

> I wept as I remembered, how often you and I
> Had tired the Sun with talking and sent him down the sky.[70]

'Mimnermus in Church' is closer to Symonds' Mimnermus than to any Christian church. The poem is agnostic about an afterlife:

> Back from that void I shrink in fear,
>   And child-like hide myself in love:
> Show me what angels feel. Till then,
>   I cling, a mere weak man, to men.[71]

The feebleness and bathos of the last line, suggesting to the irreverent modern reader some desperate homosexual embrace, is unconsciously revealing. Like Lefroy Cory relished manly exercises but could not take part himself:

> I cheer the games I cannot play;
> As stands a crippled squire
> To watch his master through the fray
> Uplifted by desire.[72]

Desire can take troublesome forms, and Cory was disturbed by sexual feelings for the young heroes of the playing-fields. His sympathy for youth made him a brilliant teacher but in the end he was forced to leave Eton under a cloud. His last days were spent rather sadly teaching classics to the ladies of Hampstead.[73]

Cory's Kingsleyan delight in military as well as sporting manliness (registered in a rollicking poem entitled 'School Fencibles') was combined with the moral manliness of Christian socialism. Along with Hughes and F. D. Maurice he was involved in the Working Men's College from the outset. He also subscribed £100 for the cooperative Association of Engineers in 1851.[74] But his temperament and instincts prevented him from being another Hughes or another Kingsley. Their robust and active religion was too much a product of their own temperaments to survive them very long.

Another distinguished Eton master, A. C. Benson, mused sadly on Cory's fate. Chaste and virtuous as befitted a son of the Archbishop of Canterbury, but aware of his homosexual inclinations, he reflected in his diary on the cultural conditioning which had helped to lead Cory astray and had corrupted Pater, as his own biographical researches had revealed:

If we give boys Greek books to read and hold up the Greek spirit and the Greek life as a model, it is very difficult to slice out one portion, which was a perfectly normal part of Greek life, and to say that it is abominable etc etc. A strongly sensuous nature – such as Pater and Symonds – with a strong instinct for beauty, and brought up at an English public school, will almost certainly go wrong . . .[75]

After reading a report of a trial for homosexual practices Benson exclaimed 'Isn't it really rather dangerous to let boys read Plato, if one is desirous that they should accept conventional moralities?'[76]

This was written in 1913. By the eve of the first world war Plato and aesthetic Hellenism seemed to have become a more potent force in public schools than the New Testament, at least for some of the more sensitive boys. But it was often claimed that by this time playing games was far more important to the majority of boys than either godliness or good learning, and that this was officially encouraged.

SCHOOLS AND SPORT

Benson was uncomfortably aware of this development, which was particularly in evidence at Eton under the headship of Edmund Warre, a fanatical sportsman. He would not have been impressed by an article in the *Public School Magazine* for 1899 about 'The Education of a Public School Boy in the Time of Socrates' which paid lip-service to the fashionable Hellenism of the day but was really a shameless glorification of athletic exercises claiming that the greatness of Greece had rested upon them and so should the coming glories of the Anglo-Saxon race.[77] Patriotic manliness could appeal strongly to Benson, who wrote the words of 'Land of Hope and Glory'. But he felt patriotism was no excuse for the deplorable sporting fanaticism shared by boys and masters which led to a prostration of the intellect before athletics and constituted a 'species of tyranny'.[78] His pupil Maurice Baring, much less bothered, blandly affirmed that when he was at school 'A boy would be thought more important for making a hundred at Lord's than for winning the Newcastle scholarship'.[79] His formulation recalls the schoolboy Philistinism of Old Brooke in *Tom Brown's Schooldays*, perhaps not accidentally: "'I'd sooner win two School-house matches running than get the Balliol scholarship any day.'"[80] The remark is all too easily detached from the serious co-operative Christian manliness which Hughes approached through sporting enthusiasms.

The whole ethos of sport and Philistinism in the public schools has been strenuously attacked in our own century, starting perhaps with E. M. Forster's unflattering picture of Sawston in *The Longest Journey* (1907). The adversaries were usually sensitive intellectuals who had been lonely and unhappy at school. Harold Nicolson, a failure at games at Wellington, sums up a whole tradition of resentment in his semi-fictional portrait of J. D. Marstock, a brilliant athletic hero, frank and manly and doomed to be an unthinking schoolboy for ever.[81] Marstock's one achievement in a rather futile life was to inspire the Etonian Cyril Connolly's self-justifying theory of permanent adolescence as a consequence of public-school education.[82]

It is not surprising that opposition to the tyranny of games and the tyranny of the public-school system has fastened on Hughes and Thomas Arnold, and to a lesser extent on Kingsley, as the villains of the piece. They have taken the blame for the degeneration of the ethos of public schools from godliness to manliness and from good learning to good form.[83] Arnold can be acquitted at once: it has already been argued that his reign at Rugby was too early and too little concerned with sport for him to influence the games-mania of later years. Hughes and Kingsley cannot be cleared so easily. The bluff and sometimes brutal heartiness they preached could be adduced in ideological justification of the incidental miseries of later school life. But they are not to blame for their unscrupulous commentators. *Westward Ho!* and *Tom Brown's Schooldays* were popular with schoolboys as they were with the reading public in general. *Tom Brown's Schooldays* effectively founded the genre of schoolboy literature, so well established by the end of the century that 'The Schoolboy in Fiction' was reported to be a favourite topic in school magazines.[84] But *Tom Brown's Schooldays* was already out of date when it first appeared in 1857, reflecting not the contemporary school situation but the author's schooldays twenty years before. By the 1850s the public schools were moving away from the model of Arnold's and Tom Brown's Rugby.

Rapid expansion was the main reason for this. More and more schools opened to educate the sons of newly rich middle-class parents. Good performances in inter-school sports, which had no place in *Tom Brown's Schooldays*, brought publicity to the new foundations and 'playing the game' began to substitute for the religious idealism of many of the established schools. Malvern in its early days was noted almost entirely for its cricket.[85] Games were soon taken much more seriously than Tom Hughes would have wished. Where *Tom Brown's Schooldays* had moved between Arnold's official programme of terrible righteousness and the attractive but manifestly inadequate rough-and-tumble sporting ethos of the informal schoolboy culture later schoolmasters negotiated a 'strategic capitulation to the "boy-culture"' as J. A. Mangan has put it.[86] Informal pleasures became part of the system. Games were exploited as a method of occupying and controlling the boys, a necessary instrument of discipline. The healthy mind in the healthy body supplanted more academic or religious objectives.

Two of the pioneers of this development, now well-documented by educational historians,[87] were Edward Thring at Uppingham and G. E. L. Cotton at Marlborough, enthusiastic athletes them-

selves. Thring admired the work of Charles Kingsley and corresponded with his widow while Cotton, once a Rugby master under
Arnold, makes a cameo appearance as the young master in *Tom
Brown's Schooldays*.[88] But neither Kingsley nor Hughes would have
welcomed the institutionalizing of games which made such a serious
business of pleasure. Hughes was frankly outraged when a later
headmaster of Rugby proudly announced that his son was away in
Ireland playing football for his country in the middle of the Oxford
term.[89]

Billy Bunter first waddled into Greyfriars School in 1908, and
stayed there for a half a century.[90] But even on his first day there he
imbibed the atmosphere of anachronism. George Orwell pointed
out that Greyfriars was more like Tom Brown's Rugby than a
modern public school. Despite the growth of the games-cult and the
Edwardian development of Officer Training Corps Greyfriars, like
early-Victorian Rugby, had neither compulsory games nor military
training.[91] After *Tom Brown's Schooldays* the history of manliness in
Victorian public schools and public-school literature crucially
involves the issues of games and militarism,[92] while Christianity
gradually drops out of the picture. But the terms in which these are
discussed owe more to contemporary circumstances than to the
perennially interesting but increasingly out-of-date adventures of
Tom Brown.

In 1913 the headmaster of Sherborne, Nowell Smith, tried to
advertize the teaching profession among undergraduates. He
realized that he had to take on the games-cult and to attack the
image of the popular schoolmaster as brainless athlete:

when everything has been admitted that can be said in praise of sport and
games as elements in the formation of a sound character in a sound body,
they do not constitute a sufficient interest for the whole life of a rational
being, let alone a man placed in the atmosphere and face to face with the
duties and ideals of a school.[93]

Gamesplaying manliness was beginning to grow threadbare. The
most devastating indictment came from one of Nowell Smith's
pupils, Alec Waugh. His novel *The Loom of Youth* (1917), written
immediately after he left school before embarking on war service, is
autobiographical and scandalously revealing, the main reason why
his younger brother Evelyn was sent to Lancing rather than
Sherborne.

Alec Waugh was a happy and successful schoolboy, popular, good
at games and competent at schoolwork. But in 1915 he was detected

in homosexual practices and obliged to leave in disgrace. This sharpened his sense of the confusions and incoherences of the public school ethos.[94] In *The Loom of Youth* Gordon Carruthers discovers at Fernhurst that 'blind worship at the shrine of the god of Athleticism' is only passport to success. 'To the athlete all things are forgiven.' But there are limits. Early in the novel the athletic Jeffries is about to be expelled for homosexuality, which seems unfair as everyone knows that there are worse offenders. Jeffries complains bitterly:

'Fernhurst taught me everything; Fernhurst made me worship games, and think that they alone mattered, and everything else could go to the deuce. I heard men say about bloods whose lives were an open scandal, "Oh, it's all right, they can play football." '[95]

The official, manly ideology that the healthy body will foster a healthy mind and a healthy morality seems increasingly wide of the mark. Gordon discovers Byron and Swinburne with delight and a sense of personal liberation, but this comes about in spite of rather than because of the objectives of his formal education. Neither individualism nor personal integrity is encouraged. The officially endorsed worship of games and the condoning of endemic cheating in the preparation of academic work involve moral distortions: schoolboys are not naturally moral or honest to start with, as Arnold had noticed long ago, and the Fernhurst system makes things worse even while professing to turn out true English gentlemen.

   For Waugh the coming of war in 1914 emphasized the emptiness and inadequacy of the whole tradition of Philistine gamesplaying as it had evolved from mid-Victorian times. Gordon gets into the Eleven but it is a hollow triumph. To be any good in the trenches you have to be good at games, runs the updated version of the gospel of manliness. But Gordon has become an unbeliever. The eccentric Ferrers, a schoolmaster-aesthete modelled on the writer S. P. B. Mais, who once taught at Sherborne, suggests persuasively that the public schools and the nation had wasted time and energy on trivial games while Germany had been preparing for war.[96]

   Kipling had said the same thing about British blundering at the time of the Boer War. Disaster threatened because the people of England were more interested in the 'Flannelled fools at the wicket and the muddied oafs at the goals'.[97] Things were just as bad in 1914. In his novel *When William Came* (1914) 'Saki' (Hector Munro) imagines an England already conquered by Germany. The patriot Yeovil holds the leisured class responsible for wasting time on sport instead of soldiering: 'one might almost assert that the German victory was won on the golf-links of Britain'.[98] There could have been some truth in this if William (the German Kaiser) had really come. Geoffrey Best has shown how in some schools the games-playing interest flatly opposed the establishing of Officer Training Corps: the fittest boys could not be spared from the playing-fields.[99]

Patriotism had been an essential component of mid-Victorian Christian manliness, reflected in the unembarrassed chauvinism of *Westward Ho!* and Hughes' active participation in the Volunteer movement. But by 1914 patriotism and religious fervour and moral strenuousness had rather dropped out of the mixture, leaving an empty shell of increasingly discredited athleticism. Waugh and Saki, and in different ways Lefroy and W. J. Cory, all testify to the instability and vulnerability of the original compound.

Attacks on public-school manliness often involved an element of literary criticism of school stories. Not surprisingly Waugh condemns Farrar's *Eric* for its unrealistic piety, its confidence in the possibility of a saintly purity at a public school. Kipling's anarchic schoolboys in *Stalky & Co.* are equally contemptuous and 'Ericking' becomes a synonym for pious twaddle. But Waugh singles out Arnold Lunn's novel *The Harrovians* (1913) for special praise because it 'stripped school life of sentiment'.[100]

Much of the sentiment Lunn attacked was available in concentrated form in an earlier Harrovian novel, H. A. Vachell's *The Hill* (1905). *The Hill* ends with the death of a Harrow boy in one of the engagements of the Boer War, so the setting is meant to be almost contemporary, but there is a deliberate attempt to establish the Harrow experience as timeless. An Harrovian cabinet minister keeps faith with his old school by sending his son there. A Field-Marshal, though an Etonian, is moved to tears at the singing of the Harrow National Anthem 'Forty Years On', written by the arch-conservative master Edward Bowen as long ago as 1872. Bowen's sentimental celebration of school games sets the tone:

> Forty years on, growing older and older
>   Shorter in wind, as in memory long,
> Feeble of foot and rheumatic of shoulder,
>   What will it help you that once you were strong?
> God give us bases to guard or beleaguer,
>   Games to play out, whether earnest or fun;
> Fights for the fearless, and goals for the eager,
>   Twenty, and thirty, and forty years on![101]

But *The Hill* is much better than one might expect. The descriptions of school life and particularly school games are vivid and exciting, warm with the author's own nostalgia for Harrow. Academic and

literary interests are not totally ignored, for the sensitive and clever
John Verney wins a Shakespeare prize. But he tells his delighted
mother ' "You look as pleased as if I'd got my Flannels." '[102] Against
this background Vachell ingeniously contrives to combine elements
of *Tom Brown's Schooldays* with Edwardian snobbery and a patriotic
militarism which comes close to suggesting that the battles of the Boer
War were won on the playing-fields of Harrow. John Verney's good
influence on his friend Caesar Desmond, comparable to Arthur's
influence on Tom Brown, is balanced by the evil influence of
'Demon' Scaife, the athletically accomplished son of an unscrupulous *nouveau-riche* contractor who is a millionaire but no gentleman.
John wins in the end, but he learns of this only after Caesar has been
killed in action, when he receives his last letter.[103]

The Hill might be described as a rearguard action on behalf of
mid-Victorian Christian manliness. But it has moved on from there.
The morality is not overtly religious. Vachell admits that games,
however enjoyable, need not be the sole interest of schoolboys. He
notes perceptively, and with regret, that school sports have almost
ceased to be simple pleasurable recreation and have become a route
to success in life, a desperately serious business if, like the ambitious
Scaife, you choose to take them that way.

Lunn's *The Harrovians*, like *The Loom of Youth*, represents a
punitive expedition against the last manly Victorian stragglers. Its
hero, Peter O'Neil, is an unsporting eccentric, an intellectual and an
individualist. He is appalled by the Philistinism, tyranny and
brutality lying at the heart of a school system which allows brainless
athletes to assume the dignity of heroes and leaders of men. Peter
succeeds in breaking the mould by becoming head of his house. His
finest hour comes when he successfully challenges the influence of
the sporting 'bloods' and personally canes the house-captain of
football and cricket for flouting his authority. Tom Brown's
Christian manliness is dismissed as muddle-headed and immature.
The school songs of Harrow, which a former headmaster affectionately described as the key to 'the essential character of that famous
school'[104] are contemptuously derided by Manson, another courageous odd-man-out who has the capacity to think for himself.
Public-school religion, culminating in the rite of confirmation, is still
part of school life as it was in Arnold's Rugby. But Peter finds this a
shallow affair, more a sanction for school discipline than a reflection
of the religion of Christ he reads about in his Bible. The author
comments sardonically:

It is easy to exaggerate the harm caused by confirmation. The average boy does not take it too seriously, and soon relapses again into cheerful paganism.[105]

The old alliance of religion and sporting manliness is in disarray. When a bishop speaks about the Harrow mission this is represented not as a Christian socialist response to social injustice but as a patronizing pre-emptive strike against socialism. To everyone's embarrassment the bishop talks down to the boys, self-consciously using cricketing and football slang in a manner that carries no conviction. Lunn would have shared A. C. Benson's contempt for the 'muscular Christian' house-master at Repton who barked at his boys during house prayers 'Here, pray up, you boys!'[106]

THE MANLINESS OF EMPIRE

The Harrovians also attacks more secular pieties. A magazine article which extols public schools as nurseries of 'the manly, clean-living men that are the rock of empire' is greeted with hoots of laughter.[107] The alliance of manliness with imperialism, reflected in popular boys' adventure-stories such as G. A. Henty's *With Clive in India, or the Beginnings of Empire* (1884), represents an extension of the mid-Victorian combination of manliness and patriotism.[108] Neither Arnold Lunn nor Alec Waugh had much time for it. Waugh complains that Sherborne and other public schools tried to turn out Brushwood Boys, potential heroes of Empire of the kind described by Kipling, who were trained to keep their pores open and their mouths shut.

In fact Kipling's story 'The Brushwood Boy', and the manliness of empire in general, is more complicated than Waugh implies. The Brushwood Boy's training had certainly 'set the public school mask upon his face, and had taught him how many were the "things no fellow can do"'. But this discipline repressed a deeper level of personality even while it prepared him to be the ideal subaltern in India and the youngest major in the army. The story is actually less about empire than about the unconscious: strange childhood dreams of the City of Sleep and Policeman Day and a Thirty Mile Ride turn out also to have formed part of the dreamlife of a girl the hero meets on leave. He recognizes her as the companion of his dreams – the Brushwood Girl. Inevitably, she marries the Brushwood Boy.[109]

Kipling's contribution to the literature of youth and empire is more sophisticated than is usually acknowledged. The manliness is tougher and much less religious than in Kingsley and Hughes but it is also more psychologically perceptive. *Stalky & Co.* (1899) is set in the United Services College and explicitly links schoolboy pranks with military cunning in India.[110] But it offers a subtle critique of militarist and imperialist ideology which it balances against sturdily anarchic individualism. Stalky sabotages a misguided attempt to set up a cadet corps in the school. Mr Raymond Martin, MP, a major in a Volunteer Regiment and a 'jelly-bellied flag-flapper', comes down to the school to speak on the subject of patriotism, blithely unaware that seventy-five per cent of the boys are sons of serving officers of the crown intending in their own time and in their own way to follow their fathers' profession. Stalky's friend M'Turk decides Martin is the original 'Gadarene swine' as he rambles on: 'In a raucous voice he cried aloud little matters, like the hope of Honour and the dream of Glory, that boys do not discuss with their most intimate equals.'[111] Kipling's heroes, like Kingsley's and Carlyle's, tend not to examine the complex emotions which animate them.

Though Waugh implies that public schools as institutions were committed to Kiplingesque ideals there is a strong element of anti-institutional anarchy in *Stalky*. Boy-life is amoral and brutal and surprisingly unregulated, like Tom Brown's early life at Rugby but very unlike the highly ordered games-dominated life of later public schools. The United Services College is emphatically not a public school but a 'limited liability company payin' four per cent'.[112] Attempts to establish a bogus sub-Etonian ethos are dismissed as 'flumdiddle' by the boys, and so are the moralistic versions of public-school life proposed in *Eric* and the *Boys' Own Paper*. The school is a recent foundation lacking the 'steadying influence of tradition', but Kipling does not seem to mind.[113] The fantastic truancies, practical jokes and covert rebellions against unwise authority, leniently observed by an idealized and improbably liberal head, prepare Stalky not for the parade-ground at Sandhurst or Simla but for highly individualistic guerilla operations.

Kipling's young imperialists out in India are morally as well as geographically remote from the conventional late-Victorian public school. Their hard-bitten and worldly air might not disqualify them from appearing in a novel by Kingsley or Hughes but would guarantee that they would be pestered into a godliness which is of no interest to Kipling. It was not Kipling but J. E. C. Welldon, former headmaster of Harrow, who defined the spirit of empire as 'a strong

and solemn consciousness thât the British Empire has been divinely
ordered as an instrument of freedom, justice and righteousness'.[114]
Kipling's private soldiers have a more realistic perception of their
situation

. . . somewhere east of Suez, where the best is like the worst,
Where there aren't no Ten Commandments an' a man can raise a thirst.[115]

So far from claiming a universal civilizing mission they are prepared
at times to concede that

      'You're a better man than I am, Gunga Din.'[116]

For Kipling as for J. R. Seeley, who observed that the British
Empire was acquired in a fit of absence of mind, Britain's overseas
possessions were a *fait accompli* which called for policing, defence and
sound administration in difficult circumstances. The White Man's
Burden was not so much the divinely ordered destiny of an Abraham
or Aeneas, as Seeley had suggested,[117] as the grim job which lies to
hand which a man can see and knows he must work at, very much in
the tradition of Carlyle's *Sartor Resartus*. Carlyle and Kipling both
had a share in the heritage of Calvinism and the Protestant ethic.
Such grim and conscientious pragmatism is very much at odds with
contemporary ideals of racial self-aggrandisement suggested by
Benjamin Kidd's *Social Evolution* (1894) or J. A. Cramb's out-
rageously chauvinistic *Origins and Destiny of Imperial Britain* (1915).[118]
The imperatives of strenuousness and service have survived from the
mid-Victorian manly Christians but stripped of the sometimes noisy
rhetoric of religion and righteousness (illustration 8).

Kipling's most 'manly' narrative, *Captains Courageous* (1897),
celebrates the character-building discomfort and harshness of life
with the Grand Banks fishing fleet. This transforms a spoilt brat of
an American millionaire's son into a resourceful and self-reliant
young man. The book was much admired by Theodore Roosevelt,
politician and roughrider, later author of *The Strenuous Life*
(1902).[119] But it had very little to do with the Christianity, the social
awareness and the quintessential Englishness of Thomas Hughes
and Charles Kingsley. Only the toughness of Christian manliness
remained.

Links between Tom Brown and the romance of empire are much
easier to find in Newbolt than in Kipling. It always comes as a slight
surprise to realize that the 'breathless hush in the Close tonight' in
Newbolt's most famous poem 'Vitaï Lampada' is at Clifton rather

8   Manliness and empire: the final repulse of the Zulus at Ginghilovo (detail) from
Illustrated London News, 2 August 1879

than Rugby. The voice of the schoolboy rallying the ranks 'Play up!
play up! and play the game!' might almost be the voice of Harry
East, who soldiered heroically in India after leaving school.[120] But
when death in Afghanistan confronts the public-school hero of 'He
fell among thieves' his thoughts go back to the School Close and the
distant tape rather than the school chapel. His dying words are a
pagan celebration of 'glorious Life, Who dwellest in earth and sun'

rather than a Christian prayer.[121] Imperial adventure is an escapist dream for the schoolmaster protagonist of 'Ionicus' who forgets the dreariness of his classroom in contemplating 'the strength and splendour of England's war'. Thomas Hughes shared his patriotic excitement but he had other interests as well which kept him too busy for dreaming: he would have promptly recruited the schoolmaster to teach in the Working Men's College.

Newbolt's schoolmaster tried to impart the romance of empire and 'faith in all the Island Race'.[122] The young Lord Jim in Conrad's novel might well have been one of the pupils. A clergyman's son, clean-living and idealistic, he embarks on a life of adventure in the South Seas. But a moment's panic when he abandons his apparently doomed ship brings about his downfall in his own eyes. This lapse from an impossibly heroic ideal confronts him wherever he goes, even when he seems to have made a romantic new life as Tuan Jim, a leader of men among the remote people of Patusan. It is interesting that this aspect of Jim's life was partly based on the adventures of Rajah Brooke of Sarawak who was one of Kingsley's favourite heroes.[123] There is an enormous gulf between the resolute adventurers of Kingsley's hero-worshipping imagination and Conrad's manly protagonists, hampered by a strange personal and moral darkness unless they are too stupid and unimaginative to think at all. Conrad's chastened and despairing romanticism drives his novella *Heart of Darkness* to a nihilistic conclusion when the magnificent Kurtz, apparently the very incarnation of humane and efficient imperialism, dies in a state of complete moral disintegration confronting 'the horror, the horror'.[124] There could be no more chilling epitaph for the manliness of imperial adventure.

John Buchan, impenitently old-fashioned, continued to sing the praises of empire and the servants of empire into the 1930s. In *The Gap in the Curtain* (1932) the dilettante Reggie Daker grudgingly admires the

'lean, hard-bitten, Empire-building breed. To listen to them you would think it was a kind of disgrace to enjoy life at home as long as there was some filthy place abroad where they could get malaria and risk their necks. . . . They . . . took it for granted that everybody but a hermaphrodite must share [their views]'[125]

But this strenuous masculinity is closer to Kipling than to Newbolt. Duty and discomfort as well as a dash of romance are the concomitants of imperial adventure as far as Buchan is concerned.

He was after all from Calvinist stock, and had stayed closer to his Calvinist heritage than Kipling. The high spirits of Tom Brown and Harry East are not much in evidence. In *A Prince of the Captivity* (1933) Adam Melfort, once a promising army-officer, is a strange and quixotic hero. He is well-disciplined in mind and body and seeks to serve and preserve the troubled postwar wasteland of Europe. But he operates not in the heroic and public fashion of an Amyas Leigh but secretly, among the shadows. A highly successful undercover agent during the war, in peacetime he works to preserve peace and order through (ultimately inadequate) hero-figures he has chosen and encouraged: a Tory-radical peer, a trade-unionist, a wealthy explorer. But all the time the man of action is possessed by a childhood dream of happiness, lost for ever.

Adam Melfort, heroic and peculiar, is perhaps Buchan's most sombre representative of the tight-lipped resourceful Empire-building breed. Sandy Arbuthnot, master of disguise, adventurer and secret agent in some of the earlier Buchan novels, is a livelier example of the type. Buchan's college friend Auberon Herbert served as a model, but so also did Lawrence of Arabia, a legend in his own lifetime and one of the strangest of heroes.[126] Lawrence also provided W. H. Auden with a model of the Truly Strong Man, compounded of heroism and self-consciousness, who had a vital role to play in the salvation and healing of the England of the 1930s 'this country of ours where no-one is well'.[127]

Buchan's Adam Melfort and Auden's Truly Strong Men seem superficially to have inherited the mantle of socially committed Victorian manliness, but this is more apparent than real. The explicitly religious element is lacking, and so is the brash optimism of old-fashioned liberal Anglicanism. For Auden at least D. H. Lawrence and psychoanalysis have demonstrated the inadequacy of romantic theories of personality. In *The Orators* (1932) Auden included an Ode to Gabriel Carritt, who once captained the Sedbergh XV. The poem invokes the spirit of gamesplaying manliness and enlists it against a mysterious Enemy. But it gradually emerges that this is all part of a whimsical literary extravaganza. The hero-worshipping athletic atmosphere is mingled with a suggestion of public-school eroticism as it was in Waugh's *Loom of Youth*: Auden had actually been in love with Carritt in 1927. In fact public-school heroics, like Icelandic saga in Auden's *Paid on Both Sides* (1930), are not taken seriously. They are a self-consciously assumed idiom, a metaphor for the much-needed decisive action which alone can rescue a sick society.[128] Kingsley and Hughes would not have recognized their bizarre offspring. Auden's generation could no longer accept Victorian manly heroism at face-value, largely because of what happened during the war. What was left of Christian manliness was desperately wounded in the trenches.

THE WOUNDS OF WAR

At first it looked as if the Great War was going to represent the climax of Victorian manliness. Rupert Brooke, who had been a magnificent athlete at Rugby, positively welcomed war as the supreme athletic opportunity:

> Now God be thanked who has matched us with His hour
>   And caught our youth, and wakened us from sleeping,
> With hand made sure, clear eye, and sharpened power,
>   To turn, as swimmers into cleanness leaping,
> Glad from a world grown old and cold and weary,
>   Leave the sick hearts that honour could not move . . .[129]

The old alliance of God and well-muscled physical vigour seemed to have been renewed in the national emergency. This theme was taken up by other poets in the early days of the war: it was still possible to glory in battle in 1914, before many battles had been fought.[130] But Rupert Brooke had really only Rugby and sport in common with Tom Brown. It was not Rugby chapel but the agnostic aestheticism of W. J. Cory and J. A. Symonds which inspired his celebrations of youth and vigour. As Christopher Hassall has shown, Brooke's unsettled iconoclasm has been obscured by the sentimental posthumous legend of the gentleman-hero and patriot.[131] In a Cambridge squib 'John Rump' he scoffed at the Victorian notion of the English gentleman which the later myth of Rupert Brooke almost brought back to life again. When John Rump meets his maker the encounter is not harmonious. Rump's shallow optimism and well-fed bourgeois complacency are a meagre response to the splendours of the world, God feels, and in exasperation he dismisses him:

> 'Perish eternally, you and your hat!'[132]

War came as a release from complex dissatisfactions, for Brooke and for others. Julian Grenfell's biographer Nicholas Mosley has brilliantly recreated the uneasy political atmosphere and the personal unhappiness and lost sense of purpose of well-born

Englishmen in the years just before the war.[133] The public schools
were trying to stop the rot on the gamesfield and in the Officer
Training Corps, as we have seen. The links between school games
and some greater game, implied in Bowen's Harrow hymn 'Forty
Years On' and made explicit in Newbolt, survived as sentiment and
did actually sustain some soldiers in battle. The influence of
Newbolt is very strong in many of the poems collected in E. B.
Osborne's wartime anthology *The Muse in Arms* (1917). Serving
officers sentimentally recalled schooldays which may not have been
very distant. Captain J. M. Rose-Troup, a prisoner-of-war in
Hessen, consoled himself with thoughts of Harrow:

> And Harrow sends a message to cheer me on my way.
> 'For good come, bad come, they came the same before,
> So heigh ho, follow the game, and show the way to more.'

Lieutenant Eric F. Wilkinson, MC, an old boy of Ilkley Grammar
School, mused

> Can you hear the call? Can you hear the call
> That drowns the roar of Krupp?
> There are many who fight and many who fall
> Where the big guns play at the Kaiser's ball,
> But hark! – can you hear it? Over all –
> Now, School! Now, School! Play up![134]

But Siegfried Sassoon strikes a different note. A former public
school cricketer, a very English fox-hunting man, he might have
been mistaken for an updated Tom Brown, the manly army officer
Newbolt urged to 'love the game beyond the prize'. For Newbolt the
emergencies of war could be assimilated to the tensions of 'Ten to
make and the match to win –' and Sassoon turns to cricket in the
midst of war as well. But Newbolt is recalled with bitterness:

> He turned to me with his kind, sleepy gaze
> And fresh face slowly brightening to the grin
> That sets my memory back to summer days
> With twenty runs to make, and the last man in.
> He told me he'd been having a bloody time
> In trenches, crouching for the crumps to burst,
> While squeeking rats scampered across the slime
> And the grey palsied weather did its worst.[135]

The tradition of manly Christianity was too naïve to withstand
the pressures of modern war. C. E. Montague's acerbic reflections
on his wartime experience may exaggerate the patronizing silliness
of would-be bluff and manly army chaplains,[136] and Woodbine

Willie at least effectively kept alive the alliance between robust Christianity and soldiering. But as the war progressed trench-fever and disenchantment took hold. The cultural tradition of the English gentleman incorporated war. The legends of chivalry of the nursery were succeeded by Homer and the siege of Troy at school. The Odes of Horace were almost inescapable as well, and it was Horace who said that it was a good thing to die for one's country, 'dulce et decorum est pro patria mori.' But Wilfred Owen's poem 'Dulce et Decorum est' savagely dismissed this familiar tag as an 'old lie'.[137] Patrick Shaw Stewart, sportsman and Etonian, Fellow of All Souls, the most dazzling of the brilliant group of friends who served with Rupert Brooke in the naval battalion on HMS *Hood*, found himself where Achilles had fought. He brooded ironically on that ancient heroism:

> O hell of ships and cities
>   Hell for men like me,
> Fatal second Helen,
>   Why must I follow thee?
>
> . . . Was it so hard, Achilles,
>   So very hard to die?
> Thou knowest and I know not –
>   So much the happier I.

By 1917, on the Western Front, he knew.[138]

Edmund Blunden had loved cricket as much as Tom Brown or Tom Hughes. But his war could only contain it as a kind of imaginative refuge, an idiom of escape. One evening after dinner, on the way to the Somme

I joyfully recollect how Millward, that famed cricketer, gave a few of us an hour's catching practice in the orchard with apples instead of cricket-balls or bombs.[139]

References to cricket and cricketers abound in his war-memories, but the tone is gentle, affectionate and unmilitary. 'The Cricketers of Flanders' by J. N. Hall strikes a different note. This rather appalling poem, published in the *Evening News* on 2 September, 1916, tries to link sporting and military manliness by linking grenades with cricket-balls:

> Full sixty yards I've seen them throw
> With all that nicety of aim
> They learned on British cricket fields.
> Ah, bombing is a Briton's game!

The author was an American volunteer who happened to be in England in 1914 and eagerly joined 'Kitchener's Mob' the moment war was declared. For him Englishness and manliness was a style and an ideal observed from outside, and he tried to appropriate the style for propagandist ends, doubtless encouraged by the War Office.[140] But no true-born Englishman, least of all Tom Hughes, would have wanted to admit that bombing was a Briton's game, or would have tolerated the degradation of cricketing skills.

The possibilities, and the ironies, of manliness in war were registered chiefly by officers. The later fortunes of mid-Victorian Christian manliness have been discussed chiefly in relation to the middle classes and the officer-class because it was from that level of society that most of the influential books and movements originated. Manliness for the million, in YMCA publications or popular fiction, tended to have bourgeois writers and values behind it. *Lord Northcliffe's War Book* was no exception. It tried to create an atmosphere of working-class patriotic manliness by talking not about Rugby football but Association football. The game had apparently been introduced in Germany only quite recently, which seemed to be yet another proof of the inferiority of the Germans, if Lord Northcliffe was to be believed. Some of the officers actually shared the interest of the other ranks in soccer and Captain W. P. Nevill and others traded on this rather more effectively than Northcliffe. At the battle of the Somme Nevill encouraged his men as they went over the top by producing a football which they dribbled over no-man's-land right into the enemy trenches.[141]

None of these wartime gestures in the direction of sport and manliness, affectionate or contemptuous, bore much relation to the religion or the serious social and moral concerns of mid-Victorian Christian manliness. Perhaps the most extended epitaph on Christian manliness is to be found in the work of Ford Madox Ford.

Even before the war Ford had been fascinated by the incompatibility of time-honoured styles of behaviour with the atmosphere and circumstances of modern life. He had personal ties with the Victorian manly Christians in that he was a grandson of Ford Madox Brown who had painted Maurice and Carlyle into *Work*. His other grandfather was German, so his perception of English traditions has both the affectionate intimacy of the native and the detachment of the outsider. In *Ladies whose Bright Eyes* (1911) the chivalry which excited the Victorians is reconstructed in a fantasy of mediaeval life into which a time-travelling modern publisher plunges in bewilderment. There is decency and absurdity in both the world of chivalry and the world of business, but in the end the publisher leaves his business and retreats as much as he can from the modern world.

The strange and enigmatic 'hero' of *The Good Soldier* (1915), observed from constantly shifting perspectives but elusive to the last, is set up as a Tom Brown figure in the first instance, a public-school man, an ex-officer and landowner with a strong sense of honour and responsibility. Yet he and his wife, his ward, his mistress and his best friend contribute to and suffer from an appalling tragedy of passion and deceit. The old ideals upon which the Good Soldier is framed cannot sustain the slings and arrows of his outrageous fortune and his own nature.

In Ford's war tetralogy *Parade's End* (1924–28) the hero is Christopher Tietjens of the Yorkshire Tietjens of Groby. He is a wooden-faced romantic idealist who represents all that is noblest and best in old England. Rather improbably, perhaps, he is a brilliant statistician in a government department when war breaks out. But spiritually he is a gallant gentleman of the eighteenth, or even the seventeenth century, as he admits himself. Self-mockingly he claims to be an arrested adolescent (anticipating J. D. Marstock and Cyril Connolly) because he has taken his public school's ethical system too seriously. At Clifton (Newbolt's school) they told him it was the vilest of sins to 'peach' to the headmaster, so he neither excuses nor explains himself when laid under the harshest calumny. Quixotic, honourable and brave, he might have been a great soldier and a great man in the public eye. But he is dogged by misfortune and misunderstanding and the malevolence of his unfaithful but possessive wife. For most of the war he is starved of love and happiness as well as success. Even in peacetime, when he can live in his beloved Groby, his wife does her best to ruin it for him by arranging to destroy Groby Great Tree. References to George Herbert's country parish at Bemerton run through *Parade's End* as a *leitmotif* of unattainable peace and holiness. Charles Kingsley had gone fishing there, thinking of Herbert and his fisherman friend Izaak Walton. The saintly poet-priest of Bemerton was his model for his own parish ministry.[142] But though Christopher bears his sufferings with Christ-like fortitude it becomes clear that he will never be a country priest like Herbert or Kingsley: 'A country parsonage was not for him'. Christian service, Christian manliness on the Victorian model, ought still to have been a possibility if

Christopher could have lived a life of social usefulness on the family estate. For Tom Brown, son of Squire Brown, the immemorial role of the English country gentleman was still worthy of respect. But Mark Tietjens, Christopher's elder brother, has never lived that kind of life and on his death-bed he registers an essentially modern impatience with the traditional modes of manliness associated with the country life: 'the old families of his country were a pretty inefficient lot that he was thankful to have done with.'[143] This can stand as the ungracious epitaph pronounced by the twentieth century on the inherited impulse to be manly and to serve which animated the Victorian manly Christians.

But are we really done with Christian manliness? Manliness at least has staying-power. Public-school games no longer enjoy their once exalted status but the games-cult took a long time to die.[144] Perhaps it lingers still. Outside the schools well-organized professional sport remains a major source of popular entertainment. The organization began in the nineteenth century not long after Kingsley and Hughes ceased to write novels.[145] It is not at all certain that they would have approved of the desperate seriousness of professional football (which dates from 1885), but the provision of playing-fields and leisure-centres for vigorous recreation might have encouraged them to think that all was not lost. There are still a few heroes of sport who can point the way to higher things. One of them, the cricketer David Sheppard, is now Bishop of Liverpool. Occasionally a modern thriller may revive the spirit of Buchan and Kipling and Kingsley by hinting at the ethic of strenuousness and service and the nobility of uncomfortable adventure. Colleen Toomey's *Bird of Prey* (1982), describing a dogged civil servant's hazardous encounter with computerized villainy, is perhaps a case in point. The 1983 centenary of the Boys' Brigade, celebrated in various parts of the world, reminds us that there are still men and boys pledged like their Victorian ancestors to strive for 'all that tends towards a true Christian Manliness'.

Notes

INTRODUCTION

1. [S. S. Pugh] *Christian Manliness*, 1867, p. 127.
2. E. B. Browning, *Aurora Leigh*, 1856, v, 152.
3. See W. L. Burn, *The Age of Equipoise*, 1964.
4. [T. C. Sandars] Review of Kingsley's *Two Years Ago*, *Saturday Review* III (Feb. 1857), p. 176; [Fitzjames Stephen] Review of *Tom Brown's Schooldays*, *Edinburgh Review* CVII (Jan. 1858), p. 190.
5. Swinburne to Rossetti, 8 August 1863, quoted in J. O. Fuller, *Swinburne, a Critical Biography*, 1968, p. 93.
6. 'Tangled Talk: Muscular Christianity', *Tait's Edinburgh Magazine* XXV (Feb. 1858), pp. 100–2.
7. [Leslie Stephen] 'Athletic Sports and University Studies', *Fraser's Magazine* n.s. II (Dec. 1870), pp. 691f; cf. K. Robinson, *Wilkie Collins*, 1951, pp. 238f.
8. Charles Kingsley, *David*, Cambridge 1865, p. 5.
9. The only serious religious and intellectual studies are Guy Kendall, *Charles Kingsley and his Ideas* and W. E. Winn '*Tom Brown's Schooldays* and the Development of "Muscular Christianity"', *Church History* XXIX (1960), pp. 64–73.
10. Owen Chadwick, *The Victorian Church*, 2 vols., 1966–70, I, pp. 462f.
11. J. H. Newman, *Certain Difficulties felt by Anglicans in Catholic Teaching* (1850), 2 vols., 1908 ed., I, p. 250.
12. See F. Darwin, ed., *Charles Darwin: his Life*, 1892, p. 228 and *The Origin of Species*, 4th ed., 1866, p. 567 for Kingsley's congratulatory letter to Darwin.
13. W. Holman Hunt, *Pre-Raphaelitism and the Pre-Raphaelite Brotherhood*, 2 vols., 1905, I, p. 355.
14. Thomas Carlyle, *On Heroes, Hero-worship and the Heroic in History*, 1844, p. 18.
15. H. W. Shrewsbury, *Brothers in Art: Studies in Wm. Holman Hunt and J. E. Millais*, 1920, pp. 153, 161; 151; Geoffrey Millais, *Sir John Everett Millais*, 1979, p. 32.
16. Ford Madox Ford, *Ford Madox Brown; a record of his life and work*, 1896, pp. 84f. See George P. Landow, *William Holman Hunt and Typological Symbolism*, New Haven and London 1979, pp. 118, 157–60.
17. Ford Madox Ford, *Ford Madox Brown*, pp. 189–93; 112.

18. [F. E. Kingsley, ed.] *Charles Kingsley: his Letters and Memories of his Life*, 2 vols. 1877 (cited hereafter as *LM*) II, p. 27; Plato, *Laws* V, 731 b, c; *Republic* IV, 440a–441b; *Timaeus*, 69d–70.

19. *Hereward the Wake* (1866), 1889 (electrotyped) ed., ch. 41. All references to Kingsley's novels will be to the Macmillan electrotyped editions.

1. VARIETIES OF MANLINESS

1. See OED s.c. 'Manly' (senses 2 and 3); s.c. 'Manliness' (sense 1).

2. Sir Walter Scott, *Waverley* (1814), Edinburgh, 1877, ed., Introduction (1829), p. 85; ch. 68.

3. Sir Leslie Stephen, *Hours in a Library*, 3rd ser., 1879, p. 62.

4. Anthony Trollope, *The Prime Minister*, 1876, ch. 60; *The Duke's Children*, 1880, ch. 50; ch. 40.

5. Charles Dickens, *Bleak House*, 1852, ch. 58.

6. Edmund Burke, *Reflections on the Revolution in France* (1790) in *Works*, World Classics ed., 6 vols, 1906–7, IV, p. 83.

7. *Don Juan* XV, xi.

8. John Morley, *Life of William Ewart Gladstone* (1903), 2 vols, 1905, I, p. 15.

9. See J. C. Reid, *Bucks and Bruisers: Pierce Egan and Regency England*, 1971, pp. 134f; 23.

10. John Milton, Preface 'To the Parliament of England' of *The Doctrine and Discipline of Divorce* in K.M. Burton, ed., *Milton's Prose Writings*, 1958, p. 250.

11. Edmund Burke, *Reflections*, *Works* IV, p. 7.

12. [T. C. Sandars] Review of *Two Years Ago*, *Saturday Review* III (Feb. 1857), p. 176.

13. See DNB s.c. 'Allardice, Robert Barclay [alias Captain Barclay], 1779–1854'.

14. Pierre de Coubertin, *L'Education en Angleterre*, Paris 1888, pp. 63–71; Hippolyte Taine, *Notes of England*, trans. W. F. Rae, 1877, pp. 49–50, 56f, 121–8; R. W. Emerson, *English Traits* (1856) in *Works*, one-vol., 1901, ed., p. 298.

15. Hugh Walpole, *Rogue Herries*, 1930, pp. 621–6. See also Montagu Shearman, *Athletics and Football*, 1887, esp. ch. 1.

16. C. L. Graves, *Life and Letters of Alexander Macmillan*, 1910, pp. 195f.

17. Maria Edgeworth, *Frank: a Sequel to 'Frank' in Early Lessons*, 3 vols., 1822, I, p. 55; Thomas Hughes, *Memoir of a Brother*, 1873, p. 15.

18. Angus Wilson, *The Naughty Nineties*, 1976, pp. 6f.

19. See, for example, Byron's *Don Juan* II, xcii; *Hints from Horace*, 1811, lines 637–40; Thomas Moore, *Tom Crib's Memorial to Congress*, 1819.

20. *Pierce Egan's Book of Sports*, 1832, pp. 49f; J. C. Reid, *Bucks and Bruisers* pp. 20f.

21. W. M. Thackeray, 'De Juventute' (1860) in *Roundabout Papers*, 1863, pp. 100, 107, 124–9.

22. Philip Guedalla, *The Duke*, 1931, p. 207.

23. William Somerville, *The Chase*, 1735, Bk 1, line 13.
24. R. S. Surtees, *Handley Cross*, 2 vols, 1843, 1, ch. 7.
25. Thomas Moore, *Complete Poetical Works*, 1869, pp. 329f; Elizabeth Longford, *Wellington, the Years of the Sword*, 1969, p. 483 and n.; J. G. Lockhart, *Memoirs of the Life of Sir Walter Scott, Bart*, 7 vols., Edinburgh and London, 1837–8, III, p. 359; *Tom Brown's Schooldays* Part I, ch. 2.
26. See, e.g., J. A. Mangan, *Athleticism in the Victorian and Edwardian Public School*, Cambridge 1981.
27. See D. C. Itzkowitz, *Peculiar Privilege: a Social History of English Foxhunting 1753–1885*, Hassocks, 1977, pp. 51–6.
28. Matthew Arnold, *Culture and Anarchy*, 1869, ch. 3 'Barbarians, Philistines, Populace'; 'An Eton Boy', *Fortnightly Review* XXXVII (June 1882), pp. 683–97, esp. p. 685.
29. G. C. G. F. Berkeley, *Life and Recollections*, 4 vols., 1865–6, 1, pp. 101, 105f; II, pp. 55–7; see also 'The Trial of Fraser vs Berkeley and another and Berkeley vs Fraser', *Fraser's Magazine* XV (Jan. 1837), pp. 100–137.
30. [G. A. Lawrence] *Guy Livingstone*, 1857, pp. 372–4.
31. G. A. Lawrence, *Sword and Gown*, 1859, pp. 31of.
32. Revd W. H. Thornton, *Reminiscences and Reflections of an Old West Country Clergyman*, Torquay, 1897, pp. 39f.
33. Henry Kingsley, *Recollections of Geoffry Hamlyn*, 3 vols., Cambridge 1859, 1, ch. 12.
34. [F. E. Smedley] *Frank Fairlegh*, 1850, ch. 21.
35. D. C. Itzkowitz, *Peculiar Privilege* pp. 143f.
36. Ibid., p. 65.
37. Discussed at length in A. J. Russell, 'A Sociological Analysis of the Clergyman's Role', Oxford D. Phil. thesis, 1970.
38. *LM* 1, pp. 349f; II, p. 463; *Hypatia* (1853), 1888 (electrotyped) ed., ch. 21; A. P. Stanley, *'Charles Kingsley', a Sermon Preached in Westminster Abbey* (1875), 3rd ed., 1875, p. 13.
39. See Mark Girouard, *The Return to Camelot: Chivalry and the English Gentleman*, 1981; John Fraser, *America and the Patterns of Chivalry*, Cambridge 1982.
40. See Malcolm Vale, *War and Chivalry*, 1981, esp. pp. 21f, 30, 166.
41. See Maurice Valency, *In Praise of Love*, New York, 1958, pp. 42–7.
42. Translated by D. G. Rossetti in *The Early Italian Poets* (1861), ed. Sally Purcell, 1981, p. 29.
43. Dante Alighieri, *Monarchy*, trans. D. Nicholl, 1954, pp. 32f; *Dante's Lyric Poetry*, ed. K. Foster and P. Boyde, 2 vols., Oxford 1967, 1, pp. 129–37.
44. Geoffrey Chaucer, *The Canterbury Tales* III(D), 1117f.
45. See, e.g., Mark Girouard, *The Return to Camelot*; J. Mordaunt Crook, *William Burges and the High Victorian Dream*, 1981 (esp. ch. 1); Alice Chandler, *A Dream of Order: the Mediaeval Ideal in Nineteenth Century English Literature*, 1970.
46. Girouard, *The Return to Camelot*, ch. 7.

47. Included in W. M. Thackeray, *Novels by Eminent Hands* 1847.
48. Anthony Trollope, *Barchester Towers*, 1857, ch. 35 and 36.
49. The Grand Staircase, for instance, was to have been dominated by a central monumental figure of an equestrian knight. See J. Mordaunt Crook, ed., *The Strange Genius of William Burges*, Cardiff, 1981, pp. 32f.
50. He painted him in *Queen Victoria and Prince Albert* (as Philippa and Edward III) (1842–6) and *Windsor Castle in Modern Times* (1841–5), discussed in Richard Ormond, *Sir Edwin Landseer*, New York and London, 1981, pp. 156f; 150–2.
51. Girouard, *The Return to Camelot*, pp. 123–5.
52. *Saturday Review* XII (Dec. 1861), p. 631.
53. First published in G. S. de M. R., ed., *Lays of the Sanctuary*, 1859, p. 49.
54. *The Book of the Courtier*, Tudor Translations XXIII, 1900, pp. 44–8, esp. p. 47.
55. Susan Chitty, *The Beast and the Monk: a life of Charles Kingsley*, 1974, p. 272.
56. Spenser's letter to Sir Walter Ralegh, prefaced to *The Faerie Queene*, ed. T. P. Roche, New Haven and London, 1981, p. 15; *Faerie Queene* III, 1, xiii.
57. Sir A. Quiller-Couch, 'The Practice of Writing' in *On the Art of Writing*, Cambridge 1916, pp. 41f.
58. R. W. Church, *Spenser* (1879), 1887 ed., pp. 71–4, 148.
59. Edward, Earl of Clarendon, *The History of the Rebellion* (1702), ed. W. D. Macray, 1888, Bk VII, par. 217.
60. F. M. Ford, *Ford Madox Brown*, pp. 126f; Roy Strong, *And when did you last see your father?*, 1979, pp., 146–8.
61. *Hansard's Parliamentary Debates*, 3rd ser. cxv cols. 325, 595f.
62. M. C. Battestin, *The Moral Basis of Fielding's Art*, Middletown, Connecticut, 1959, ch. 2; see, e.g., some of the sermons of Isaac Barrow in his *Theological Works*, ed. A. Napier, 9 vols, Cambridge 1859, I, pp. 3–96; II, pp. 524–45; II, pp. 320–36, etc.
63. M. A. Doody, *A Natural Passion. A Study of the Novels of Samuel Richardson*, Oxford 1974, p. 250.
64. Ibid., p. 263.
65. There seem to have been some 14 editions or abridgements published in England in the nineteenth century (*British Library Catalogue; National Union Catalog*).
66. C. M. Yonge, *The Heir of Redclyffe*, 1855, ch. 3; ch. 34.
67. George Meredith, *The Ordeal of Richard Feverel* (1859), 2nd ed., 1875, ch. 19.
68. Richard Shannon, *The Crisis of Imperialism 1865–1915* (1974), 1976 ed. pp. 82–5; J. S. Mill, *Considerations of Representative Government* (1861) ed. H. B. Acton, 1972, ch. 14 esp. pp. 335–46.
69. Mrs Craik, *John Halifax, Gentleman*, 1856, ch. 29.
70. Philippians 3 v.14; I Timothy 6 v.12; compare Hebrews 12 v.1; I Corinthians 9 v.24.

71. C. H. Spurgeon, *A Good Start: a book for young men and women*, 1898, p. 16; compare Revd H. R. Heywood, *Manliness: a sermon*, Manchester 1877; Revd H. S. Brown, *Manliness, a lecture*, YMCA Exeter Hall Lectures 1857–8.

72. C. Newman Hall, *Wellington and War*, 1852, p. 11; see also Revd D. J. Harrison, *Greatness, Godliness, Glory; a sermon on the death of Wellington*, 1852; J. Jefferson, *The funeral of the Duke of Wellington: its lessons for this world and the next*, 1852.

73. Edward Hawkins, *The Duty of Moral Courage: a sermon preached before the University of Oxford*, 1852.

74. *LM* I, p. 440.

75. Discussed in Olive Anderson, 'The Growth of Christian Militarism in mid-Victorian Britain', *English Historical Review* LXXXVI (1971), pp. 46–72; see, e.g., T. Teignmouth Shore, *War and Christianity*, 1878, p. 18 (Havelock); Catherine Marsh, *Memorials of Captain Hedley Vicars*, 1855; Seton Churchill, *General Gordon: a Christian Hero*, 1890; Thain Davidson, D.D., 'Pious Patriotism', *Family Friend* XXVII (1896), pp. 134f (Gordon).

76. *Yeast* (1851), 1888 (electrotyped) ed., Preface (first added to 4th ed., 1859), p. xii.

2. STURDINESS AND THE SAINTS

1. See R. B. Martin, *The Dust of Combat. A Life of Charles Kingsley*, 1959, pp. 19–21; Thomas Hughes, *Memoir of a Brother*, 1873, pp. 12f.

2. M. F. Thorp, *Charles Kingsley (1819–1875)*, Princeton, 1937, pp. 10, 12; Susan Chitty, *The Beast and the Monk. A Life of Charles Kingsley*, 1974, p. 75; *LM* II. pp. 159, 183; see Walter Houghton, 'The Issue between Kingsley and Newman' in R. O. Preyer, ed., *Victorian Literature, Selected Essays*, New York, 1967, pp. 13–36.

3. *LM* I, pp. 143f. 'Manichee' was Kingsley's favourite term of abuse, especially in correspondence: see, e.g., *LM* I, pp. 105, 143f, 191, 219, 251f, 256, 272; II, pp. 31f.

4. *LM* I, pp. 81, 325; II, pp. 31f; cf. M. F. Thorp, *Charles Kingsley (1819–1875)*, p. 20.

5. See Owen Chadwick, ed., *Western Asceticism*, 1958, pp. 14f.

6. Geo Widengren, *Mani and Manichaeism*, Eng. trans. 1965, pp. 43ff.

7. See G. Bonner, *The Warfare of Christ*, 1962, 'The Two Cities', pp. 65–96, esp. pp. 66–8 where he distinguishes the Augustinian concept of the earthly and the heavenly cities from Manichaean dualism as Kingsley completely failed to do.

8. S. T. Coleridge, *Conciones ad Populum* (1795), *Collected Works*, Bollingen edition (1969–) I, pp. 65f; 'Essay on Fasts', *The Watchman* (1796), *Works* II, pp. 51ff; R. Southey, *The Book of the Church*, 2 vols., 1824, I, pp. 301–14; cf. *Sir Thomas More*, 2 vols., 1829, I, p. 29.

9. Review of J. A. Froude's *History of England, Macmillan's Magazine* IX (Jan. 1864), p. 216.

10. *Phaethon,* Cambridge, 1852, pp. 41f.

11. See, e.g., Revd R. P. Blakeney, *Awful Disclosures of the Iniquitous Principles taught by the Church of Rome* 1846; Revd F. Meyrick, *But isn't Kingsley right after all?*, 1864. The theological issue is reviewed in G. Egner, *Apologia pro Charles Kingsley,* 1969.

12. *Theologia Moralis,* Book 4, Tract 2, ch.2; Book 3, Tract 1, ch.3; available in the Mechlin, 1845–6, edition, 10 vols, ed. P. Mich. Heilig, II, pp. 316–26; II, pp. 116f.

13. J. H. Newman, 'Position of my mind since 1845', *Apologia pro Vita Sua* (1865), ed. M. J. Svaglic, Oxford 1967, pp. 244–9; 304–6. This edition, cited hereafter as 'Svaglic', reprints Kingsley's side of the controversy as well.

14. M. F. Thorp, *Charles Kingsley* p. 22; *LM* I, pp. 48–53.

15. H. Venn, *The Complete Duty of Man* (1763), ed. 1841, p. 52.

16. Ibid., Introduction p. xx.

17. *Evangelical Magazine* VIII (Dec. 1800) p. 526, quoted M. Quinlan, *Victorian Prelude,* New York 1941, p. 114f.

18. E. C. Gaskell, *Life of Charlotte Bronte,* 2 vols, 1857, I, pp. 64–6.

19. *The Friendly Visitor* XXX (Kirkby Lonsdale, Nov. 1848), pp. 172, 179–83.

20. H. Venn, *The Complete Duty of Man,* Introduction p. viii.

21. *Evangelical Magazine,* VIII (Dec. 1800). Pleasure-seeking, especially on the Lord's Day, merits the same negative position on the 'spiritual barometer' as profanity, adultery and drunkness.

22. *The Friendly Visitor* XXVI (Feb. 1844), p. 30.

23. Maurice Kauffman, *Charles Kingsley, Christian Socialist and Social Reformer,* 1892, p. 208; *Yeast,* Preface to 4th ed. (1859), p. ix.

24. C. H. Spurgeon, *A Good Start* (posthumously published 1898), pp. 22, 289. Cf. S. S. Pugh, *Christian Manliness,* p. 222.

25. *The Record,* 25 Jan. 1856, p. 2, cols. 2–3.

26. J. H. Newman, *Apologia pro Vita Sua,* Svaglic, pp. 15–18.

27. J. H. Newman, *Parochial Sermons* III (1836), pp. 350f.

28. E. B. Pusey, *Thoughts on the Benefits of the System of Fasting, Enjoined by our Church* (1833), 2nd ed. 1840, *Tracts for the Times* no. 18, p. 17; *Sermons . . . from Advent to Whitsuntide,* 1848, pp. 299–305.

29. F. W. Faber, *Life of St Ebba,* printed with *Life of St Paulinus,* etc, 1844, p. 108f. For attributions see Appendix II of the 1900–1 collected edition of the *Lives of the English Saints,* vol. VI, pp. 399f.

30. *Sermons bearing on Subjects of the Day,* 1843, no. 7, pp. 90–92; 98f.

31. *Sermons bearing on Subjects of the Day,* no. 8, p. 120; *The Saint's Tragedy,* 1848, IV, i, p. 181.

32. *Sermons bearing on Subjects of the Day,* no. 20, p. 339. See *Apologia,* Note C, Svaglic, pp. 276f, where he explains the circumstances of the sermon.

33. 'Mr Kingsley and Dr Newman: a Correspondence', Svaglic, p. 342.

34. *Thoughts on the . . . System of Fasting*, esp. pp. 1,26f.

35. *LM* I, p. 56.

36. J. A. Froude, *History of England from the Fall of Wolsey to the Defeat of the Spanish Armada*, vols. VII and VIII (*The Reign of Elizabeth*, vols. I and II), 1863.

37. *Macmillan's Magazine* IX (Jan. 1864), p. 216.

38. Advertisement prefixed to 'Mr Kingsley and Dr Newman', Svaglic, p. 339; cf. p. 407.

39. U. Pope-Hennessy, *Canon Charles Kingsley*, 1948, pp. 22f, 88f.

40. Ibid., p. 39.

41. Chitty, *The Beast and the Monk*, pp. 57–86 supplies detailed information about Kingsley's sexuality on the basis of hitherto discreetly unpublished materials.

42. *LM* I, pp. 255f; see F. D. Maurice, *The Church a Family*, 1850, etc.

43. *The Saint's Tragedy*, 1848, Introduction pp. xxii–xxiii, etc.

44. See *Oxford Dictionary of the Christian Church*, 2nd ed. 1974, s.c. 'Original Sin', pp. 1010f.

45. *Sermons on Subjects of the Day*, no. 19, p. 328: cf. Newman's *The Church of the Fathers*, 1840, p. 122 for a rather unfair contrast between the average married, domestic Anglican incumbent and the penitentially celibate SS Basil and Gregory.

46. *What, then, does Dr Newman Mean?*, Svaglic, pp. 358f, 380.

47. Svaglic, p. 20. Compare Newman's semi-autobiographical novel *Loss and Gain* (1848), ed. 1874, pp. 188–193. Kingsley acknowledges the practical argument when he amusingly defends the statutory celibacy of Cambridge fellows on the grounds that the alternative would breed an undesirable race of 'pedantlets and pedanticulets' – Letter of 23 Feb. 1857, CUL Add. 725, f.314.

48. T. Mozley, *Reminiscences of Oriel College and the Oxford Movement*, 2nd ed., 2 vols, 1882, I, p. 307. Cf. *Loss and Gain* pp. 349–52 where Newman wittily ridicules the marriage of a clergyman to a beautiful but witless young girl and his celibate hero who observes them is physically nauseated. See also Newman's 'The Married and the Single', *Verses on Various Occasions*, 1867, pp. 176–81.

49. Svaglic, p. 34; G. V. Cox, *Recollections of Oxford* (1868), 2nd ed. 1870, pp. 346f; W. Ward, *William George Ward and the Oxford Movement*, 1889, p. 348.

50. R. Chapman, *Father Faber*, 1961, p. 100; cf. 'First Love' and 'Birthday Thoughts', F. W. Faber, *The Cherwell Water Lily, and other Poems*, 1840, pp. 266ff, 190f.

51. [M. Pattison] *Life of St Ninian*, 1845, pp. 21f. This relates to the 144,000 male virgins mentioned in the Book of Revelation, 14 vv. 3–4.

52. [F. W. Faber] *Life of St Ebba*, printed with *Life of St. Paulinus*, 1844, pp. 113f.

53. R. Southey, *Vindicia Ecclesiae Anglicanae*, 1826, pp. 290ff, 337.

54. E. J. Whately, *Maude, or, The Anglican Sister of Mercy*, 1869, pp.

115f. This novel is based on actual correspondence relating to the
writer's sister-in-law. See K. M. Denison, 'The Sisterhood
Movement', Cambridge Ph.D. thesis, 1970, pp. 149–53, etc.

55. *LM* I, p. 250.

56. See, e.g., *LM* I, p. 100: '"Every creature of God is good, if it be
sanctified with prayer and thanksgiving"'.

57. *LM* I, p. 249.

58. *Tracts for the Times* no. 21 (1833); cf. no. 18, Pusey's *Thoughts on the
. . . System of Fasting*. See also Newman's *Parochial Sermons* III, no. 11,
'Bodily Suffering', esp. 164f.

59. R. Chapman, *Father Faber*, pp. 98, 100.

60. R. H. Froude, *Remains*, 1st ser., 2 vols., 1838, II, pp. 295–334.

61. See e.g. *British Critic* XXX (October 1841), pp. 389–91, which praises
the Abbess Angélique's love of mortifications.

62. K. M. Denison, 'The Sisterhood Movement' pp. 185–9; E. J.
Whately, *Maude* pp. 54–7.

63. See, e.g., *The Awful Disclosures of Maria Monk*, New York 1836 etc;
E. Harris, *From Oxford to Rome*, 1847, esp. pp. 40, 51–3, 177.

64. R. Southey, *Commonplace Book*, ed. J. Warter, 2nd ser. 1849, pp.
368–401. By an irony of history the Park Village sisterhood which
had once attracted Mrs Kingsley was set up partly in Southey's
memory as he had once advocated Protestant Sisterhoods, though
based on very different principles. *Life and Correspondence*, ed. C. C.
Southey, 6 vols., 1849, II, pp. 51f; cf. *Sir Thomas More*, II, pp.
195–234.

65. See, e.g., W. Walsh, *The Secret History of the Oxford Movement*,
(1897), 6th ed. 1899, p. 189.

66. *LM* I, p. 246.

67. *What, then, does Dr Newman mean?*, Svaglic, p. 377.

68. E. J. Whately, *Maude*, pp. 92f; *Quarterly Review* CIII (Jan. 1858), pp.
161–3; *Record* 7 Jan. 1856, p. 2, col. 2; *LM* I, pp. 80f.

69. A. R. Ashwell, R. G. Wilberforce, *Life of the Rt. Rev. Samuel
Wilberforce*, 3 vols., 1880–2, II, p. 367.

70. W. O. Chadwick, *The Founding of Cuddesdon*, Oxford 1954, pp. 22f,
27f, 38–40.

71. Ibid., pp. 92f; Ashwell and Wilberforce, *Life of Wilberforce* II, 368.

72. *British Critic* XXVII (Jan. 1840), pp. 88f; *Apologia*, Svaglic, pp. 119f.

73. See, e.g., *Protestantism and Popery . . . by a Staunch Protestant* (1864),
2nd ed. 1865, pp. 4f; E. Harris, *Rest in the Church*, 1848, esp. p. 342;
E. R. Norman, *Anti-Catholicism in Victorian England*, 1968, esp. pp.
57, 172–4; W. P. Lyon, *Christianity the Weal of England; Popery and
Infidelity the Weal of France*, Tunbridge Wells 1851; M. Tupper,
Half-a-Dozen No-Popery Ballads, 1851, esp. no. 5, p. 4, 'Rise
Britannia!'.

3. LIBERAL RELIGION

1. J. A. Froude, *Thomas Carlyle. A History of his Life in London 1834–1881*, 2 vols., 1884, II, 73.
2. C. R. Sanders, *Coleridge and the Broad Church Movement*, Durham, North Carolina, 1942, esp. pp. 146, 156–62, 176.
3. OED s.c. 'Broad'; [W. J. Conybeare] 'Church Parties', *Edinburgh Review* XCVIII (Oct. 1853), 273–342.
4. See for example H. R. Haweis, *The Broad Church, or What is Coming*, 1890.
5. *LM* II, pp. 393f; I, 327.
6. J. H. Newman, *Apologia pro Vita Sua*, ed. M. Svaglic, p. 42.
7. Best accounts of Maurice in A. R. Vidler, *F. D. Maurice and Company*, 1966; Torben Christenson, *The Divine Order: A Study in F. D. Maurice's Theology*, Leiden, 1973.
8. David Newsome, *Godliness and Good Learning*, p. 12.
9. Matthew Arnold, *Culture and Anarchy* (1869), ed. J. Dover Wilson, Cambridge 1935, 'Conclusion' p. 203.
10. See Bernard Semmel, *The Governor Eyre Crisis*, 1962; Thomas Carlyle, 'Occasional Discourse on the Negro Question', *Fraser's Magazine* XL (Dec. 1849), pp. 670–79, reprinted as a pamphlet *Occasional Discourse on the Nigger Question*, 1853.
11. Frederick Maurice, ed., *The Life of Frederick Denison Maurice* (1884), 2nd ed., 2 vols., 1884, II, p. 172.
12. Ibid, II, p. 497.
13. *Don Juan* III, xciii, lines 5f.; x, xiii.
14. J. A. Froude, *Thomas Carlyle* I, p. 45; letter from Charles Lamb to William Wordsworth, 26 April 1816, *Letters of Charles Lamb*, ed. Alfred Ainger, 2 vols., 1888, I, p. 305.
15. A. P. Stanley, *Life and Correspondence of Thomas Arnold, D.D.*, 2 vols, 1844, II p. 56; see F. R. Leavis, ed., *Mill on Bentham and Coleridge*, 1950; David Newsome, *Two Classes of Men: Platonism in English Romantic Thought*, 1974, ch. 4.
16. David Newsome, *Godliness and Good Learning*, p. 197.
17. The episode is wittily reconstructed by E. M. Forster, 'Trooper Silas Tomkyn Comberbacke', *Abinger Harvest* (1936), 1967 Penguin ed., pp. 244–50.
18. Quoted by Una Pope-Hennessy, *Canon Charles Kingsley*, p. 26.
19. 'Lines on Having Left a Place of Retirement' (1795), *Complete Poetical Works*, ed. E. H. Coleridge, Oxford, 1912, p. 108, line 63.
20. *Aids to Reflection* (1825), 1884 ed., pp. 267f.
21. Ibid., p. 269.
22. Ibid., p. 121.
23. Ibid., pp. 4, 143, 92.
24. Ibid., p. 5. Coleridge slightly misquotes Daniel's 'To the Ladie Margaret, Countess of Cumberland', *Poetical Works*, ed. A. B. Grosart, 5 vols., 1885, I, p. 206, lines 98f.

25. *Aids to Reflection* pp. 24, 128f.
26. *Tom Brown at Oxford* (1861), electrotyped one-vol. ed. 1889, ch. 11.
27. *Aids to Reflection* p. 6, quoting II Peter 1 v.5; *arete* is linked with *Ares* in the earlier editions of H. G. Liddell and R. Scott, *A Greek-English Lexicon* (Oxford 1843 etc) but not in the revised 9th ed. (Oxford 1940) nor in G. W. H. Lampe's *Patristic Greek Lexicon*, Oxford 1961.
28. *The Friend* in *Collected Works of Samuel Taylor Coleridge*, Bollingen ed., Princeton and London, 1969 –, IV (1), p. 516, essay of 1809 repr. 1818.
29. Coleridge to Rev. Edward Coleridge, 25 Oct. 1826, *Collected Letters*, ed. E. L. Griggs, 6 vols., Oxford 1956–71, VI, 641.
30. *Lectures on Revealed Religion, Collected Works* I, 225.
31. *Conciones ad Populum: On the Present War, Collected Works* I, pp. 65f.
32. For a full discussion see J. W. Burrow, *A Liberal Descent: Victorian Historians and the English Past*, Cambridge 1981, ch.2, esp. pp. 13, 34f.
33. *On the Constitution of Church and State* (1830), ed. John Barrell, 1972, ch. 7 'Regrets and Apprehensions', esp. pp. 49–51.
34. Robert Southey, *Sir Thomas More; or, Colloquies on the Progress and Prospects of Society*, 2 vols., 1829, esp. II, 173–99; T.B. Macaulay, 'Southey's Colloquies on Society', *Edinburgh Review* L (Jan. 1830), 528–65.
35. 'A Moral and Political Lecture' (Feb.? 1795), *Collected Works* I, p. 12.
36. *On the Constitution of Church and State*, p. 58.
37. Ibid., p. 59.
38. Ibid., pp. 64f, 120.
39. *Aurora Leigh* V, 152.
40. Thomas Hughes, *Early Memories for the Children*, 1889, pp. 51f.
41. Letter from Maurice to Hughes published in *Working Men's College Magazine* II (May 1860), pp. 75–8; there is an account of the Sayers–Heenan fight in Hugh Walpole's novel *The Fortress*, 1932, Part IV 'The Fight'.
42. *Life* I, 127.
43. Letter from Maurice to Kingsley in *Life* II, 262.
44. DNB s.c. 'Maurice, Sir Frederick Barton, 1871–1951'.
45. A. Tennyson, 'To F. D. Maurice', *Poems*, ed. Christopher Ricks, 1969, p. 1024, lines 37–40.
46. *Life* I, pp. 482f.
47. Enclosed in letter from Macmillan to Hughes, 16 Oct. 1856, Macmillan Archive, BL Add. MS 54917 f.6v. The reader was Joseph Mayor, Cambridge don and Old Rugbeian.
48. *LM* I, p. 127.
49. *LM* I, pp. 371f.
50. F. D. Maurice, *The Kingdom of Christ* (1838), ed. A. R. Vidler (from text of 2nd ed., 1842), 2 vols, 1958, II, pp. 248, 268.

51. F. D. Maurice, *The Gospel of St John*, Cambridge, 1857, p. 253.

52. F. D. Maurice, *The Prayer Book*, 1849, pp. 111f; *The Kingdom of Christ* I, pp. 68, 272f; *The Church a Family*, 1850, p. 93.

53. *Theological Essays*, Cambridge 1853, p. 117.

54. *Life* I, p. 446.

55. *The Kingdom of Christ* I, pp. 227–9.

56. For a comprehensive survey see Geoffrey Rowell, *Hell and the Victorians*, Oxford 1974.

57. *The Prayer Book* pp. 297f.

58. *Life* I, p. 150; the influence of Stephenson is assessed in F. M. McClain, *Maurice, Man and Moralist*, 1972, esp. pp. 54–62.

59. F. D. Maurice, *Reasons for Co-operation*, 1851, p. 23; *The Kingdom of Christ*, I, p. 201.

60. Charles Kingsley, 'Robert Southey on Owenism', *The Christian Socialist* I (30 Nov. 1850), pp. 38f; see Robert Southey, 'Owen of Lanark', *Sir Thomas More* II, pp. 132–45.

61. See Neville Masterman, *John Malcolm Ludlow, the Builder of Christian Socialism*, Cambridge, 1963.

62. Karl Marx and Friedrich Engels, *Manifesto of the Communist Party* (1848), ed. H. J. Laski, 1948, III, p. 148.

63. *Life* II, p. 41.

64. *Eustace Conway*, 3 vols., 1834, I, pp. 162f.

65. *Life* II, p. 497.

66. *Life* II, pp. 404f.

67. John 17 v.3; *Theological Essays* p. 474.

68. *Theological Essays* pp. 465f: see John Locke, *An Essay Concerning Humane Understanding*, 1690, Bk II, ch. xvii and R. I. Aaron, *John Locke*, 1937, pp. 160–4.

69. *Aids to Reflection* pp. xii, 44; *On the Constitution of Church and State*, p. 54.

70. *Life* II p. 481.

71. *Theological Essays* p. 474, and pp. 158f.

72. *Alton Locke*, ch. 36.

73. Letter from Hughes to Viscount Goderich, 8 Dec. 1856, Ripon Papers, BL Add. MS 43547 ff.288–9; letter from Hughes to Macmillan, 15 Dec. 1856, Macmillan Archive, BL Add. MS 54918 f.8.

74. John Bunyan, *The Pilgrim's Progress*, ed. J. B. Wharey, 1928, pp. 318f, 325; A. P. Stanley, *Life of Arnold* II, pp. 64f.

75. F. D. Maurice, *The Doctrine of Sacrifice*, Cambridge 1854, pp. 301f, 315, 322.

76. Ibid. pp. 307f, 313; see Rosemary Woolf, 'The Theme of Christ the Lover-Knight in Mediaeval English Literature', *Review of English Studies* n.s. XIII (1962), pp. 1–16.

77. G. S. de M. R., ed., *Lays of the Sanctuary*, 1859, p. 49; see also W. M. Furneaux, *A Companion to the Public School Hymn Book*, 1903, p. 44.

78. C. C. J. Bunsen, *Hippolytus and his Age*, 4 vols., 1852, II, p. 23,

quoted with approval to define Kingsley's own outlook, *LM* I, pp. 85f.

79. *LM* I, pp. 20–2; Susan Chitty, *The Beast and the Monk* pp. 40f.
80. George Rudé and Eric Hobsbawm, *Captain Swing*, 1969, p. 140.
81. In 'Occasional Discourse on the Negro Question', *Fraser's Magazine* XL (Dec. 1849), p. 673.
82. *LM* I, p. 22.
83. Thomas Hughes, *Memoir of a Brother* pp. 88–91; E. E. Brown, ed., *True Manliness*, Boston, 1880, Preface (autobiographical letter from Hughes to J. R. Lowell), pp. xiif.
84. Una Pope-Hennessy, *Canon Charles Kingsley* pp. 40f.
85. *LM* I, pp. 244f.
86. *Sartor Resartus* (1834), 1838 ed., Bk II, ch. 8.
87. Ibid. pp. 169f, 201. Carlyle's adaptations of Fichte are discussed in C. F. Harrold, *Carlyle and German Thought*, New Haven, 1934.
88. Kingsley to Carlyle, 20 April 1849, quoted in M. F. Thorp, *Charles Kingsley* p. 22.
89. Ibid., p. 93; E. C. Mack and W. H. G. Armytage, *Thomas Hughes*, 1952, p. 35.
90. *Life of Frederick Denison Maurice* II, pp. 261f.
91. J. A. Froude, *Thomas Carlyle* I, p. 54.
92. *The Tempest* IV, i, lines 156f; *Sartor Resartus* pp. 54, 276–9, etc.
93. *Faust* I, ll.508f; *Sartor Resartus* pp. 54, 278.
94. 'Intimations of Immortality' ll.203f; *Sartor Resartus* pp. 72, 66.
95. Charles Kingsley, *Scientific Lectures and Essays*, 1880, p. 249.
96. Thomas Hughes, *Alfred the Great*, 1869, p.7.
97. *LM* I, p. 119; *LM*, abridged ed. (which has some extra material), 1884, pp. 49f.
98. Una Pope-Hennessy, *Canon Charles Kingsley* p. 127.
99. Thomas Carlyle, *The French Revolution: A History*, 3 vols., 1837–9, I, pp. 68f.
100. Ibid., I, p. 297.
101. Thomas Carlyle, ed., *Oliver Cromwell's Letters and Speeches*, 2 vols., 1845, Introduction, I, p. 61.
102. *On Heroes, Hero-worship and the Heroic in History*, 1844, p. 20.
103. *Past and Present*, 1843, p. 48.
104. J. G. Fichte, *The Nature of the Scholar* in *Popular Works*, trans. W. Smith, 2 vols., 1848, I, pp. 247, 253, 312.
105. *On Heroes* pp. 87, 108, 337f, 388f; ibid. p. 106.
106. Ibid., p. 69; *Cromwell* I, p. 20.
107. *Cromwell* I, pp. 15f.
108. *On Heroes* p. 353.
109. Charles Kingsley, *The Heroes*, Cambridge 1856, p. 58; Thomas Hughes, *David Livingstone*, 1889.
110. Roy Strong, *And when did you last see your father?* p. 149.
111. See e.g. W. R. Greg, 'Kingsley and Carlyle', *Literary and Social Judgements*, 1869, pp. 122, 124; Justin McCarthy, *Reminiscences*, 2 vols., 1899, I, p. 264.

112. See Norman Vance, 'Anythingarianism', *Notes and Queries* n.s. XXII (March 1975), pp. 108f.
113. 'Novalis' [Friedrich von Hardenberg], 'Hymns of Night' no. 3 in *Hymns and Thoughts on Religion*, trans. W. Hastie, Edinburgh 1888, pp. 7f.
114. Discussed more fully in Norman Vance, 'Heroic Myth and Women in Victorian Literature', *Yearbook of English Studies* XII (1982), pp. 169–85.
115. [Fitzjames Stephen] '*Tom Brown's Schooldays*', *Edinburgh Review* CVII (Jan. 1858), pp. 172–93, esp. p. 183; Matthew Arnold, 'Rugby Chapel' line 161. The origins of the poem are discussed by Kenneth Allott in his edition of Arnold's *Poems*, 1965, p. 444.
116. David Newsome, *Godliness and Good Learning* p. 37.
117. E. E. Brown, ed., *True Manliness* pp. x-xi; Thomas Hughes, *The Manliness of Christ* (1879), 1894 ed. pp. 215f; Thomas Hughes, *Memoir of a Brother* pp. 17, 32–41.
118. See e.g. A. P. Stanley, *Life of Arnold* I, p. 165.
119. *LM* I, p. 22.
120. *LM* I, p. 143, letter of Dec. 1846: Stanley's *Life* was published in 1844.
121. *The Manliness of Christ* p. 221.
122. Lytton Strachey, *Eminent Victorians* (1918), 1921 ed. p. 207.
123. *Tom Brown's Schooldays* Part I, ch. 5.
124. Stanley, *Life of Arnold* I, p. 163; I, p. 117; Plato, *Republic* III, 41C.
125. Note on Thucydides II, 93 in his edition of *The History of the Peloponnesian War*, 3 vols, Oxford 1830–5, I, p. 385.
126. Stanley, *Life of Arnold* I, pp. 103–5; II, p. 137.
127. Thomas Arnold, 'On the Discipline of Public Schools', *Quarterly Journal of Education*, repr. in *Miscellaneous Works*, 1845, pp. 369f.
128. Stanley, *Life of Arnold* I, pp. 99f.
129. Stanley, *Life of Arnold* I, pp. 126f.
130. Thomas Arnold, 'Christian Schools' in *Christian Life, its Hopes, its Fears and its Close*, 1842, pp. 66f; the overstrain argument is advanced by, e.g., Dean Lake in Katherine Lake, ed., *Memorials of William Charles Lake*, 1901, p. 12.
131. *Eminent Victorians* pp. 201f.
132. Thomas Arnold, *Sermons*, 3 vols, 1829–34, II, p. 122.
133. Thomas Arnold, *Christian Life, its Course, its Hindrance and its Helps*, 1841, p. 30.
134. Stanley, *Life of Arnold*, I, pp. 103–5.
135. *Christian Life, its Hopes* p. 83.
136. *Tom Brown's Schooldays* Part I, ch.6.
137. Stanley, *Life of Arnold* I, p. 287.
138. [Thomas Arnold] 'The Oxford Malignants and Dr Hampden', *Edinburgh Review* LXIII (April 1836), pp. 225–39. The title was not actually chosen by Arnold. For Newman's attitude to Hampden see *Apologia* pp. 61f.

139. Thomas Arnold, Letter to the *Hertford Reformer*, 2 Feb. 1839, repr. in *Miscellaneous Works* p. 470.
140. *Brief Observations of the Political and Religious Sentiments of the Late Rev. Dr Arnold . . . extracted from The Record newspaper*, 1845, p. 7.
141. *Miscellaneous Works* p. 182
142. Thomas Arnold, *History of the Later Roman Commonwealth* (1845), 2 vols., 1857 ed., II, pp. 14f. and n.
143. Note on Thucydides VIII, 81, *Peloponnesian War* III, p. 459; *Roman Commonwealth* I, p. 68.
144. Stanley, *Life of Arnold* I, p. 351; *Christian Life, its Course* Introduction p. lxvi.
145. *Advancement of Learning* (1605), Bk II, in *Works*, ed. J. Spedding, R. L. Ellis and D. D. Heath, 12 vols, 1858–69, III, p. 421, slightly misquoted in Stanley *Life of Arnold* I, p. 176.
146. *The Manliness of Christ* pp. 198–201; Stanley *Life of Arnold* II, p. 340.
147. Discussed in E. L. Williamson, *The Liberalism of Thomas Arnold*, Alabama 1964, p. 60
148. Stanley, *Life of Arnold* I, p. 351.
149. *History of Rome* (1838), 3 vols., 1857 ed., I, p. 421.
150. Stanley II, p. 362. There is an imaginative reconstruction of Hermann's victory in Robert Graves' novel *I, Claudius*, 1934, ch.12.
151. *Introductory Lectures on Modern History*, 1842, pp. 178f.
152. *History of Rome* I, p. 385.
153. *Sermons* III, Introduction, p. xvi.

4. KINGSLEYAN MANLINESS(I): ITS LIFE AND TIMES

1. Letter to J. M. Ludlow, 1848, *LM* I, p. 180.
2. Preface to fourth edition of *Yeast*, 1859, pp. xi–xiv.
3. Discussed by Stephen Prickett in *Victorian Fantasy*, Hassocks, 1979, pp. 153f.
4. Susan Chitty, *The Beast and the Monk* pp. 116f; Kingsley to Macmillan, 2nd Nov. 1854, Macmillan Archive, BL Add. MS 54911 f.40. The order of the first two chapters of *Hypatia*, for example, is reversed between serial publication (*Fraser's Magazine* XLV (Jan. 1852)) and first edition (2 vols, 1853).
5. Emerson's lectures, *The Mind and Manners of the Nineteenth Century*, were delivered on June 6–17; his second lecture was on the Kingsleyan theme of the 'Relation of Intellect to Natural Science'. *Letters of R. W. Emerson*, ed. R. L. Rusk, 6 vols., New York and London, 1939, IV, p. 84n.
6. *LM* I, p. 180.
7. 'Letters to Chartists No. 1', *LM* I, p. 163.
8. Discussed by Sheila Smith, 'Blue Books and Novelists', *Review of English Studies* n.s. XXI (1970), 23–40; see also Sheila Smith, *The Other Nation*, Oxford 1980.

9. See, e.g., Louis Cazamian, *Le Roman Social en Angleterre*, Paris 1903; A. J. Hartley, *The Novels of Charles Kingsley. A Christian Social Interpretation*, Folkestone 1977. For Christian socialism see the studies of Charles Raven (1920) and Torben Christenson (Aarhus 1962).

10. Louis Cazamian, *Kingsley et Thomas Cooper, Étude sur une Source d'Alton Locke*, Paris 1903.

11. *Address to the Jury, by Thomas Cooper, the Leicester Chartist, at the Stafford Special Assizes*, Leicester 1843.

12. *LM* I, p. 215.

13. Una Pope-Hennessy, *Canon Charles Kingsley* p. 16; 'Who causes Pestilence' (three sermons) published in *Sermons on National Subjects*, 1st ser., 1852.

14. *Morning Chronicle*, 24 Sept. 1849, p. 4, cols 1–3; *LM* I, p. 216; *Alton Locke* ch.35.

15. *LM* I, p. 224; *Morning Chronicle* 11, 14, 18 Dec. 1849, repr. in E. P. Thompson and Eileen Yeo, eds., *The Unknown Mayhew*, 1971.

16. World's Classics series, Oxford 1983.

17. *LM* I, p. 127; the New Mill meeting-house at Eversley, connected with Wokingham Baptist Church, had been built in 1804 and survived until 1881, after Kingsley's death. Private communication from Revd Lawrence H. Jones of Wokingham Baptist Church.

18. Ludlow to Kingsley, 26th Aug. 1850, Ludlow Papers, CUL Add. 7348/16 no. 36 f.2v. Kingsley included *Mary Barton* in his review of 'Recent Novels' in *Fraser's Magazine* XXXIX (April 1848), pp. 417–32.

19. 'Corn-Law Rhymes', *Edinburgh Review* LV (July 1832), pp. 338–62; *Alton Locke* ch.27.

20. Kingsley to Hughes, spring 1852, BL Add. MS 41298 f.62; *Hypatia* ch.22; Benjamin Disraeli, Speech in the House of Commons, 15 March 1838, *Hansard's Parliamentary Debates* 3rd ser. XLI, col. 910.

21. Kingsley to Hughes, spring 1852, BL Add. MS 41298 f.62; see also *LM* I, p. 162, 257.

22. See Thomas Arnold, *Sermons*, vol. III, Introduction p. xvi.

23. Edward Gibbon, *History of the Decline and Fall of the Roman Empire* (1776–88), ed. H. H. Milman, 2nd ed., 6 vols, 1846, IV, ch.47, pp. 338–50.

24. Maurice to Kingsley, 4 August 1855, *Life of Frederick Maurice* II, pp. 261f.

25. Susan Chitty, *The Beast and the Monk*, p. 43.

26. Kingsley to Hughes, spring 1852, BL Add. MS 41298 f.62; R. B. Martin, *The Dust of Combat* p. 143.

27. *LM* I, pp. 296f.

28. Kingsley to Max Müller, 5 May 1852, Bod. MS Dep. d. 171 f.IV, 2r.

29. *Westminster Review* LVIII (July 1852), pp. 32–67; *Fraser's Magazine*

XLVIII (1853), pp. 371–87; 489–501, repr. in *Short Studies on Great Subjects*, 4 vols, 1891, I, pp. 443–501. See Charles Mansfield, *Paraguay, Brazil and the River Plate. Letters written in 1852–3. With a sketch of the author's life by the Rev. Charles Kingsley*, Cambridge 1856.

30. Kingsley to Macmillan, 17 Feb. 1853, Macmillan Archive, BL Add. MS 54911 f.19r.

31. Owen Chadwick, *The Victorian Church*, I, pp. 290–309; *Morning Chronicle*, 9 Feb. 1853, p.4, cols. 1–2; *Daily News* 29 Jan. 1853, p. 4, cols. 1–2.

32. J. P. T. Bury, ed., *The Zenith of European Power, 1830–70*, Cambridge 1960, p. 565; *Daily News*, 23 Dec. 1852, p. 4, col. 5; *Times*, 12 March 1853, p. 6 col. 6.

33. A. J. Kirwan in *Fraser's Magazine* XLVI (Dec. 1852), p. 711.

34. *Morning Chronicle*, 28 Jan. 1853, p. 4, cols 1–2; A. J. Kirwan, 'Napoleon III – Invasion – French Pamphlets and the English Press', *Fraser's Magazine* XLVII (Feb. 1853), pp. 135–48.

35. The rally lasted for three days, 27–29 January; *Times*, 1 Feb. 1853, p. 4, col. 2.

36. Kingsley to Macmillan, 1 June 1854, Macmillan Archive, BL Add. MS 54911 f. 26r.

37. *Brave Words* in F. E. Kingsley, ed., *True Words for Brave Men*, 1878, pp. 205f.

38. *Westward Ho!* ch.29.

39. See Olive Anderson, 'The Reactions of Church and Dissent towards the Crimean War', *Journal of Ecclesiastical History* XVI (Oct. 1965), pp. 209–20.

40. Edwin Hodder, *The Life and Work of the Seventh Earl of Shaftesbury, K. G.*, 3 vols., 1886–7, II, pp. 461–3.

41. J. H. Newman, *Lectures on the History of the Turks* (1854), originally delivered in Liverpool 17 Oct. – 3 Nov. 1853, repr. in *Historical Sketches*, 3 vols., 1908, I, p. xii, p. 225.

42. J. H. Newman, 'Who's to Blame?', *Catholic Standard* 3 March–21 April 1855, repr. in *Discussions and Arguments on Various Subjects* (1872), 1911 ed., pp. 362, 306–11, 326, 361.

43. Kingsley to A. G. Stapleton, 16 Aug. 1855, in R. B. Martin, ed., 'An Edition of the Correspondence and Private Papers of Charles Kingsley', Oxford B. Litt. thesis 1950, no. 282, p. 617

44. *On the Constitution of Church and State* pp. 64f, 120.

45. Henry Kingsley, *Ravenshoe*, 1862; G. A. Lawrence, *Sword and Gown*, 1859.

46. Susan Chitty, *The Beast and the Monk* p. 182; see G. H. Kingsley, *Notes on Sport and Travel*, 1900.

47. *LM* I, p. 428.

48. *LM* I, p. 422.

49. Evelyn Ashley, *Life and Correspondence of Henry John Temple, Viscount Palmerston*, 2 vols, 1879, II, p. 266; Charles Kingsley, 'Lord Palmerston and the Presbytery of Edinburgh', *Fraser's Magazine* XLIX (Jan. 1854), pp. 47–53.

50. B. W. Richardson, *The Health of Nations: a Review of the Work of Edwin Chadwick*, 2 vols, 1887, I, p. xxvii.
51. *LM* II, p. 15.
52. 'Thoughts on Shelley and Byron', *Fraser's Magazine* XLVIII (Nov. 1853); 'Alexander Smith and Alexander Pope', *Fraser's Magazine* XLVIII (Oct. 1853), both repr. in *Miscellanies*, 2 vols, 1859: see I, p. 311; I, pp. 285f, 292, 295.
53. For the 'spasmodic' poets see M. A. Weinstein, *William Edmonstone Aytoun and the Spasmodic Controversy*, New Haven, 1968.
54. *LM* I, p. 181; Kingsley reviewed the poem in *Fraser's Magazine* XXXIX (Jan. 1849), 103–110.
55. 'Thoughts on Shelley and Byron' *Miscellanies* I, pp. 318f.
56. Edward Fitzgerald, *Euphranor* (1851), *Complete Works*, 6 vols., New York 1967, I, pp. 143f.
57. *LM* I, p. 292.
58. M. F. Thorp, *Charles Kingsley*, pp. 135f.
59. Susan Chitty, *The Beast and the Monk* pp. 24, 242.
60. R. B. Martin, *The Dust of Combat* pp. 257f.
61. *The Water-Babies* ch.4; ch.7; there is a reference to the difficulty of foretelling 'the end of President Lincoln's policy' in the serial version of ch.7 in *Macmillan's Magazine* VII (Feb. 1863), p. 326, which was deleted in the first edition.
62. See Arthur Johnson's informative article '*The Water-Babies*: Kingsley's Debt to Darwin', *English* XII (1959), pp. 215–19.
63. Hodder, *Earl of Shaftesbury* III, pp. 153–8.
64. Susan Chitty *The Beast and the Monk* pp. 251f.
65. *The Water-Babies* ch.7; W. S. Gilbert, *The Savoy Operas*, 1926, p. 231; see John Keble, *Against Profane Dealing with Holy Matrimony*, Oxford 1849, discussed in 'Marriage with a Deceased Wife's Sister', *Christian Remembrancer* XXIX (April 1855), pp. 458–77.
66. See J. R. Moore, *The Post-Darwinian Controversies*, Cambridge 1979; Owen Chadwick, *The Selwyn Lectures: Religion and Science in Victorian England*, Auckland 1968.
67. *The Water-Babies* ch.4; Leonard Huxley, *Life and Letters of Thomas Henry Huxley*, 2 vols., 1900, I, pp. 179–89.
68. *The Water-Babies* ch.4, ch.6; Leonard Huxley, *Life* I, pp. 178–80, 190–2; see T. H. Huxley, *Evidence as to Man's Place in Nature*, 1863.
69. Leonard Huxley, *Life*, I, p. 217; see also pp. 242–4.
70. Kingsley to Maurice n.d. [? 1863], BL Add. MS 41297 f.147.
71. T. H. Huxley, *Lectures to Working Men, on our knowledge of the causes of the phenomena of organic nature*, 1863, pp. 152–4; *LM* II, pp. 171f.
72. *The Water-Babies* ch.6.
73. *Spectator* 23 May 1863, p. 2138.
74. Susan Chitty, *The Beast and the Monk* p. 193.
75. Kingsley to Max Müller, 10 May 1852, Bod. MS Dep. d. 171 f.4v.
76. Maria Cummins, *The Lamplighter*, 1854, ch. 48 'Anchors for World-tried Souls'; 'E. Wetherell' [Susan Warner] *Queechy*, 1852, esp. ch.52 'The Last Summer There'.

77. Kingsley to Maurice, [1863], BL Add. MS 41297 f.147.
78. Thomas Wright, 'Adventures of Hereward the Saxon' in *Essays on the Literature, Superstitions and History of England in the Middle Ages*, 2 vols., 1846, II, pp. 91–120.
79. Susan Chitty, *The Beast and the Monk* p. 26.
80. J. Earle, ed., *Two of the Anglo-Saxon Chronicles Parallel*, Oxford 1865, p. 207; *Genealogical Roll of the Lords of Bourne and Deeping* in F. Michel, ed., *Chroniques Anglo-Normandes*, 3 vols., Rouen 1836–40, I, pp. xii–xiv. See Ludwig Dicke, *Charles Kingsleys "Hereward the Wake": Eine Quellenuntersuchung*, Münster, Westphalia, 1906.
81. *Hereward the Wake*, Prelude 'Of the Fens'.
82. *LM* I pp. 222, 369f; II, p. 235.
83. Described in N. Pevsner, *The Buildings of England: Berkshire*, 1962, p. 295.
84. John Burrow, *A Liberal Descent* p. 209.
85. Discussed by Christopher Hill, 'The Norman Yoke' in *Puritanism and Revolution*, 1962 ed., pp. 50–172.
86. [E. A. Freeman] Reviews in *Saturday Review* XVII (April 1864), pp. 446–8; *Saturday Review* XXI (May 1866), pp. 594f.
87. Augustin Thierry, *Histoire de la Conquête de l'Angleterre par les Normands, de ses causes et de ses suites jusqu'à nos jours, en Angleterre, en Ecosse, en Irlande et sur le continent*, Paris, 3 vols., 1825, English tr. by C. C. Hamilton, 1841.
88. John Burrow, *A Liberal Descent* p. 162.
89. *LM* I, p. 201; referred to in *Hereward* ch.18.
90. *Harold* Bk XII, ch.5, ch.7.
91. J. M. Kemble, *The Saxons in England*, 2 vols., 1849; E. A. Freeman in *Saturday Review* XVII (May 1864), p. 622.
92. E. A. Freeman, *The Chief Periods of History*, Oxford 1886, p. 622.
93. R. B. Martin, *The Dust of Combat* p. 19.
94. *LM* I, p. 201.
95. *Frederick the Great*, 6 vols., 1858–65, I, p. 415.
96. See e.g. *Past and Present* pp. 259f; for Stubbs' attitude see Burrow pp. 143f.
97. W. C. Sellar and R. J. Yeatman, *1066 and All That*, 1930, ch.35 'Charles I and the Civil War'.
98. *LM* I, p. 201.
99. Susan Chitty, *The Beast and the Monk*, p. 214; L. Woodward, *The Age of Reform*, 2nd ed. 1962, pp. 317–24.
100. Kingsley to Max Müller, 16 Nov. 1866, *LM* II, p. 238.

5. KINGSLEYAN MANLINESS (II): SOME VERSIONS OF VIRTUE

1. [Leslie Stephen] *Sketches from Cambridge*, Cambridge 1865, pp. 22f.
2. *LM* I, p. 296; Susan Chitty *The Beast and the Monk* p. 150
3. R. B. Martin, *The Dust of Combat* pp. 218f; 67.
4. R. B. Martin, ibid., pp. 275–7; Susan Chitty *The Beast and the Monk* p. 239n, 279.

5. Susan Chitty, ibid., p.27.
6. Dedication to *Hypatia*.
7. J. Butler, *Analogy of Religion* (1736), new ed. 1844.
8. William Whewell, *The Philosophy of the Inductive Sciences*, 2 vols., 1840, esp. Preface p. xiv; II, p. 407; see also *LM* II, pp. 101, 227.
9. R. B. Martin *The Dust of Combat* p. 276.
10. See A. N. Sherwin-White, *Racial Prejudice in Ancient Rome*, Cambridge 1967, ch.2, esp. p. 57; compare the racial stereotyping in the review of Eugene Sue's *The Rival Races* (1863), *Anthropological Review* I (Nov. 1863), p. 482.
11. *Westward Ho!* ch.2; Henry Brooke, *The Fool of Quality* (1766–70), 2 vols., 1859, I, pp. 95–9.
12. *Westward Ho!* ch.7; J. Prince, *Worthies of Devon* (1697), 1810 ed. p. 444; cf J. A. Froude, 'England's Forgotten Worthies', *Short Studies on Great Subjects* I, p. 500.
13. See R. R. Chope, *The Historical Basis of Kingsley's "Westward Ho!"*, Bristol 1912, p. 19.
14. *Hereward* ch.37; compare S. H. Miller and W. D. Sweeting, ed. and trans., *De Gestis Herewardi Saxonis*, Peterborough 1895, ch.32, pp. 66f; see also L. Dicke, *Charles Kingsleys "Hereward the Wake"*, pp. 38f.
15. In the thirteenth-century *Vita Sanctae Elizabethae* by Theodoric of Thuringia Walter is simply one of a group of supporters of Elizabeth, all 'viri utique omni prudentia praediti, et honestate conspicui': see J. Basnage, ed., *Thesaurus Monumentorum Ecclesiasticorum et Historicorum*, 6 vols., Antwerp 1725, IV, p. 137.
16. *The Saint's Tragedy*, 1848, I, ii, p. 51.
17. *Elizabeth of Hungary*, BL Add. MS 41296 f.11.
18. Kingsley to Froude, 11 Sept. 1863, BL Add. MS 41298 ff.138–41, referring to A. K. H. Boyd's article in *Fraser's Magazine* LXVIII (Sept. 1863), p. 356. Froude was the current editor of *Fraser's*.
19. Text in PL LXXIII. Kingsley asked Froude for information about this: see W. E. Dunn, *James Anthony Froude*, 2 vols., 1961–3, I, p. 187.
20. Susan Chitty, *The Beast and the Monk* p. 154.
21. Surveyed in P. Bernardus Merker, *Die historischen Quellen zu Kingsleys Roman "Hypatia"*, Heiligenstadt (Eichsfeld) 1908.
22. *LM* I, p. 249.
23. [Robert Chambers] *Vestiges of the Natural History of Creation* (1844), 6th ed. 1847; J. C. Pritchard, *The Natural History of Man*, 2nd ed., 1845, esp. Section xviii 'Of the Arian Race'.
24. Sir William Jones, *Works* ed. Lord Teignmouth, 13 vols, 1807, III, pp. 34f; 125; C. C. J. Bunsen, 'On the Results of the recent Egyptian researches in reference to Asiatic and African Ethnology' in *Three Linguistic Dissertations read at the meeting of the British Association in Oxford*, 1848, pp. 262f; J. G. Grimm, *Geschichte der Deutschen Sprache*, 2 vols, Leipzig 1848, I, pp. 266f where the family-

names in thirty Indo-European languages are presented in a
comparative table.

25. See H. H. Milman, *History of Latin Christianity*, 6 vols, 1854–5, I, pp.
6, 76f; J. M. Kemble, *The Saxons in England* II, pp. 439, etc.
Discussed in Duncan Forbes, *The Liberal Anglican Idea of History*,
Cambridge 1952, pp. 76, 166.

26. See F. Stenton, *Anglo-Saxon England*, 3rd ed., 1971, pp. 586, 658;
Hereward ch.32.

27. *Saint's Tragedy* IV, i, pp. 181f; 185f.

28. *Hypatia* ch.16; ch.22; Horace, *Odes* III, xxvi, 5; IV, xi, 15; see H.
Usener, *Legenden der Pelagia*, Bonn 1879, esp. pp. xx–xxii.

29. Jacobus Diaconus, *Vita S. Pelagiae Meretricis*, PL LXXIII, cols.
663–72.

30. *Hypatia*, Preface p. xiv; *Suda*, ed. A. Adler, 5 vols., Leipzig, 1929–
38, IV, p. 644; see also Damascius, *Vita Isidori*, epitomized in
Photius, *Bibliotheca*, PG CIII, col. 1285.

31. J. Grimm, *Deutsche Mythologie*, Götingen, 1835, pp. 64, 227f; see also
F. Panzer, *Beitrag zur Deutschen Mythologie*, Munich, 1848, pp. 1,
250f, 369. For a more detailed discussion of the origins and
significance of the 'Alruna' figure see my article 'Heroic Myth and
Women in Victorian Literature'.

32. *Yeast*, Preface to fourth edition, p. 12.

33. For a general discussion see Eric Trudgill, *Madonnas and Magdalens*,
1976, esp. ch.2.

34. Ludlow to Kingsley, 26 Aug. 1850, Ludlow Papers, CUL Add.
7348/16, no. 36, f.IV.

35. V. Martineau, *John Martineau, the Pupil of Kingsley*, 1921, p. 155.

36. *Saint's Tragedy* IV, i, p. 188.

37. Letter to his daughter in Berlin, quoted in T. Martin, *Life of the
Prince Consort*, 5 vols., 5th ed., 1879, IV, p. 340.

38. *Saint's Tragedy* IV, iii, pp. 202f.

39. *Hypatia* ch.25; Plotinus, *Enneads* I, vi, 5–9.

40. *Westward Ho!* ch.1; ch.7; see R. Hakluyt, ed., *Principle Navigations,
Voyages, Traffiques and Discoveries of the English Nation* (1599), 5 vols,
1809–12 ed., IV, pp. 2–4 (Oxenham); *Westward Ho!* ch.1, ch.5; see
T. Fuller, *The History of the Worthies of England* (1662), ed. P. A.
Nuttall, 3 vols, 1840, I, pp. 414f; see also DNB s.c. 'Stucley,
Thomas'.

41. Susan Chitty, *The Beast and the Monk* p. 272.

42. 'Palinodia, 1841', *Poems*, 1872, p. 266.

43. *Yeast* ch.1; compare R. W. Emerson, *Nature* ch.1, *Works* pp. 548f;
see my article 'Anythingarianism' in *Notes and Queries* n.s. XXII
(March 1975), pp. 108f.

44. R. W. Emerson, 'Self-Reliance', *Essays* 1st ser., *Works* pp. 11f.

45. Francis Bacon, *Novum Organum* I, Aphorism iii, cxxix, *Works* I, pp.
157, 222.

46. *LM* I, pp. 280–2.

47. 'Elegiacs', in a letter to J. M. Ludlow, February 1849, *LM* I, p. 197.
48. E. M. Forster, *A Passage to India*, 1924, ch.37.
49. See esp. J. D. Coleridge's review in the *Guardian* (a high-church paper, *not* the *Manchester Guardian*), 7 May 1851, pp. 331f.
50. Preface to 1859 edition of Henry Brooke's *The Fool of Quality*, p. xlix; *The Heroes*, Cambridge 1856, Preface p. xviii.
51. See, e.g., his Preface to *Theologia Germanica*, trans. Susan Winkworth (1854), 1893 ed. pp. xii–xiii where he defends the notion of man as *vergottet*, 'deified'. See also his lecture 'Heroism' in *Health and Education*, 1874, pp. 204–8.
52. *The Heroes* p. 58.
53. Preface to 1860 edition of John Bunyan's *The Pilgrim's Progress* pp. vii–xvi; *Yeast* 'Epilogue'.
54. Preface to *Pilgrim's Progress* p. xv.
55. *Hereward* ch.1; compare *De Gestis Herewardi* II, p. 10.
56. Preface to *Pilgrim's Progress* p. xv.

6. TOM BROWN'S MANLINESS

1. *Times*, 9 Oct. 1857, p. 10 cols. 1–3; *Edinburgh Review* CVII (Jan. 1858), pp. 593f.
2. E. C. Mack and W. H. G. Armytage, *Thomas Hughes* p. 49.
3. *Tom Brown at Oxford* (1861), electrotyped one-vol. ed., 1889, 'Introductory'.
4. See S. M. Ellis, 'Literary Associations of White Horse Hill' in *Wilkie Collins, Le Fanu and Others*, 1931, p. 214; Mary A. Hughes, *Letters and Recollections of Sir Walter Scott*, ed. H. G. Hutchinson, 1904.
5. Mack and Armytage *Thomas Hughes* p. 41.
6. Quoted, e.g., in Thomas Hughes, *Vacation Rambles*, 1895, pp. 7, 344. The Durandarte legend goes back to sixteenth-century Spanish ballads and features in *Don Quixote* but this particular expression of it, 'Durandarte and Belerma', is by M. G. Lewis, incorporated in his novel *The Monk*, 1796, ch.2.
7. John Hughes, ed., *The Boscobel Tracts*, 1830.
8. Thomas Hughes, *Memoir of a Brother* pp. 140–3.
9. *Proceedings of the Oxford Union Society*, Oxford 1842, p. 23; 1845, p. 25.
10. *Memoir of a Brother* pp. 88–91.
11. Byron, 'The Age of Bronze' (1823), xiv, lines 572f.
12. Hughes to Ludlow, 11 Oct. 1853, Ludlow Papers, CUL Add 7348/6 no. 30 f.2.
13. *Tom Brown's Schooldays* Part II ch.8; S. Selfe, *Chapters from the History of Rugby School*, Rugby 1910, pp. 144–6.
14. Mack and Armytage *Thomas Hughes* pp. 28f, 79f.

15. There are slightly varying accounts of this: see e.g. Mack and
    Armytage pp. 118f; Owen Chadwick, *The Victorian Church* I, pp.
    497–501.
16. Mack and Armytage *Thomas Hughes* pp. 66f.
17. Ibid., pp. 80f.
18. Ibid., p. 167.
19. *Tom Brown's Schooldays* Part I ch.8 'The War of Independence'
    (Lowell's 'Stanzas on Freedom'); Part II ch.1 'How the Tide
    Turned' (Lowell's 'The Present Crisis'); Part III ch.2; Part II ch.7.
20. See F. J. Woodward, *The Doctor's Disciples*, 1954, pp.180–228;
    Hughes alludes to a letter received from W. D. Arnold in India in a
    letter to A. H. Clough, 6 Jan. 1859, Bod. Eng. Lett. e.75 f. 78; see
    DNB s.c. 'Arnold, William Delafield (1828–1859)' and 'Arnold,
    Thomas (1823–1900)'.
21. See his Preface to *G.T.T. Gone to Texas* (letters from his nephews in
    Texas), 1884, p. xii.
22. The fullest account is Marguerite B. Hamer, 'Thomas Hughes and
    his American Rugby', *North Carolina Historical Review* V (Oct. 1928),
    pp. 391–413.
23. Mack and Armytage *Thomas Hughes* p. 54; E. L. Woodward, *The
    Age of Reform* p. 237.
24. See Asa Briggs, *The Age of Improvement 1783–1867* (1959), 1979 ed.
    pp. 379f, 391.
25. See [George Dodd] *The History of the Indian Revolt and of the
    expeditions to Persia, China and Japan 1856–7–8*, 1859, pp. 578–84;
    Times, 16 Dec. 1856, p. 6.
26. Thomas Hughes, 'Hodson of Hodson's Horse', *Fraser's Magazine* LIX
    (Feb. 1859), p. 131.
27. See, e.g., his *Ode . . . on the visit of the Prince Regent and the foreign
    Potentates* [i.e. leaders of Britain's allies in the war against France],
    Oxford [1814].
28. R. B. Litchfield, 'Thomas Hughes', *Working Men's College Journal* IV
    (May 1896), p. 70; text available in (for example) *The Universal
    Songster* (1825–7), 3 vols., 1832 ed., III, p. 24.
29. See, e.g., Thomas Hughes, 'The Last of Nelson's Captains',
    Macmillan's Magazine XIX (Feb. 1869), pp. 353f.
30. Thomas Hughes, 'The Volunteer's Catechism', *Macmillan's
    Magazine* II (July 1860), p. 193.
31. Mack and Armytage *Thomas Hughes* pp. 116f.
32. Hughes to Macmillan, 11 Oct. 1856, Macmillan Archive, BL Add.
    MS 54918 f.2r.
33. [S. S. Pugh] *Christian Manliness* p. 127; W. Holman Hunt, *Pre-
    Raphaelitism* I, p. 355, etc; discussed in the Introduction to the
    present work.
34. His own Private School experiences were much happier: Mack and
    Armytage *Thomas Hughes* p. 13.
35. Hughes to Macmillan, 20 Oct. 1856, Macmillan Archive, BL Add.
    MS 54918 f.4r; Mack and Armytage *Thomas Hughes* pp. 150, 144f.

36. Part II ch.8 quoting A. H. Clough's 'Ambarvalia'.
37. Hughes to Macmillan, 11 Oct. 1856, Macmillan Archive, BL Add. MS 54918 f.2.
38. Mack and Armytage *Thomas Hughes* pp. 88, 104.
39. Cyril Connolly, *Enemies of Promise*, 1938, ch.24.
40. *Saturday Review* XII (Dec. 1861), pp. 611–3.
41. *Tom Brown at Oxford* 'Introductory'.
42. Thomas Hughes, *James Fraser, Second Bishop of Manchester. A Memoir 1818–1885*, 1887.
43. See J. C. Reid, *Bucks and Bruisers* pp. 128f.
44. Ibid. pp. 187–91.
45. Macmillan to Hughes, 16 Oct. 1856, Macmillan Archive, BL Add. MS 54917 f.4; Revd T. Whytehead, *College Life: Letters to an Undergraduate* (1845), 2nd ed. (the one recommended by Macmillan), 1856, esp. pp. ii–ix, p. 12.
46. Hughes to Ludlow, 21 Aug. 1851, Ludlow Papers, CUL Add. 7348/6 no. 3.
47. W. M. Thackeray, *The History of Pendennis*, 1849–50; J. G. Lockhart, *Reginald Dalton*, Edinburgh 1823; A Graduate, *Oxford Unmasked*, Oxford 1842; An Anxious Father, *A Few Plain Facts and Observations Relative to the Two Universities of Oxford and Cambridge*, 1850; Anon, *Honesty the Best Policy*, Oxford 1854.
48. Thomas Hughes, *Memoir of a Brother* pp. 93–7.
49. *Tom Brown at Oxford* antedates the published versions of the story in E. J. Whately, *Life and Correspondence of Richard Whately*, 2 vols., 1866, I, pp. 16f and W. Tuckwell, *Pre-Tractarian Oxford*, 1909, p. 60.
50. *Unto this Last* appeared between August and November in the *Cornhill* (vol. II); chapters 26–32 of *Tom Brown at Oxford* appeared simultaneously in *Macmillan's Magazine* (vol. II).
51. Hughes to Macmillan, 3 Oct. 1860, Macmillan Archive, BL Add. MS 54918 f.99.
52. Mack and Armytage *Thomas Hughes* pp. 54f.
53. G. S. de M. R., ed., *Lays of the Sanctuary*, 1859, p. 49.
54. ch.28; A. P. Stanley, 'The Freedom of the Gospel' in *Freedom and Labour, Two Sermons*, Oxford 1860.
55. See Benjamin Jowett, 'Difficulties of Faith and their Solution' (1852 or 3) in W. H. Fremantle, ed., *College Sermons by the late Benjamin Jowett, M.A.*, 1895, p. 18 and Benjamin Jowett, *Epistles of Paul to the Thessalonians, Galatians* (1855), 2nd ed., 2 vols., 1859, II, pp. 248f, both linking Plato with the moral significance of the religious life.
56. Hughes to H. R. Jennings, Secretary of the Working Men's College, 10 Feb. 1881, offering to lecture on the *Apology* of Socrates, Working Men's College Papers Box 1 no. 69.

7. THE UNMANNING OF MANLINESS

1. *Tom Brown's Schooldays* sold 11,000 copies in its first nine months. *Westward Ho!* sold 500,000 copies of the cheap (1889 and later)

edition. Before 1889 there were 5 editions and 27 reprints of *Westward Ho!* and at least 5 editions and 11 reprints of Kingsley's other novels except *Hereward* (3 editions and 11 reprints). In the same period *Tom Brown's Schooldays* ran through 14 editions and 35 reprints and *Tom Brown at Oxford* had 3 editions and 11 reprints. See R. D. Altick. *The English Common Reader* (1957), Chicago, 1963, ed., p. 385; *Bibliographical Catalogue of Macmillan's Publications from 1843 to 1889*, 1891.

2. E. M. Forster, 'Notes on the English Character' (1920) in *Abinger Harvest* (1936), Penguin ed., 1967, p. 15.

3. Clyde Binfield, *George Williams and the Y.M.C.A.*, 1973, pp. 26f.

4. Ibid., pp. 288f.

5. Henry Venn, *The Complete Duty of Man* (1763), 1841 ed. with *Memoir*, p. vii.

6. P. G. Scott, 'Cricket and the Religious World in the Victorian Period', *Church Quarterly* III (Oct. 1970), pp. 134–44.

7. In *Twenty-Six Stories of the Backwoods*, Religious Tract Society, n.d. [c. 1927], pp. 107–29.

8. D. P. Thomson, *Scotland's Greatest Athlete: the Eric Liddell Story*, Crieff 1970, p. 45.

9. *Glasgow Evening News* obituary, 1945, quoted in D. P. Thomson, *Eric Liddell*, 1945, p. 37.

10. *Times*, 12 July 1924, p. 14.

11. *British Weekly*, 17 July 1924, p. 349.

12. See e.g. *The Scotsman*, 19 July 1924, p. 8, p. 11; *Glasgow Herald*, 14 July 1924, p. 10.

13. *British Weekly*, 10 May 1945, p. 77.

14. *Sunday Times*, 20 May 1945, p. 8.

15. Owen Chadwick, *The Victorian Church* I, p. 458.

16. The best account of the origins and history of the Boys' Brigade is J. O. Springhall, ed., *Sure and Stedfast. A History of the Boys' Brigade 1883–1983*, 1983; see also R. S. Peacock, *Pioneer of Boyhood: the Story of Sir William Alexander Smith*, 1954.

17. He worked with a Manchester Boys' Club and contributed an essay on 'Lads' Clubs and the Secondary School' to Cyril Norwood and A. H. Hope, eds., *The Higher Education of Boys in England*, 1909.

18. F. P. Gibbon, *Comrades under Canvas* [1907], pp. 134, 304f, 140f.

19. See e.g. F. P. Gibbon, *William A. Smith of the Boys' Brigade*, 1934, p. 137; E. E. Reynolds, *Baden-Powell*, 1942, pp. 137–9.

20. See Basil Willey, *More Nineteenth Century Studies* (1956), Cambridge 1980, pp. 146f.

21. E. E. Reynolds, *Baden-Powell* p. 12.

22. Gertrude Himmelfarb, 'John Buchan, the Last Victorian' in *Victorian Minds*, 1968, p. 235.

23. John Buchan, *Mr Standfast*, 1919, ch.42.

24. John Buchan, '"Divus Johnson"' in *The Runagates Club*, 1928, p. 158.

25. John Buchan, *Memory Hold-the-Door*, 1940, p. 166.
26. Ibid., p. 164.
27. See Janet Adam Smith, *John Buchan. A Biography*, 1965, pp. 13–7.
28. [G. A. Studdert-Kennedy] *Rough Rhymes of a Padre*, 1918, p. 25.
29. W. Purcell, *Woodbine Willie*, 1962, pp. 175–7, 186f.
30. See H. Scott Holland, *The Labour Movement*, 1896, p. 23.
31. Melvin Richter, *The Politics of Conscience: T. H. Green and his Age*, 1964, pp. 126–9.
32. Discussed in P. D'A. Jones, *The Christian Socialist Revival 1877–1914*, Princeton 1968, esp. ch.6 'The Christian Social Union 1884–1919'.
33. See B. M. G. Reardon's Introduction to *Henry Scott Holland. A Selection from his Writings*, 1962, p. 3.
34. [Charles Gore, ed.] *Lux Mundi*, 1889, p. 322.
35. Quoted by B. M. G. Reardon, *Henry Scott Holland* p. 18.
36. Hughes to Ludlow, 31 Dec. 1895, Ludlow Papers, CUL Add. 7348/6 no. 84 f.2v; see J. M. Ludlow, 'Some of the Christian Socialists of 1848 and the following years', *Economic Review* III (Oct. 1893), pp. 486–500; 'Thomas Hughes and Septimus Hansard', *Economic Review* VI (July 1896), pp. 297–316.
37. Melvin Richter, *T. H. Green* p. 128.
38. J. A. Mangan, *Athleticism in the Victorian and Edwardian Public School*, Cambridge 1981, pp. 38–40.
39. Compton Mackenzie, *The Altar Steps*, 1922, p. 349; *Parson's Progress*, 1923, pp. 230–3.
40. See DNB s.c. 'Knox, Wilfred Lawrence (1886–1950)'; Graham Davies, 'Squires in the East End?', *Theology* LXXXVI (July 1983), pp. 249–59.
41. Mrs Humphry Ward, *Robert Elsmere*, 1888, ch.25.
42. Ibid., ch.12.
43. Ibid., ch.51.
44. See DNB. He was the author of numerous books, including *American Humorists* (1889) and *My Musical Life* (4th ed. 1888).
45. H. R. Haweis, *The Broad Church, or What is Coming*, 1890, pp. 25f, 37.
46. Ibid., pp. 159, 173.
47. Joseph McCabe, *Life and Letters of George Jacob Holyoake*, 2 vols., 1908, II, p. 169; Mack and Armytage pp. 144–6 etc.
48. R. J. Campbell, *A Spiritual Pilgrimage*, 1916, pp. 53, 104, 135, 193.
49. Rose Macaulay, *Told by an Idiot*, 1923, pp. 251, 264.
50. Shaw's 1912 addition to *The Quintessence of Ibsenism* (1891), ed. J. L. Wisenthal, Toronto etc, 1979, p. 115.
51. Cyril Norwood, *The English Tradition of Education*, 1929, pp. 101–15.
52. See Werner Picht, *Toynbee Hall and the English Settlement Movement*, rev. ed. trans. Lilian A. Cowell, 1914.
53. Letter to R. W. Dixon, 12 Oct. 1881, in C. C. Abbott, ed., *The Correspondence of Gerard Manley Hopkins and Richard Watson Dixon*, 1935, p. 74.

54. See his DNB articles on Maurice and Kingsley and *Some Early Impressions*, 1924 pp. 42–5, 64f.
55. *The Science of Ethics*, 1882, pp. 57–9.
56. Bruce Haley, *The Healthy Body and Victorian Culture*, Cambridge, Mass., 1978 esp. p. 230; see also T. H. Graber, '"Scientific" education and *Richard Feverel*', *Victorian Studies* XIV (Dec. 1970), 129–41.
57. George Meredith, *Lord Ormont and his Aminta*, 1893, ch.30, ch.24.
58. A. J. Balfour, *The Foundations of Belief*, 1895, quoted in Max Egremont, *Balfour*, 1980, p. 341.
59. James Lee-Milne, *Harold Nicolson. A Biography 1886–1929*, 1980, p. 341.
60. E. T. Raymond, *Mr Balfour. A Biography*, 1920, p. 7.
61. Matthew Arnold, *Literature and Dogma*, 1873, pp. 18, 22.
62. See Richard Jenkyns, *The Victorians and Ancient Greece*, Oxford 1980, esp. pp. 280–97.
63. Walter Pater, 'Conclusion' to *The Renaissance* (1873), 1912 ed. pp. 249f.
64. J. A. Symonds, *Studies of the Greek Poets*, 1st and 2nd ser. (1873–6), 2nd ed. 1877–9, I, pp. 75–7, 186f, II, pp. 378f.
65. J. A. Symonds, 'Edward Cracroft Lefroy' in *In the Key of Blue*, 1893, pp. 87–110.
66. E. C. Lefroy, 'Muscular Christianity', *Oxford and Cambridge Undergraduates' Journal*, 31 May 1877, p. 451.
67. Quoted in W. A. Gill, *Edward Cracroft Lefroy. His Life and Poems*, 1897, p. 51; 'A Palaestral Study', p. 110; 'Bill: a Portrait', p. 112.
68. Gill, ibid., p. 49.
69. Ibid., p. 18.
70. T. F. Higham and C. M. Bowra, eds., *The Oxford Book of Greek Verse in Translation*, Oxford 1938, p. 513.
71. W. J. Cory, *Ionica* (1858), 3rd ed. 1905 p. 5.
72. W. J. Cory, 'Academus', *Ionica* p. 26.
73. See DNB s.c. 'Cory, William Johnson'.
74. Charles Raven, *Christian Socialism*, 1920, pp. 378f; 251; *The Christian Socialist* I, no. 16 (Feb. 1850), p. 128.
75. David Newsome, *On the Edge of Paradise*, 1980, p. 192.
76. Ibid., p. 194.
77. Athol Forbes, 'The Education of a Public School Boy in the Time of Socrates', *Public School Magazine* IV (1899), pp. 401–5.
78. Newsome *Paradise* pp. 69f; A. C. Benson, *The Leaves of the Tree*, 1911, pp. 79–81.
79. Maurice Baring, *The Fruits of Experience*, 1932, pp. 21f.
80. *Tom Brown's Schooldays* Part I, ch. 6.
81. Harold Nicolson, *Some People*, 1927, ch.2.
82. Cyril Connolly, *Enemies of Promise* ch.24.
83. See, e.g., David Newsome, *Godliness and Good Learning*, pp. 197–9; W. E. Winn, '*Tom Brown's Schooldays*, and the Development of Muscular Christianity', *Church History* XXIX (1960), 64–73;

Kenneth Allsop, 'A Coupon for Instant Tradition. On *Tom Brown's Schooldays*', *Encounter* xxv (Nov. 1965), pp. 60–3.

84. *Public School Magazine* vii (August 1901), p. 142.
85. Ralph Blumenau, *A History of Malvern College 1865–1965*, 1965, pp. 50–2.
86. 'Athleticism: a Case Study of the Evolution of an Educational Ideology' in Brian Simon and Ian Bradley, eds, *The Victorian Public School*, Dublin 1975, p. 152.
87. See esp. J. A. Mangan, *Athleticism in the Victorian Public School*; J. R. de S. Honey, *Tom Brown's Universe*, 1977.
88. See Cormac Rigby, 'The Life and Influence of Edward Thring', Oxford D.Phil. thesis, 1968, ch.11 'The Rise and Fall of Philathleticism', esp. pp. 267–73.
89. O. F. Christie, *Clifton School Days 1879–85*, 1930, p. 28n.
90. The first stories appeared in the *Magnet*: see W. O. G. Lofts and D. J. Adley, *The Men Behind Boys' Fiction*, 1970, p. 17.
91. George Orwell, 'Boys' Weeklies' (1940), *Collected Essays, Journalism and Letters* vol. i, 1968, pp. 465f.
92. Discussed by Geoffrey Best, 'Militarism and the Victorian Public School' in Simon and Bradley, *The Victorian Public School* pp. 129–46.
93. Nowell Smith, *Public Schoolmastering as a Profession*, Oxford 1913, p. 13.
94. Alec Waugh, *The Early Years of Alec Waugh*, New York, 1963, pp. 48f, 63, 73.
95. Alec Waugh, *The Loom of Youth*, 1917, Bk ii, ch.3; Bk i, ch.1, ch.5.
96. *The Loom of Youth* Bk iv, ch.4.
97. Rudyard Kipling, 'The Islanders' (1902), *The Definitive Edition of Rudyard Kipling's Verse*, 1940, p. 302.
98. 'Saki' [H. H. Munro], *When William Came*, 1914, ch.7. Kipling's charge against games-playing Englishmen seems to have become almost a commonplace: see e.g. Theodore Roosevelt, *The Strenuous Life*, 1902, p. 117; E. F. Benson, *Mike*, 1916, ch.4, etc.
99. Geoffrey Best, 'Militarism' pp. 134f.
100. Alec Waugh, *The Loom of Youth* Bk ii, ch.3; *Stalky & Co*, ch.2, ch.4, ch.5; *The Loom of Youth* Bk iii, ch.1.
101. H. A. Vachell, *The Hill*, 1905, ch.6.
102. *The Hill* ch.9.
103. *The Hill* ch.14.
104. J. E. C. Welldon, *Recollections and Reflections*, 1915, p. 131.
105. Arnold Lunn, *The Harrovians*, 1913, ch.8.
106. David Newsome, *On the Edge of Paradise*, p. 212 (this was in 1906).
107. *The Harrovians* ch.4.
108. See Louis James, 'Tom Brown's Imperialist Sons', *Victorian Studies* xvii (Sept. 1973) 89–99; J. O. Springhall, *Youth, Empire and Society*, 1977, chs. 1 and 2.
109. Rudyard Kipling, 'The Brushwood Boy' in *The Day's Work* (Calcutta 1888), 1898 ed. pp. 338–81.

110. Rudyard Kipling, *Stalky & Co.* ch.2 and ch.9, 'Slaves of the Lamp' Part I and II.
111. *Stalky* ch.7 'The Flag of their Country'.
112. *Stalky* ch.6.
113. Ibid. ch.6.
114. J. E. C. Welldon, Preface to Agnes Maude Machar, *Stories of the British Empire*, 1913, p. vii.
115. Rudyard Kipling, 'Mandalay', *Verse* p. 420.
116. 'Gunga Din', ibid. p. 408.
117. J. R. Seeley, *The Expansion of England* (1883), 2nd ed., 1895, p. 157.
118. Discussed in Bernard Semmel, *Imperialism and Social Reform*, 1960, pp. 32f, 51f, 65f.
119. Theodore Roosevelt, *Letters*, ed. E. E. Morison, 8 vols., Cambridge, Mass., 1951–4, I, p. 707.
120. Henry Newbolt, 'Vitaï Lampada' in *Collected Poems 1897–1907* [1910], p. 132.
121. Ibid., pp. 117–22.
122. Ibid., pp. 123, 125.
123. See Cedric Watts, *A Preface to Conrad*, 1982, pp. 65f.
124. 'Heart of Darkness' (1899) in *Youth, Heart of Darkness and The End of the Tether, Collected Edition of the Works of Joseph Conrad*, 1946, pp. 156, 161.
125. John Buchan, *The Gap in the Curtain*, 1932, ch.4.
126. See S. Weintraub's letter 'Buchan's Heroes' in *Times Literary Supplement*, 11 Nov. 1983, p. 1247.
127. W. H. Auden, review of B. H. Liddell Hart's *T. E. Lawrence* (1934) in Edward Mendelson, *The English Auden*, 1977, pp. 320f.
128. *The English Auden* pp. 96–8; see Humphry Carpenter, *W. H. Auden. A Biography* (1981), 1983 ed. pp. 120–30, 221.
129. Rupert Brooke, '1914: I. Peace', *Poetical Works*, ed. G. Keynes, 1970, p. 19.
130. See *Songs and Sonnets for England in Wartime*, 1914, esp. the poems by R. E. Vernede and Harold E. Goad, pp. 65–7, 80.
131. Christopher Hassall, *Rupert Brooke. A Biography*, 1964.
132. Quoted in Edward Marsh, *A Number of People*, 1939, p. 318.
133. Nicholas Mosley, *Julian Grenfell*, 1976.
134. E. B. Osborn, ed., *The Muse in Arms*, 1917, pp. 176, 210.
135. Henry Newbolt, 'Vitaï Lampada', *Collected Poems* p. 131.
136. C. E. Montague, *Disenchantment*, 1922, ch.5; for a more favourable scholarly assessment see Alan Wilkinson, *The Church of England and the First World War*, 1978, pp. 117f.
137. Horace, *Odes* II, ii, 13; Wilfred Owen, 'Dulce et Decorum est', *Collected Poems*, ed. C. Day Lewis, 1963, p. 55.
138. Ronald Knox, *Patrick Shaw Stewart*, 1920, pp. 113, 160, 204f.
139. Edmund Blunden, *Undertones of War* (1925), Penguin ed. 1982, p. 87.

140. See J. N. Hall, *Kitchener's Mob. The Adventures of an American in the British Army*, 1916, pp. 1–3, 133, 198.

141. Paul Fussell, *The Great War and Modern Memory* (1975), 1977 ed. pp. 26–8.

142. *LM* I, p. 118; Susan Chitty, *The Beast and the Monk* p. 97.

143. F. M. Ford, *Parade's End* (1924–8), one-vol. Penguin ed. 1982, pp. 490, 603, 651, 719.

144. J. Gathorne-Hardy, *The Public School Phenomenon 1597–1977*, 1977, pp. 395f, maintains this lingered into the 1950s.

145. See Sir Charles Tennyson, 'They Taught the World to Play', *Victorian Studies* II (March 1959), pp. 211–22.

Index